AN ANNOTATED STUDY OF

# THE
# MUSLIM
## PROGRAM

DEMETRIC MUHAMMAD

## An Annotated Study Of The Muslim Program

Copyright **2024** Demetric Muhammad

www.ResearchMinister.Com

Ordering Information:

Quantity sales. Special discounts are available on quantity purchases by corporations, associations, and others. For details, contact the publisher at the address above.

Cover Art: Khadir Yasin Muhammad

Printed in the Nation of Islam

**ISBN- 978-1-7375613-6-1**

# CONTENTS

THE PROGRAM of the Honorable Elijah Muhammad, presented in the form of a huge blow-up of a page from Muhammad Speaks newspaper, occupies part of the speaker's platform during a huge outdoor rally sponsored by Muhammad's Mosque No. 7, in New York City. Thousands attending the Harlem rally were familiarized with the teachings of the Messenger of Allah and received first hand reports of the struggle for freedom across the country. Minister Malcolm X (right) was among the principal speakers.

Archival photo of The Honorable Minister Louis Farrakhan and Minister Malcolm X and an unnamed Brother from the Fruit of Islam class presenting The Muslim Program of the Most Honorable Elijah Muhammad to a rally audience in New York City-image publication date October 11, 1963

# The Messenger Presents

# The Muslim Program

## What the Muslims Want

This is the question asked most frequently by both the whites and the blacks. The answers to this question I shall state as simply as possible.

1. We want freedom. We want a full and complete freedom.

2. We want justice. Equal justice under the law. We want justice applied equally to all, regardless of creed or class or color.

3. We want equality of opportunity. We want equal membership in society with the best in civilized society.

4. We want our people in America whose parents or grandparents were descendants from slaves, to be allowed to establish a separate state or territory of their own— either on this continent or elsewhere. We believe that our former slave masters are obligated to provide such land and that the area must be fertile and minerally rich. We believe that our former slave masters are obligated to maintain and supply our needs in this separate territory for the next 20 to 25 years — until we are able to produce and supply our own needs.

Since we cannot get along with them in peace and equality, after giving them 400 years of our sweat and blood and receiving in return some of the worst treatment human beings have ever experienced, we believe our contributions to this land and the suffering forced upon us by white America, justifies our demand for complete separation in a state or territory of our own.

5. We want freedom for all Believers of Islam now held in federal prisons. We want freedom for all black men and women now under death sentence in innumerable prisons in the North as well as the South.

We want every black man and woman to have the freedom to accept or reject being separated from the slave master's children and establish a land of their own.

We know that the above plan for the solution of the black and white conflict is the best and only answer to the problem between two people.

6. We want an immediate end to the police brutality and mob attacks against the so-called Negro throughout the United States. We believe that the Federal government should intercede to see that black men and women tried in white courts receive justice in accordance with the laws of the land — or allow us to build a new nation for ourselves, dedicated to justice, freedom and liberty.

7. As long as we are not allowed to establish a state or territory of our own, we demand not only equal justice under the laws of the United States, but equal employment opportunities—NOW!

We do not believe that after 400 years of free or nearly free labor, sweat and blood, which has helped America become rich and powerful, that so many thousands of black people should have to subsist on relief, charity or live in poor houses.

8. We want the government of the United States to exempt our people from ALL taxation as long as we are deprived of equal justice under the laws of the land.

9. We want equal education — but separate schools up to 16 for boys and 18 for girls on the condition that the girls be sent to women's colleges and universities. We want all black children educated, taught and trained by their own teachers.

Under such schooling system we believe we will make a better nation of people. The United States government should provide, free, all necessary text books and equipment, schools and college buildings. The Muslim teachers shall be left free to teach and train their people in the way of righteousness, decency and self respect.

10. We believe that intermarriage or race mixing should be prohibited. We want the religion of Islam taught without hinderance or suppression.

Those are some of the things that we, the Muslims, want for our people in North America.

## What the Muslims Believe

1. WE BELIEVE in the One God Whose proper Name is Allah.

2. WE BELIEVE in the Holy Qura-an and in the Scriptures of all the Prophets of God.

3. WE BELIEVE in the truth of the Bible, but we believe that it has been tampered with and must be reinterpreted so that mankind will not be snared by the falsehoods that have been added to it.

4. WE BELIEVE in Allah's Prophets and the Scriptures they brought to the people.

5. WE BELIEVE in the resurrection of the dead—not in physical resurrection—but in mental resurrection. We believe that the so-called Negroes are most in need of mental resurrection; therefore, they will be resurrected first.

Furthermore, we believe we are the people of God's choice, as it has been written, that God would choose the rejected and the despised. We can find no other persons fitting this description in these last days more than the so-called Negroes in America. We believe in the resurrection of the righteous.

6. WE BELIEVE in the judgement; we believe this first judgement will take place, as God revealed, in America. . . .

7. WE BELIEVE this is the time in history for the separation of the so-called Negroes and the so-called white Americans. We believe the black man should be freed in name as well as in fact. By this we mean that he should be freed from the names imposed upon him by his former slave masters. Names which identified him as being the slave master's slave. We believe that if we are free indeed, we should go in our own people's names—the blac kpeoples of the earth.

8. WE BELIEVE in justice for all, whether in God or not; we believe as others, that we are due equal justice as human beings. We believe in equality—as a nation—of equals. We do not believe that we are equal with our slave masters in the status of "freed slaves."

We recognize and respect American citizens as independent peoples and we respect their laws which govern this nation.

9. WE BELIEVE that the offer of integration is hypocritical and is made by those who are trying to deceive the black peoples into believing that their 400-year-old open enemies of freedom, justice and equality are, all of a sudden, their "friends." Furthermore, we believe that such deception is intended to prevent black people from realizing that the time in history has arrived for the separation from the whites of this nation.

If the white people are truthful about their professed friendship toward the so-called Negro, they can prove it by dividing up America with their slaves.

We do not believe that America will ever be able to furnish enough jobs for her own millions of unemployed, in addition to jobs for the 20,000,000 black people as well.

10. WE BELIEVE that we who declared ourselves to be righteous Muslims, should not participate in wars which takes the lives of humans. We do not believe this nation should force us to take part in such wars, for we have nothing to gain from it unless America agrees to give us the necessary territory wherein we may have something to fight for.

11. WE BELIEVE our women should be respected and protected as the women of other nationalities are respected and protected.

12. WE BELIEVE that Allah (God) appeared in the Person of Master W. Fard Muhammad, July, 1930; the long-awaited "Messiah" of the Christians and the "Mahdi" of the Muslims.

We believe further and lastly that Allah is God and besides HIM there is no God and He will bring about a universal government of peace wherein we all can live in peace together.

Honorable Elijah Muhammad

August 16, 1963 edition of the Muhammad Speaks Newspaper is one of the earliest times that the Muslim Program was printed for public view and placed on the back page of the Nation of Islam's national news organ

# FOREWORD

Brother Student Minister Demetric Muhammad is a Muslim, researcher, scholar, and extraordinary human being, with a voracious appetite for knowledge, keen analytical skills, and an unmitigated determination to preserve, protect, and defend the character of the Honorable Minister Louis Farrakhan. As our Minister works to re-establish the Nation of Islam and prove once again the efficacy of the theological underpinnings of the Teachings of our Eternal Leader the Most Honorable Elijah Muhammad as revealed to him by Allah (God) in Person Master Fard Muhammad, Brother Demetric has been one of his chief defenders in our Student Ministry Class. Of the many scholarly books, articles, and lectures Brother Demetric has produced and delivered, this book – **An Annotated Study of The Muslim Program** – may turn out to be one of his most consequential endeavors.

## Every Nation Has A Term

We are witnessing the unraveling of a great nation, the United States of America, and the world order she has dominated since the end of World War II. In times of uncertainty such as these, people yearn for what is visionary, aspirational, and extraordinary, as well as that which is tangible, solid, and material. No matter how difficult or precarious a situation may be, people find solace and the strength to endure when they see the light at the end of the proverbial tunnel. What could be more visionary, aspirational, and extraordinary than *a universal government of peace wherein we all can live in peace together* as stated in **What the Muslims Believe**? What could be more tangible, solid, and material for an oppressed people than *to be allowed to establish a separate state or territory of their own* as stated in **What the Muslims Want**?

## The Government Shall Be Upon His Shoulders

**The Muslim Program, What the Muslims Want and What the Muslims Believe**, is the Nation of Islam's constitution. A constitution is defined as "a body of fundamental principles or established precedents according to which a state or other organization is acknowledged to be governed." The aspirational principles of "full and complete freedom; equal justice under the law; and equality of opportunity" among others articulated in **The Muslim Program** can only be achieved when we render them unto ourselves. These divine rights will not be granted to us by our former slave masters' children because it is not in their nature to do so. Over four and one-half centuries of history have proven this to be a fact.

## Read In The Name Of Thy Lord Who Creates

Within the pages of this book, we will find that Brother Demetric has provided us with a solid head start toward the goal of implementing **The Muslim Program**. The task before us today is to read, study, parse, and organize institutions for the sovereignty of our posterity. May Allah (God) bless us with the Light of His Understanding along with the wisdom and courage to act accordingly.

**-Brother Abdul Haleem Muhammad, Ph.D.**
**Southwest Regional Student Minister, Nation of Islam**

# INTRODUCTION

## The Inspiration

The genesis of this book is words from the Most Honorable Minister Louis Farrakhan several years ago when he spoke of the value of the Muslim Program. The Muslim Program that officially adorned the back page of The Muhammad Speaks newspaper during the years 1963-1975 and has adorned back page of the, The Final Call newspaper since its beginning in 1979, is comprised of 2 primary sections; What The Muslims Want and What The Muslims Believe. At that time, I drafted an outline for a book that would present the Muslim Program as an annotated book, where each annotation would contain supporting research and commentary for each one of the line item points contained within both sections; What The Muslims Want and What The Muslims Believe. However due to other commitments to more urgent projects, I shelved that book project until a date undetermined.

I am grateful to the Honorable Minister Louis Farrakhan for the words he spoke during the livestreamed Nubian Leadership Circle conference on October 14, 2023. The Minister's powerful words reminded me of the idea and outline that I had shelved. I interpreted the Minister's words during the Nubian Leadership Circle conference as an indication that now was the time to re-visit the idea of creating An Annotated Study of The Muslim Program and bring it to fruition.

During that very important conference that comprised a very diverse array of conscientious brothers and sisters from throughout Black America, the Honorable Minister Louis Farrakhan presented the Muslim Program, authored by the Most Honorable Elijah Muhammad, as the guiding sacred document that should be studied and acted upon in order to create a new reality for the Black man and woman of America and for all human beings who seek the path of righteousness; true freedom, justice and equality. Among the Minister's divinely inspired words, spoken during the Nubian Leadership Circle, he said the following that exists as the inspiration for the completion of this modest book project:

"As a student of the Honorable Elijah Muhammad, he developed a program for us that was on the back page of Muhammad Speaks newspaper back in the 60's. There's no way that I could think to bring back his teaching, his way, the culture of Islam, without starting from the program that he brought us which is the very constitution of the Nation of Islam. And when we talk about laying a foundation for a Black Nation you couldn't lay a foundation for that nation unless you understood that the foundation of it should be a part of the very nature of those of us who were created by Allah and now coming back to ourselves we want to be a Nation.... **I want you to do me a favor. Just take the paper, get it, I'll give it to you, but I want you to take this paper, get to the back page and it says what the Muslims want. I want each of you to study a program that Allah gave to the Honorable Elijah Muhammad for all of us.** It's not just for Black, it's not just for Brown, it's not just for Muslims, it's for every human being. I want to go through a few of the steps of the program just to let you see how valuable it is. It starts with "What do you want?". Every time we said we wanted to separate from white people the first thing they wanted to ask was "What do you want?". If you don't know what you want then you don't know how to learn what to do to get what you want. Now look at this, the first want. ...**I want you to study this program. I want you to look deeply into each word and see if it doesn't make sense.**"

## Black People Are Muslims According To Our Nature

There may be some within the larger community of Black people in America who would look at the title **"The Muslim Program"** and think that such a reference is for those who self-identify as being members of the Islamic religion. However, it was revealed to the Most Honorable Elijah Muhammad by Allah, who appeared in the person of Master W. Fard Muhammad, that the Black man and woman of America are Muslims by nature. And the Most Honorable Elijah Muhammad and His National Representative-The Honorable Minister Louis Farrakhan-has profoundly taught this for many years. It doesn't matter how any particular brother or sister self-identifies in terms of his or her religion, it is the view of Allah (God), that we are all Muslim by nature. Consider the following sacrosanct words of The Most Honorable Elijah Muhammad in his illuminating series of articles entitled **"What is Islam, What Is A Muslim"**.

He writes on May 9, 1969

> "We make religion by agreeing on various beliefs and ways of worship. But, Islam did not come to us in the way of a belief. **Islam came to us in a way of the very nature in which we were created**. And, since it is the nature in which God created us, then God Himself is referred to as being the Author of Islam; and Islam is the Nature of God.
> **So, I want you to understand that there has never been a concept of belief between the Creator and the creation. It is the very Law of Nature that takes over; since we are from God, and by nature we were created by God, and by nature we are of God, we can see that what we worship is of the Law of Nature; in which we were created; in that we are Muslims or we are Islamic People, because we were born to submit to God who is the Author and Creator of us.** Then, we have no alternative but to submit to our Maker. So, Islam cannot be referred to as a religion. A religion is made by groups of people and its decisions are of people.
> So, let us get down to the real meaning of Islam. Islam cannot be a religion if it is the nature of us, because religions are organized and they are not made according to the nature in which we were created."

He continues July 17, 1970:

> "ISLAM IS RIGHTEOUSNESS, ISLAM IS JUSTICE. ISLAM IS EQUALITY, ISLAM IS FREEDOM. Islam is everything that the created man needs.
> **THE BLACK PEOPLE in America are by nature, born Muslim.** The enemy, slave-making devil deprived the Black Man in America of the knowledge of himself. Accordingly, they have deprived the Black Man in countries other than America of the knowledge of self.... **WHAT IS MUSLIM? As I have foresaid, Allah, (God) in Peron of Master Fard Muhammad, to Whom Praises are due forever has taught me that all Black Men, Black Women and Black Children are Muslims by nature. They are from the righteous.** This is why the

Bible teaches you under the name of Israel that they will all be saved. Naturally the white man would not teach you that this is referring to the Black slave, the Black Man of America.

Also, in the Bible, you have the parable of the bones waking up and uniting together and assembling a frame of bones. Then the lessons teach you that they all did live. THE HOLY QURAN a later Book than the Bible verifies the Bible parable by teaching you and me that Allah (God) Gave Life to all. He called them once and they all stood up. The Bible has it symbolically that when the loud trumpet sounded, they all will wake up.

BLACK BROTHER AND Black sister, you are by nature one of the righteous but you have been robbed of your righteousness and made to live unrighteousness until now you will be whipped into submission, by Divine Will and Power. You will be made to accept yourself. THERE is no limit to the Nation of the Black Man. The Black Man will endure forever. God Himself is With us. Let us Submit to Allah (God) and live forever.

PEACE Be with you. The Mercy of Allah (God) and His Blessings to he who believes and accepts his own.... ISLAM AND THE MUSLIMS."

In his August 7, 1970 installment of What Is Islam he states:

**"SO, we the Black People are that by nature and we have a Lesson English C-1, from Master Fard Muhammad, to Whom Praises is due forever. In this Lesson C-1 He Declares us to be righteous Muslims, but we did not know it because the enemy caused us to eat the wrong food."**

THE WRONG FOOD, referred to here is "following and practicing evil." And we can take it literally. The white race did teach us to eat the wrong food. The physical food that he taught us to eat is the food that Allah (God) cursed, (the pig, snakes, scavengers of the sea and wild birds and wild animals)."

## Historical Influence

The Muslim Program written by the Most Honorable Elijah Muhammad is really one of the first times in history that the Black man and woman in America has developed and presented to the world what it is that we want, and what we deserve, and having done so without the paternalistic intervention of white thinkers and writers. This -The Muslim Program-is a divinely inspired document that is presented forthrightly and unabashedly without any self-censoring concerns for what the white power structure in America may be willing to give us as a people. For certainly, when Allah (God) places a demand on behalf of the suffering of His people, that demand stands independent of what the wicked may or may not be willing to give.

### The Muslim Program Inspired the Black Panthers

It should be noted that all within the Black community should be motivated and sincerely interested in a careful study and reappraisal of the Most Honorable Elijah Muhammad, the Honorable Minister Louis Farrakhan and the Nation of Islam. Numerous sources reveal to us how impactful and influential the Nation of Islam has been in the positive development of the Black community throughout America.

When Louis Masseh conducted his **"Eyes On The Prize"** interview with Black Panther Party leader Huey P. Newton, he asked him about the Nation of Islam's influence in the development of the Black Panther Party, he stated:

> "I came in contact with the Black Muslims. I was very impressed with Malcolm X and, Malcolm X's program, or the Honorable Elijah Muhammad's program that Malcolm X followed; the program, it was like a Ten Point Program. **Matter of fact, our Ten Point program was structured after and patterned after the Black Muslim program. It was just minus the religion**."

According to Michael Gillender in his 2014 dissertation entitled The Influence of the Nation of Islam (NOI) on the Black Panther Party (BPP) in the USA:

> **"The NOI had a significant degree of influence on the establishment of BPP aims and values, as well as providing a certain amount of inspiration for the actions of the Party in their prime, particularly social and economic programs, and policies of recruitment.** This thesis has explored this measure of influence from the perspective of the development of the ideologies of the Party leadership, focusing specifically on Huey Newton, David Hilliard and Eldridge Cleaver, as well as using the examples set by

the two groups' respective publications, The Black Panther and Muhammad Speaks. **Newton's admiration of Malcolm X, a Muslim minister, as well as Cleaver's past as a NOI convert in prison have led to the BPP's policies to have a certain Muslim tinge to them; most notably, their objective of economic self- determination and self-discipline, as well as using both the prison system and utilizing the neighborhood to recruit and organize their actions."**

October 1966

Black Panther Party
Platform and Program

# What We Want
# What We Believe

*Huey P. Newton Minister of Defense Black Panther Party*

**1. We want freedom. We want power to determine the destiny of our Black Community.**

We believe that black people will not be free until we are able to determine our destiny.

**2. We want full employment for our people.**

We believe that the federal government is responsible and obligated to give every man employment or a guaranteed income. We believe that if the white American businessmen will not give full employment, then the means of production should be taken from the businessmen and placed in the community so that the people of the community can organize and employ all of its people and give a high standard of living.

**3. We want an end to the robbery by the CAPITALIST of our Black Community.**

We believe that this racist government has robbed us and now we are demanding the overdue debt of forty acres and two mules. Forty acres and two mules was promised 100 years ago as restitution for slave labor and mass murder of black people. We will accept the payment in currency which will be distributed to our many communities. The Germans are now aiding the Jews in Israel for the genocide of the Jewish people. The Germans murdered six million Jews. The American racist has taken part in the slaughter of over fifty million black people; therefore, we feel that this is a modest demand that we make.

**4. We want decent housing, fit for shelter of human beings.**

We believe that if the white landlords will not give decent housing to our black community, then the housing and the land should be made into cooperatives so that our community, with government aid, can build and make decent housing for its people.

**5. We want education for our people that exposes the true nature of this decadent American society. We want education that teaches us our true history and our role in the present-day society.**

We believe in an educational system that will give to our people a knowledge of self. If a man does not have knowledge of himself and his position in society and the world, then he has little chance to relate to anything else.

**6. We want all black men to be exempt from military service.**

We believe that Black people should not be forced to fight in the military service to defend a racist government that does not protect us. We will not fight and kill other people of color in the world who, like black people, are being victimized by the white racist government of America. We will protect ourselves from the force and violence of the racist police and the racist military, by whatever means necessary.

**7. We want an immediate end to POLICE BRUTALITY and MURDER of black people.**

We believe we can end police brutality in our black community by organizing black self-defense groups that are dedicated to defending our black community from racist police oppression and brutality. The Second Amendment to the Constitution of the United States gives a right to bear arms. We therefore believe that all black people should arm themselves for self-defense.

**8. We want freedom for all black men held in federal, state, county and city prisons and jails.**

We believe that all black people should be released from the many jails and prisons because they have not received a fair and impartial trial.

**9. We want all black people when brought to trial to be tried in court by a jury of their peer group or people from their black communities, as defined by the Constitution of the United States.**

We believe that the courts should follow the United States Constitution so that black people will receive fair trials. The 14th Amendment of the U.S. Constitution gives a man a right to be tried by his peer group. A peer is a person from a similar economic, social, religious, geographical, environmental, historical and racial background. To do this the court will be forced to select a jury from the black community from which the black defendant came. We have been, and are being tried by all-white juries that have no understanding of the "average reasoning man" of the black community.

**10. We want land, bread, housing, education, clothing, justice and peace. And as our major political objective, a United Nations-supervised plebiscite to be held throughout the black colony in which only black colonial subjects will be allowed to participate, for the purpose of determining the will of black people as to their national destiny.**

When, in the course of human events, it becomes necessary for one people to dissolve the political bands which have connected them with another, and to assume, among the powers of the earth, the separate and equal station to which the laws of nature and nature's God entitle them, a decent respect to the opinions of mankind requires that they should declare the causes which impel them to the separation.

We hold these truths to be self-evident, that all men are created equal; that they are endowed by their Creator with certain unalienable rights; that among these are life, liberty, and the pursuit of happiness. That, to secure these rights, governments are instituted among men, deriving their just powers from the consent of the governed; that, whenever any form of government becomes destructive of these ends, it is the right of the people to alter or to abolish it, and to institute a new government, laying its foundation on such principles, and organizing its powers in such form, as to them shall seem most likely to effect their safety and happiness. Prudence, indeed, will dictate that governments long established should not be changed for light and transient causes; and, accordingly, all experience hath shown, that mankind are more disposed to suffer, while evils are sufferable, than to right themselves by abolishing the forms to which they are accustomed. But, when a long train of abuses and usurpations, pursuing invariably the same object, evinces a design to reduce them under absolute despotism, it is their right, it is their duty, to throw off such government, and to provide new guards for their future security.

## Inspired The Development Of Black Theology

According to Marjorie Corbman in her 2020 article entitled **"The Creation of the Devil and the End of the White Man's Rule: The Theological Influence of the Nation of Islam on Early Black Theology",** the theology of the Most Honorable Elijah Muhammad and the Nation of Islam helped the Black church sever its ties from its entanglement with the white supremacy inside traditional Christianity.  She writes:

> "This article examines the emergence of the Black Theology movement in the late 1960s and early 1970s in the context of the religiously diverse milieu of Black political movements during the same period. **In particular, the theology of the Nation of Islam was widely understood by contemporary commentators as a major source of the confrontational rhetoric and tactics of the Black Power movement. Drawing upon the writings of the radical Black nationalist minister Albert B. Cleage, Jr., this article examines the importance of what Cleage termed the Nation of Islam's "Black cultural mythology" in providing the possibility of a break in identification with white Christianity. In particular, it traces the influence of the Nation of Islam's proclamation of God's imminent apocalyptic destruction of white America on the theology of James H. Cone and Cleage.** In doing so, this article argues for the importance of examining questions of racial and religious difference in American history alongside one another. It was precisely through creative appropriation of a non-Christian framework of biblical interpretation, rooted in faith in God's complete identification with Black humanity and the consequent imminent judgment of white America, that early (Christian) Black Theologians were able to retain their Christian identity and sever its entanglement with white supremacy."

Corbman continues by noting Professor James H. Cone's enthusiasm over the Nation of Islam and its influence in the development of Black Liberation Theology:

> "In his groundbreaking 1969 text, Black Theology & Black Power, the theologian James H. Cone judged both the "Black Church" and the "White Church" as having betrayed the gospel of Jesus Christ. In contrast, it was Black Power, the slogan increasingly

embraced since 1966 by more radical participants in Black social movements, that was "Christ's central message to twentieth-century America" .... It would be easy to interpret this assessment as a description of a religious thinker incorporating nonreligious communal and political concerns into his work. This interpretation, however, is belied by Cone's enthusiasm, expressed in Black Theology & Black Power, for two religious communities that he did not categorize within the "Black Church" he criticized. **"Black Muslims," he wrote, "through allegiance to Islam, have demonstrated more than any existing black religious community, the relationship between religion and the suffering of black people"**. Similarly, he praised the Rev. Albert B. Cleage, Jr., a Detroit-based Black Christian nationalist minister heavily influenced by the Nation of Islam, for "seeking to reorient the church community on the basis" of Black Power. **Cleage described the syncretistic, Black nationalist1 "cultural mythology" of the Nation of Islam as enabling a new self-understanding among Black Americans, divorced from a religious worldview steeped in the American Christian mythology of white supremacy....the Nation of Islam's "messianic-nationalist" proclamation of imminent judgment for white America and imminent exaltation of Black America, a theology rooted in the apocalyptic and prophetic narratives of both Christianity and Islam, was profoundly influential on the political rhetoric of the Black Power movement and the theological production of the (Christian) Black Theology movement."**

## "How Elijah Muhammad Won"

According to anti-Nation of Islam critic Daniel Pipes, the Most Honorable Elijah Muhammad is worthy of study and examination because despite tremendous opposition, history reveals Muhammad's victory over his opponents! He writes in his June 2000 article entitled **"How Elijah Muhammad Won"** the following:

"In the early 1930's, when the Nation of Islam had just come into existence, its founder made the bold prediction that, one day, Islam would replace Christianity as the primary faith of black

Americans. At the time, this assertion must have sounded incredible, if not slightly mad; not only was the Islamic faith broadly despised in the United States, but African-Americans who were Muslim numbered at that time only in the dozens. Is there a single figure most responsible for the remarkable career of Islam among African-Americans? Undoubtedly, the most common reply to this question would name the man who was born as Malcolm Little and died as El-Hajj Malik El-Shabazz, and is best known as Malcolm X (1925-65). In the final analysis, it was another man, Malcolm X's mentor, who had the greater impact on establishing Islam among African-Americans. This was the uncharismatic, inarticulate, heterodox, and long-lived Elijah Muhammad. But this, too, must be counted as part of the legacy of the redoubtable Elijah Muhammad.... he clearly altered the course of black culture and politics. As Clegg notes: The Muslims were "black" before it became fashionable to be labeled as such, and the Black Power Movement and all subsequent African-American protest styles, from the rhymes of the nationalistic rap group Public Enemy to the raison d'être of the Million Man March, are undeniably offshoots of the legacy of Elijah Muhammad. but all African-American Muslims today can claim him as their patron, for nearly every one of them has a direct connection, personal or familial, to the Nation of Islam. Without Muhammad, the million or so African-Americans who are now Muslims would almost certainly still be Christians. It does not take much imagination to see that, should Islam in fact replace Christianity as the primary religion of African-Americans, this will have vast significance for all Americans, affecting everything from race relations to foreign policy, from popular culture to issues of religion and state. Eric Lincoln, a leading authority on African-American Islam, once wrote that the Nation of Islam might "well change the course of history in the West." Should that come to pass, the credit, or blame, will belong above all to the "squeaky little man teaching hate," Elijah Muhammad."

Throughout this text you will see each of the points of the Muslim Program with accompanying notes, supporting passages from the Holy Qur'an and Bible. This arrangement has been inspired by the great pioneering translator of the Holy Qur'an into the English language, Maulana Muhammad Ali. He presents to us the words of Allah (God) and supports the sacred ayats with commentary and explanatory notes. We have attempted to do the same in our presentation of the Muslim Program of the Most Honorable Elijah Muhammad. Additionally, we pray that the reader will appreciate and benefit from the supplemental sections as well as the complete glossary of each word contained within the Muslim Program.

Thanks, and sincere love and devotion to the Honorable Minister Louis Farrakhan, my family and to all the believers. All Praise Belongs To Allah (God)!-**Demetric Muhammad, January 2024**

# The Most Hon. Elijah Muhammad & His "Message To The Blackman" Equal Keys To Group Wealth & Power

"It is foolish to the Jews, who ask for signs from heaven. And it is foolish to the Greeks, who seek human wisdom.... This foolish plan of God is wiser than the wisest of human plans, and God's weakness is stronger than the greatest of human strength. Remember, dear brothers and sisters, that few of you were wise in the world's eyes or powerful or wealthy when God called you. Instead, God chose things the world considers foolish in order to shame those who think they are wise. And he chose things that are powerless to shame those who are powerful. God chose things despised by the world, things counted as nothing at all, and used them to bring to nothing what the world considers important."
-1 Corinthians 1:22,25-28

Many politically astute news conscious Black folk have recently become outraged as a result of statements made by Arkansas Governor Sarah Huckabee. Her administration, similar to Florida Gov. Ron DeSantis' administration, has ushered forth a vigilance against what it has been dubbed "woke" public school curriculums. Gov. Huckabee has instructed her department of education to drop AP African American Studies classes and she has stated:

"We cannot perpetuate a lie to our students and push this propaganda leftist agenda teaching our kids **to hate America and hate one another**."

The Governor's juxtaposition of the teaching of Black (African American) History with the teaching of hate is a false equivalency. But it is not a new or novel reaction to the sharing of Black History with Black people. It is reminiscent of the criticisms of the Most Hon. Elijah Muhammad and his "Message To The Black People of America". The powerful and transformative life-giving teachings of the Most Hon. Elijah Muhammad have been falsely labeled as "hate teachings" for many years by those who are afraid of what

Black people will do, if the masses of us ever realized the severity of what was done to us in America during slavery and beyond.

The Most Hon. Elijah Muhamad's best student and national representative, the Hon. Min. Louis Farrakhan has offered as insight into this kind of toxic reaction to the teaching of true Black History to our people in the following profound statement. The Minister has stated that

> "The white man of America is possessed of the mind of Cain. For when Cain killed Abel, he said to himself 'Now every man that sees me will slay me.'"

So just as Cain became deathly afraid of his sins being exposed, the white ruling class in America is afraid of their sins being exposed to Black people; they are all but consumed by the fear of retaliation.

Yet over and over again, the Most Hon. Elijah Muhammad and Min. Farrakhan have successfully channeled any negative emotions that have arisen among our people, as a result of learning the truth of our suffering, into the constructive work of self-development and the building of an independent Nation. Juxtapose the mass rallies conducted by the Nation of Islam to the January 6th siege of the U.S. Capitol by former President Trump and his supporters. They lost an election and organized to retaliate against the seat of the American government. This is something never seen in the aftermath of any of the Nation of Islam's mass gatherings.

Recently I purchased a book, written by 2 Yale Law School professors. The book is written by the married duo of Professors Amy Chua and Jed Rubenfeld. The couple, who are both attorneys, Ivy League professors, and legal scholars, published a controversial best-seller back in 2015 titled **"The Triple Package: How 3 Unlikely Traits Explain the Rise and Fall of Cultural Groups in America."**

I am drawn to their research findings and conclusions because they offer a rather important vindication of the Most Hon. Elijah Muhammad's message that students of Minister Farrakhan who love the Mot Hon. Elijah Muhammad may use to defend it against the charge that Muhammad's message is "hate teachings" or that Muhammad is guilty of teaching "Black supremacy".

According to Chua and Rubenfeld:

> "It may be taboo to say so, but some groups in this country do better than others. Mormons, Cuban, Nigerian, and Chinese Americans have all recently achieved astonishing business success. Why do these groups and other groups come out on top? That certain groups do much better in America than others- as measured by income, occupational status, test scores, and so on-is difficult to talk about. In large part this is because the topic feels racially charged."

The research findings of Chua and Rubenfeld have identified The Triple Package of cultural traits that are responsible for collective group success and upward mobility in American society as being: a superiority complex; insecurity and impulse control.

Chua and Rubenfeld write powerfully:

> "Superiority Complex: This element of the Triple Package is the easiest to define; a deeply internalized belief in your group's specialness, exceptionality, or superiority. This belief can derive from widely varying sources. It can be religious...it can be rooted in a story about the magnificence of your people's history and civilization...it can be based on identity defining social distinctions that most Americans have never even heard of...or it can be a mix.... A crucial point about the Superiority Complex is that it is anti-thetical to mainstream liberal thinking, which teaches us to refrain from judging any individual or any life to be better than another. Everyone is equal to everyone else. And if individual superiority judgments are frowned on, group superiority judgments are anathema. Group superiority is the stuff of racism, colonialism, imperialism, Nazism. Yet every one of America's extremely successful groups fosters a belief in its own superiority."

How does these findings relate to the majestic message of the Most Hon. Elijah Muhammad? His teachings are falsely labeled as "hate teachings" and sometimes as "Black Supremacy." Yet according to these esteemed researchers the most successful groups in America maintain a private teaching and resulting belief in their superiority over others and they are never labeled as "supremacists." In fact, they are sometimes a part of the "model minority" stereotype; but in no public way are immigrant groups condemned for their beliefs like the Most Hon. Elijah Muhammad and his followers are. They are allowed to practice and benefit from their respective teachings that uplift and empower their people. But it is the Most Hon. Elijah Muhammad and Min. Farrakhan who are condemned and slandered when they teach the divinely revealed message of the uplift of the Black man and woman of America.

What the Most Hon. Elijah Muhammad teaches to his beloved Black people in America is divine truth revealed to Him by Allah, who appeared in the person of Master W. Fard Muhammad! It is not Black Supremacy or racism and has not ever produced anything approaching colonialism, imperialism or Nazism. He has taught us that we are the Original People of the planet earth. He teaches that the Original Man-the first human being- is Allah (God) Himself, the Maker, the Owner, the Cream of the Planet Earth and God of the Universe; and that we descend directly from Allah (God)! He has taught to the Black people in America that we are in fact the Asiatic Black People and are the Creator's Nation! Muhammad has taught that we as a people are the fathers and mothers of civilization!

His teachings, though falsely dubbed as "Black supremacy' are in fact a verifiable body of divine wisdom and truth. At the heart of the criticisms of His divine message is the fact that they serve as powerful iconoclasts to the notion that Black people descend from Ham, the cursed son of the Prophet Noah. His teachings necessarily break the mind enslaving teachings that the Black people of America were saved from a life of savagery in Africa by God fearing Christian white folks who brought us to America. His teachings provide the accurate history of the Black man before we were enslaved in America, and before we conquered the jungles of Africa; His message is the root knowledge from which many branch fields of study exist.

The Most Hon. Elijah Muhamad writes on page 32 of Message To The Blackman:

"We are the mighty, the wise, the best, but do not know it."

If we are to believe Chua and Rubenfeld, we have to conclude that what the Most Hon. Elijah Muhammad has given to Black people in America is the kind of knowledge wisdom and understanding that is the key to Black People's collective achievement of wealth and power.

However, as they point out, what successful groups teach and believe about themselves conflicts with popular and widely accepted liberal thinking, something of a "pollyanna-ish" concoction meant to inhibit Black empowerment instead of facilitating it! This reminds me of when J. Edgar Hoover looked at the Rev. Dr. Martin Luther King Jr. as a candidate for the role of Messiah among Black People. He felt that Dr. King could only fulfill that role if he abandoned his obedience to white liberal doctrines.

Space constraints do not permit me to show how the other 2 elements of what Chua and Rubenfeld call the Triple Package are also component parts of the message of the Most Hon. Elijah Muhammad, however it most likely will be included in one of my next lectures.

As we celebrate the 126th birth anniversary of the Most Hon. Elijah Muhammad we should reflect on the power of what he gave to us, and apply it in every area of our lives. Many once called Muhammad's Message foolishness, hate teaching and Black Supremacy, yet nowadays we can easily see how Allah (God) is causing time and circumstances to band together in a grand conspiracy to vindicate the Most Hon. Elijah Muhammad and his bold teaching, while exposing it as the path that the masses of Black people need to follow. We are now some 59 years since integration. And yet metrics that measure quality of life and success show the Black community's continued endurance of the unending problems of police brutality; a widening wealth gap; a lack of access to quality health care; rising infant mortality rates; disproportionate jail and imprisonment rates among our males.

We thank Allah (God) for giving to us the Most Hon. Elijah Muhammad, whose great commission has been made known by His best student and helper the Hon. Min. Louis Farrakhan! Black leaders throughout America should now sit with Min. Farrakhan and carve out a plan to make Muhammad's life-giving and life-saving message the widely spread and implemented program that it must needs be, in order for the survival of our people into the future!

# EXPLANATION OF WHAT MUSLIMS WANT AND BELIEVE

### By The Most Honorable Elijah Muhammad

(Extracted From Message To The Blackman In America, pages 164-169)

I would like to put a little emphasis on some of what the Muslims want. If we ask you (meaning the white American slave-master) for freedom in deed, I think that we are right. We use the words IN DEED, as we have been your subjects for now 400 years. That is a long time to be subject to a people or the slave of a people. Three hundred of those years we worked for you for nothing. And those 300 years we were treated like your own herd of cattle. You have no regard for our human rights, no more than you did your animals. You slashed the backs of my fathers and my mothers without any mercy. You killed them whenever you felt you wanted to, and you sweet hearted with my grandparents. Truth hurts. You went into our grandmothers, had children by them and then put them on the block for sale, and today you are still crossing over to our women.

This should show you why we want to take leave of you today. In those days you sold her children, who were your own sons and daughters. I am telling you what my own grandparents told me. My father's mother told me her father was a white man, and she looked it.

Today our women are all subject to your biddings. You take their sons and bash their brains in with your club and blow their brains out with your gun-throughout the country without due process of the law that you already put here before them. You have in words trodden us under foot in the name of civilization and now today you stand as our chief adversary to prevent us from escaping your evil and unjust doings to our people whose sweat and blood has helped to build the greatest country and government on the earth.

You are so rich today that you are able to feed almost every mouth in Europe. You are so rich that you can now give away billions of dollars to nations in order to get their friendship. You are so powerful that you can command the high seas, the air, the land, even the ice caps of the poles of the earth. All this we helped you do. Some of us went to your wars, shooting down your enemy as you pointed them out to us and we were being shot down also.

If we cry out for justice you twist it and make it look as though we are the real enemies of justice. If we say that you are evil, you want to make a case against us for "falsely" accusing you, when you know that you have never been good to us.

Today you are trying to deceive the poor once-servant slaves of yours by telling them that you will now show a little friendship. I will let you ride beside me on my best transportation; I will also allow you to work in my office. I am going to put you in the government. What is that going to do for us and our children in the future? Will this help us to make a great future for our people and own what you still own, which is a place we can call our own?

WHY HINDER US?

Your dog is more classified as a citizen in the land than we so-called Negroes. If the dog wants freedom, if the dog whines in the night because he is uncomfortable, you will get up and try to comfort it. But if you hear a million Negroes crying and suffering from the brutal treatment at your hand and the hand of your people, you will laugh. I am here with the truth. Take the words, turn them over and examine them, put them on the scale of facts and weigh them, and if I am not teaching you the truth I say come up here and prove it and I will lay down my head on the floor and let you chop it off. We want freedom IN DEED. Why should we not want to leave a people who have lynched and burned us. Why continue to send our own brother out there falling under the blows of so-call peace officers and falling from a bullet from his gun. I have seen police vex our people to try and make them say something so they can beat or kill them.

You say you want to help us. Help us to do what? If you do not want to help us leave you with a good sendoff, then what are you going to help us do if we stay here? I have lived with you all my life. I was born in the South. I have looked upon the evil treatment of our people day and night. I have shed tears for you many times. No justice whatsoever. I have seen people kicked about who asked for a fair salary. I have heard it said to a brother, "You take what I say, you don't figure behind me, Nigger." We are 20 million people who have come (according to the old prophets) through "toil and tribulations." We are here today asking for equal justice under YOUR OWN LAW.

We are asking for freedom that you claim you have given to us. Freedom to do for ourselves. We do not want to be beggars. But if we are given freedom IN DEED we can build for ourselves the same things that you have. Our people who are educated in your colleges and universities, our technicians and engineers of all kinds, why shouldn't they go and make a way for their own people as a nation, build and construct a government for their people as your fathers did for you when they crossed the Atlantic? They may be a little lazy and want to start at the top first, but you were not able to start (at the top). You have put it in their minds that they cannot go for themselves. How educated were your fathers when they crossed the Atlantic and started working for their freedom? They were not wise politicians and senators as you are today, but, nevertheless, they kept digging and turning the soil, felling trees, pacing the country for a place for themselves. Today they have made a nation.

They were not satisfied with trying to do this alone, they had to go across the Atlantic and get our fathers to help them. If you wanted to be your lily-white self, why did you go and get black people to come here? Why would you mix your blood with the black people and yet deprive them of equal justice? We built your railroads with our own sweat. We plowed your farms and plantations. We cut down the underbrush and trees, and now today you have replaced that kind of labor with mechanical labor and you do not have anything for us to do. With just two or three men you can cultivate hundreds of acres of land with machine operations. You pick your cotton with a mechanical machine. Everything is done mechanically today. Why don't you want us to leave you?

Especially when you do not want us to do anything but labor. Why shouldn't we want some of this earth where we can start building a government for the future of our people so that they will not be just a people who labor, year after year, for another people and all their labor still be subject to the brutal treatment? You should be ashamed of yourself today to lynch and kill so-called Negroes while you have an army full of Negroes helping you to fight and protect and maintain the government. You should be ashamed of it. Especially when that same man's father slaved for your fathers for nothing, and now you will go and take him before your own judges and give him an unjust judgment.

This is a sham. Do you think you are going to get away with it forever?

We say Allah is God. We say in the Arabic language, Allahu-Akbar. We say in the Arabic language, "LA ILAHA ILLALLAH MUHAMMAD RASULULLAH".  We that say that in your midst today should make you tremble and go off and commit suicide.  Those babies crying in the Name of Allah (they were never taught by you to worship), you know that your time must be short. Today, I say you see all of these things, hear all of them as the Bible teaches even of being plagued with divine plagues, and you still will not worship the God of truth and justice.

The white race has never believed in God -not the God of freedom, justice and equality.  The man of sin does not want to hear the poor so-called Negroes who are under your feet-he does not want them to seek help from God because he is guilty and he knows he has mistreated us. We called on the God that you said was the right one for a long time. For a hundred years we have been calling on your God and the Son, both.  I am sure today that God and his Son that you are presenting to us have been for white people, surely, they were not friends of ours. He never heard us. He must have been off somewhere in conversation over your future and did not have time to hear our prayers. But Allah hears, Allah acts.

Never any more will you fool us to bow and pray to a dead Jesus any more than Moses or any other dead prophet and hope that my people believe that there is a Jesus killed and buried but still sitting receiving their prayers. I hope that they wake up and know that they haven't been heard since the day he was killed.  Those who represent that Jesus to you do not wait for Jesus to answer their prayers, they answer their own prayers. Get out of that kind of stuff. There is no such thing as dying and coming up out of the earth, meeting your friends and meeting those who died before you. I say, get out of such slavery teachings. It keeps you blind, deaf and dumb to reality. Get out of it, for if you depend on such, you will not believe in yourself. When you are dead, you are DEAD. I have proof of that. Do you have proof of that which you say-they will come back? No! I say to you my friend, the mentally dead are awakening. Your slave-masters have deceived you. They want you to remain deceived.

They hate anyone of you that will try to teach facts. They hate anyone of you that want to become equal. They hate any one of you that want justice. They do not want that, yet, they will tell you that they want to hc1p you and they want to give you justice. You do not get it. We want freedom, indeed, and we want to be human beings along with other humans. We want the world to know that we love to be respected as other people who are now being respected. I say to you my beloved, freedom indeed is what we want. Freedom to do for ourselves as we think best. That is what they (white race) are fighting for themselves. To be free to do as they want to, and they are fighting to the death for it. You and I should fight to the death to be free to do what we want. You know and I know how much these people hate me because I am teaching the truth, and they know I am doing a better job with you than anyone of, those who ever appeared among you. If the white circle leaders want to keep their circle white, I say keep it white. If the K u Klux Klan want to keep their race white, I say, help yourself, go to it. Now when I say to keep mine black-white Circle League German Nazi-keep your mouth out of it.

We want to build a nation that will be recognized as a nation that will be self-respecting and receive respect of the other nations of the earth. I say we have a God that will make a place here for us. "What the Muslims want for the whole black nation of our people is freedom, justice and equality-that is what we want for you. We cannot exercise or enjoy freedom, justice and equality unless we have a home on this earth that we call our own.

# The Muslim Program

Annotated With Supporting Ayats From The Holy Qur'an, The Bible & The History of Black People's Struggle For Freedom, Justice & Equality in America

# What the Muslims Want

## 1. We want freedom. We want a full and complete freedom.

**POINT NO.1 Notes:** The Most Honorable Elijah Muhammad has taught us that the first of our fore parents were brought to the shores of America in the year 1555. According to the book "**Slaves and Englishmen: Human Bondage in the Early Modern Atlantic World**" by Michael Guasco p. 67, we see the following documenting the English slave trade in the year 1555,

> "an expedition under the command of John Lok reportedly returned to England with "certayne blacke slaves" in 1555."

Our lack of freedom in the modern era may be also noted in the fact that the vast majority of Black people in America are still identified by "slave names" as their surname. These names identify us as being the property of the slave masters who once owned our ancestors. The Most Hon. Elijah Muhammad insists that we must give up our former slave masters names and be called by one of the names of Allah (God). According to Time magazine, in an article entitled, **"How Did Washington Become The Blackest Name In America?"**, the following is true:

> "George Washington's name is inseparable from America, and not only from the nation's history. It identifies countless streets, buildings, mountains, bridges, monuments, cities — and people. In a puzzling twist, most of these people are black. The 2000 U.S. Census counted 163,036 people with the surname Washington. Ninety percent of them were African-American, a far higher black percentage than for any other common name."

The Hon. Min. Louis Farrakhan has said that **"freedom"** is an entirely different idea than that of **"license."** He has stated on page 205-206 of the book **Closing The Gap** the following:

> "But freedom is not license. Freedom has to be within the sphere of a law that regulates the behavior of the creature so that it does not destroy the life that it has been given. So, there is no love without freedom and there is no freedom without love that restricts us from that which is destructive of our being and that would disallow us to justify our existence, thus making us equal to all things in creation. "So, love is life and life is love. There is no life without freedom, justice, and equality. And there is no love without the same."

And bearing witness to what the Minister has stated are insightful comments from the **Catholic Education Resource Center**, which states:

> "Freedom is taking responsibility for our own life. Insofar as it is compatible with the common good, people should be allowed to choose freely how they want to live. Freedom, within the context of mutual respect, leads to independent and energetic action.... self-discipline and responsibility are required if the freedom is to be fruitful. License is the throwing off of all responsibility. It is a carte blanche to do as we feel. As such, it is incompatible with virtue and destroys community. License, as the throwing off of all responsibility, leads to absurd and dangerous action. On the personal level, license leads to moral chaos. If my actions are based merely on whim or the impulse of the moment, they are completely unpredictable, even to me. License can cause damage in the very places where freedom enriches. License abandons personal responsibility and so loses the creative energy and fruitfulness of freedom."

**Support From The Holy Qur'an**-Surah 90:11-17 And what will make thee comprehend what the uphill road is? It is to free a slave, Or to feed in a day of hunger, An orphan nearly related, Or the poor man lying in the dust, Then he is of those who believe and exhort one another to patience, and exhort one another to mercy.

Surah 2:177 - It is not righteousness that you turn your faces towards the East and the West, but righteous is the one who believes in Allah, and the Last Day, and the angels and the Book and the prophets, and gives away wealth out of love for Him to the near of kin and the orphans and the needy and the wayfarer and to those who ask and to set slaves free and keeps up prayer and pays the poor-rate; and the performers of their promise when they make a promise, and the patient in distress and affliction and in the time of conflict. These are they who are truthful; and these are they who keep their duty.

**Support From The Bible**- "Now the Lord is the Spirit, and where the Spirit of the Lord is, there is freedom."-2 Corinthians 3:17

"For you were called to freedom, brothers. Only do not use your freedom as an opportunity for the flesh, but through love serve one another."-Galatians 5:13

"Live as people who are free, not using your freedom as a cover-up for evil, but living as servants of God."-1Peter 2:16

"The Spirit of the Lord God is upon me, because the Lord has anointed me to bring good news to the poor; he has sent me to bind up the brokenhearted, to proclaim liberty to the captives, and the opening of the prison to those who are bound;"-Isaiah:61:1

# 2. We want justice. Equal justice under the law. We want justice applied equally to all regardless of creed, class, or color.

**POINT NO. 2 Notes:** In an article written by the Most Hon. Elijah Muhammad entitled Separation of Death he writes:

> "If the Negro leadership was only wise to the clock of time and the slave master's code of laws for their Black slaves, they would be as I-seeking separation and a home of our own; somewhere on the Planet Earth which our Father created for us.... The laws are unequal. Free social worship and religious instruction prohibited. The legal recognition of the Negroes' rights is ignored. Submission is required of all so-called Negroes to all White devils,

as written in the slave code of laws, as enforced in many parts of the United States of America over Negroes and Indians, or any people of color. Adequate protection for the lost-founds (so-called Negroes) under the devil's is almost impossible...According to the **American Slave Code of Law, by William Goodell**—page 304, under the above title, the Negroes may be used as breeders, prostitutes, concubines, pimps, tapsters, attendants at the gaming table and as subjects of medical and surgical experiments for the benefit of science."

These words from the Most Hon. Elijah Muhammad highlight the history of injustice in America as it relates to the treatment of Black People. William Goodell's legendary book cited in the above by the Most Hon. Elijah Muhammad meticulously traverses the American legal system presenting what has become known as the "slave codes." Judge William Jay writing in the front matter to the author, Goodell, makes this important Biblical reference that compares the state of injustice suffered by the Black man and woman of America to that suffered by the "Children of Israel" in the Bible:

"Surely never before has mischief been framed by law with more diabolical ingenuity than in this infernal code."

Judge Jay's reference is to the 94th Psalms. In the 94th Psalms, the Psalmist cries out unto God as a result of suffering injustice and states:

"Shall the throne of iniquity, which devises evil by law, Have fellowship with You?"-Psalms 94:20

Compare the history of the slave codes and Psalms 94:20 with the prevailing conditions of the Black man and woman in America in today's modern times.

Some examples to consider include the following as cited within the ACLU's 2006 report entitled **"Cracks In The System, 20 Years Of The Unjust Federal Crack Cocaine Law"**, which states:

"Congress passed the Anti-Drug Abuse Act of 1986, establishing

for the first time mandatory minimum sentences triggered by specific quantities of cocaine. Congress also established much tougher sentences for crack cocaine offenses than for powder cocaine cases. For example, distribution of just 5 grams of crack carries a minimum 5-year federal prison sentence, while for powder cocaine, distribution of 500 grams – 100 times the amount of crack cocaine – carries the same sentence. First, the current 100:1 drug quantity ratio promotes unwarranted disparities based on race. Because of its relative low cost,
crack cocaine is more accessible for poor Americans, many of whom are African Americans. Conversely, powder cocaine is much more expensive and tends to be used by more affluent white Americans. Nationwide statistics compiled by the Sentencing Commission reveal that African Americans are more likely to be convicted of crack cocaine offenses, while whites are more likely to be convicted of powder cocaine offenses.
Thus, the sentencing disparities punishing crack cocaine offenses more harshly than powder cocaine offenses unjustly and disproportionately penalize African American defendants for drug trafficking comparable to that of white defendants. Compounding the problem is the fact that whites are disproportionately less likely to be prosecuted for drug offenses in the first place; when prosecuted, are more likely to be acquitted; and even if convicted, are much less likely to be sent to prison.[6] Recent data indicates that African Americans make up 15% of the country's drug users, yet they comprise 37% of those arrested for drug violations, 59% of those convicted, and 74% of those sentenced to prison for a drug offense. Specifically, with regard to crack, more than 80% of the defendants sentenced for crack offenses are African American, despite the fact that more than 66% of crack users are white or Hispanic."

And according to **The Sentencing Project**:

"People of color—particularly African Americans—experience imprisonment at a far higher rate than whites.... In 2021, Black Americans were imprisoned at 5.0 times the rate of whites, while American Indians and Latinx people were imprisoned at 4.2 times and 2.4 times the white rate, respectively. These disparities are even more stark in seven states that imprison their Black residents at over 9 times the rate of their white residents: California,

Connecticut, Iowa, Minnesota, New Jersey, Maine, and Wisconsin. These national trends represent both persistent injustices which must be corrected, as well as dramatic progress in the past two decades.26 While all major racial and ethnic groups experienced decarceration since reaching their peak levels, the Black prison population has downsized the most. Reforms to drug-related law enforcement, charging, and sentencing, especially in urban areas which are disproportionately home to communities of color, have helped to drive decarceration for Black Americans.27 While the total U.S. prison population has downsized by 25% since reaching its peak level in 2009, the Black prison population has downsized by 39% since its peak in 2002.28 As shown next, this trend has narrowed, but not eliminated, disparities.

**Dred Scott Decision**

*Roger B. Taney*

"The framers of the Constitution, Justice Taney wrote, believed that blacks "had no rights which the white man was bound to respect; and that the negro might justly and lawfully be reduced to slavery for his benefit. He was bought and sold and treated as an ordinary article of merchandise and traffic, whenever profit could be made by it."

**Support From The Holy Qur'an**-Surah 3: 108 - These are the messages of Allah which We recite to thee with truth. And Allah desires no injustice to (His) creatures.

Surah 4: 135 - O you who believe, be maintainers of justice, bearers of witness for Allah, even though it be against your own selves or (your) parents or near relatives — whether he be rich or poor, Allah has a better right over them both. So, follow not (your) low desires, lest you deviate. And if you distort or turn away from (truth), surely Allah is ever Aware of what you do.

Surah 5: 8 - O you who believe, be upright for Allah, bearers of witness with justice; and let not hatred of a people incite you not to act equitably. Be just; that is nearer to observance of duty. And keep your duty to Allah. Surely Allah is Aware of what you do.

Surah 16:90 - Surely Allah enjoins justice and the doing of good (to others) and the giving to the kindred, and He forbids indecency and evil and rebellion. He admonishes you that you may be mindful.

Surah 60: 8 - Allah forbids you not respecting those who fight you not for religion, nor drive you forth from your homes, that you show them kindness and deal with them justly. Surely Allah loves the doers of justice.

**Support From The Bible-** "In the multitude of my thoughts within me thy comforts delight my soul. Shall the throne of iniquity have fellowship with thee, which frameth mischief by a law? They gather themselves together against the soul of the righteous, and condemn the innocent blood. But the LORD is my defense; and my God is the rock of my refuge. And he shall bring upon them their own iniquity, and shall cut them off in their own wickedness; yea, the LORD our God shall cut them off."-Psalms 94:19-23

# 3. We want equality of opportunity. We want equal membership in society with the best in civilized society.

**POINT NO. 3 Notes:** According to a February 20, 2020 article in Time magazine entitled **"Nearly 6 Decades After the Civil Rights Act, Why Do Black Workers Still Have to Hustle to Get Ahead?"** by writer Tressie McMillan Cottom, the following is true for Black workers:

> "But black Americans have to hustle more. A white family of four living at the poverty line has about $18,000 in wealth. A black family at that threshold has negligible wealth. Everyone is hustling, but poor black Americans are literally hustling from zero. For middle-class black people, the trends aren't much better. Again, it's not just income but also wealth that reproduces racial inequalities, so being "middle class" when you are black is not nearly as secure a position as it is for other racial groups. The black

middle class takes on more debt for education, earns less for their educational achievements and struggles more to repay their student loans than their white peers."

Doug Irving of the Rand Corporation writes in his essay entitled **"What Would It Take to Close America's Black-White Wealth Gap?"** the following that highlights the glaring truth that even in 2023, Black people in America do not have equality of opportunity. His article states:

"The median wealth gap in America—the difference between the middle Black household and the middle White household—is around $164,000. The average wealth gap? Around $840,000. Using that as the measure, the researchers found it would take $7.5 trillion to halve the wealth gap, and $15 trillion to eliminate it."

**Support From The Holy Qur'an**-Surah 8:58 - And if thou fear treachery on the part of a people, throw back to them (their treaty) on terms of equality. Surely Allah loves not the treacherous.

Surah 33:35 - Surely the men who submit and the women who submit, and the believing men and the believing women, and the truthful men and the truthful women, and the patient men and the patient women, and the humble men and the humble women, and the charitable men and the charitable women, and the fasting men and the fasting women, and the men who guard their chastity and the women who guard, and the men who remember Allah much and the women who remember — Allah has prepared for them forgiveness and a mighty reward.

Surah 28:77 - And seek the abode of the Hereafter by means of what Allah has given thee, and neglect not thy portion of the world, and do good (to others) as Allah has done good to thee, and seek not to make mischief in the land. Surely Allah loves not the mischief-makers.

**Support From The Bible**- "For all of you who were baptized into Christ have clothed yourselves with Christ. There is neither Jew nor Greek, slave nor free, male nor female, for you are all one in Christ Jesus."-Galatians 3:27-28

"He has told you, O man, what is good; and what does the LORD require of you but to do justice, and to love kindness, and to walk humbly with your God?"-Micah 6:8

"Woe to you, scribes and Pharisees, hypocrites! For you tithe mint and dill and cumin, and have neglected the weightier matters of the law: justice and mercy and faithfulness. These you ought to have done, without neglecting the others."- Matthew 23:23

"Thus, says the LORD: Do justice and righteousness, and deliver from the hand of the oppressor him who has been robbed. And do no wrong or violence to the resident alien, the fatherless, and the widow, nor shed innocent blood in this place."-Jeremiah 22:3

"Moreover, I saw under the sun that in the place of justice, even there was wickedness, and in the place of righteousness, even there was wickedness. I said in my heart, God will judge the righteous and the wicked, for there is a time for every matter and for every work."-Ecclesiastes 3:16-17

---

4. We want our people in America whose parents or grandparents were descendants from slaves to be allowed, to establish separate state or territory of their own -- either on this continent or elsewhere. We believe that our former slave-masters are obligated to provide such land and that the area must be fertile and minerally rich. We believe that our former slave-masters are obligated to maintain and supply our needs in this separate territory for the next 20 or 25 years until we are able to produce and supply our own needs. Since we cannot get along with them in peace and equality after giving them 400 years of our sweat and blood and receiving in return some of the worst treatment human beings have ever experienced, we believe our contributions to this land and the suffering forced upon us by white America justifies our demand for complete separation in a state or territory of our own.

**POINT NO. 4 Notes:** Numerous reports abound that document the failure of integration. The Rev. Dr. Martin Luther King Jr. told his beloved friend Harry Belafonte the following:

> "I've come upon something that disturbs me deeply. We have fought hard and long for integration, as I believe we should have, and I know we will win, but I have come to believe that we are integrating into a burning house. I'm afraid that America has lost the moral vision she may have had, and I'm afraid that even as we integrate, we are walking into a place that does not understand that this nation needs to be deeply concerned with the plight of the poor and disenfranchised. Until we commit ourselves to ensuring that the underclass is given justice and opportunity, we will continue to perpetuate the anger and violence that tears the soul of this nation. I fear I am integrating my people into a burning house."

The daily indicators of the failure of integration make the call for separation made by the Most Honorable Elijah Muhammad more and more relevant.

The Health Services Research Journal issued a special report in October, 2019 entitled **"Discrimination in the United States: Experiences of black Americans".** It documents the continuing experience of the Black man and woman of America with discrimation and practices that express that American society continues to harbor disdain and hatred for the descendants of her former servitude/chattel slaves. In this report we read the following:

> "About one-third of blacks (32 percent) reported experiencing discrimination in clinical encounters, while 22 percent avoided seeking health care for themselves or family members due to anticipated discrimination. A majority of black adults reported experiencing discrimination in employment (57 percent in obtaining equal pay/promotions; 56 percent in applying for jobs), police interactions (60 percent reported being stopped/unfairly treated by police), and hearing microaggressions (52 percent) and racial slurs (51 percent). The extent of reported discrimination across several areas of life suggests a broad pattern of discrimination against blacks in America, beyond isolated

experiences. **Black-white disparities exist on nearly all dimensions of experiences with public and private institutions, including health care and the police.**"

There are many who consider the divine idea of "separation" as a pipe dream or that which is un-achievable. However, we should consider the activities of our enslaved foreparents after the days of chattel slavery were ended by the Civil War. They left the plantation and had the mind of independence. The went forth to buy land and create more than 80 Black towns and settlements throughout the country. Our ancestors understood the fundamental truth expressed by the Most Honorable Elijah Muhammad when he stated that 'as long as we live with the white man, we will live under the white man.'

Consider the following image that maps our "striking a blow for freedom."

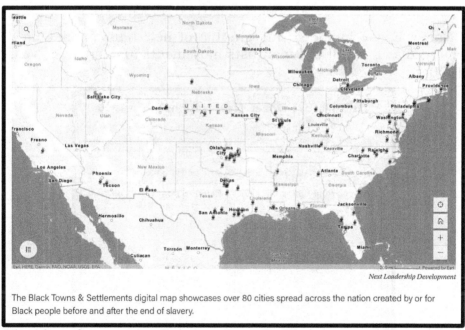

*Next Leadership Development*

The Black Towns & Settlements digital map showcases over 80 cities spread across the nation created by or for Black people before and after the end of slavery.

The idea of separation is strengthened when we expand our sights to consider global trends among the nations of the Earth. Researcher Brian Beary writes in his excellent report **'SEPARATISTS MOVEMENTS WORLDWIDE: Should Nations Have The Right To Self-Determination"** the following:

"When Kosovo declared its independence on Feb. 17, 2008, thousands of angry Serbs took to the streets to protest the breakaway region's secession from Serbia. Less than a month later, Chinese authorities battled Buddhist monks in Lhasa, the legendary capital of Tibet, where separatist resentments have been simmering since China occupied the Himalayan region more than 50 years ago. The protests were the latest flashpoints in s01me two dozen separatist "hot spots" - the most active of roughly 70 such movements around the globe. They are part of a post-World War II independence trend that has produced a nearly fourfold jump in the number of countries worldwide, with 26 of those new countries e1nerging just since 1990. Some nations, like the far-flung Kurds and the Sri Lankan Tamils, are fighting fiercely to establish a homeland, while others - like Canada's Quebecois - see1n content with local autonomy. A handful have become de facto states that are as yet- unrecognized by the U.N., including Somaliland, Taiwan, South Ossetia and Nagorno-Karabakh."

Bleary's Essay includes this graphic of new nations that have emerged as a result of separatists movements just since the year 1990:

**Support From The Holy Qur'an**-Surah 7:10 - And certainly We established you in the earth and made therein means of livelihood for you; little it is that you give thanks!

Surah 24: 41 - Those who, if We establish them in the land, will keep up prayer and pay the poor-rate and enjoin good and forbid evil. And Allah's is the end of affairs.

Surah 7:74 - And remember when He made you successors after 'Ad and settled you in the land — you make mansions on its plains and hew out houses in the mountains. So, remember Allah's bounties and act not corruptly in the land, making mischief.

Surah 14:6 - And when Moses said to his people: Call to mind Allah's favour to you, when He delivered you from Pharaoh's people, who subjected you to severe torment, and slew your sons and spared your women. And therein was a great trial from your Lord.

Surah 4:75 - And what reason have you not to fight in the way of Allah, and of the weak among the men and the women and the children, who say: Our Lord, take us out of this town, whose people are oppressors, and grant us from Thee a friend, and grant us from Thee a helper!

**Support From The Bible**- "May He also give you the blessing of Abraham, to you and to your descendants with you, that you may possess the land of your sojournings, which God gave to Abraham."-Genesis 28:4

"I will establish my people in the land and make them prosper. I will show love to those who were called "Unloved," and to those who were called "Not-My-People" I will say, "You are my people," and they will answer, "You are our God.""-Hosea 2:23

"And after you have suffered for a little while, the God of all grace, who has called you to His eternal glory in Christ, will Himself restore you, secure you, strengthen you, and establish you."

-I Peter 5:10

"'Look, I am giving all this land to you! Go in and occupy it, for it is the land the LORD swore to give to your ancestors Abraham,

An Annotated Study Of The Muslim Program

Isaac, and Jacob, and to all their descendants.""-Deuteronomy 1:8

"You will live in the land that I gave to your forefathers; so, you will be My people, and I will be your God."-Ezekiel 36:28

---

# 5. We want freedom for all Believers of Islam now held in federal prisons. We want freedom for all black men and women now under death sentence in innumerable prisons in the North as well as the South. We want every black man and woman to have the freedom to accept or reject being separated from the slave master's children and establish a land of their own. We know that the above plan for the solution of the black and white conflict is the best and only answer to the problem between two people.

---

**POINT NO. 5 Notes:** According to the book "Bound for America: The Transportation of British Convicts to the Colonies, 1718-1775" by J. Roger Ekirch, we note the following history of British convicts being sent to America during her colonial era:

> "During the 18th century, transportation to the colonies became Britain's foremost criminal punishment. From 1718 to 1775, British courts banished fifty thousand convicts. They formed the largest body of emigrants after African slaves ever compelled to go to America."

According to the History In Charts article entitled **"Discover the Penal Colonies of the British Empire",** we learn the following:

Page 46-Demetric Muhammad

"During the colonial age, many of the newly established empires sent criminals to penal colonies.... With the establishment of new colonies all over the world, the British sought two outcomes: First, a solution for the dangerous overcrowding of prisons on the British Isles. Industrialization had led to a huge rise in city populations and crime rates with it. Prisons were so overcrowded that old, decommissioned warships were being used to house prisoners. To help with this problem the British government decided to exile these prisoners and send them to far off lands – away and out of the sight. Secondly, the British needed settlers in their new colonies. The empire hoped that once the prisoners' sentences were up, the distance and isolation of their new location would persuade them to stay and settle the lands."

These important episodes from the history of America help us to see the practicality of the call of the Most hon. Elijah Muhammad in this Point No.5 of What The Muslims Want. America should consider doing for Black people what England did for her; open up the prisons and give the incarcerated Black men and women

the chance to go and settle a new society in an independent land that will become a nation for all Blacks who seek independence from White oppression.

Moreover, the Nation of Islam has a long and very strong record of reforming the so-called 'criminal" population within Black America. According to the book entitled, **"Islam In American Prisons: Black Muslims Challenge To American Penology"** by Hamid Reza Kusha we learn the following:

> "The success of the Nation of Islam, as we shall explore in this book, is due to two interconnected factors. First, the Nation of Islam has provided an effective prison-bound mechanism of protection to those who convert to its brand of Islam. Second, the literature of the Nation of Islam claims that not only has it converted a large number of inmates to Islam, but has also successfully reintegrated them into its social and economic infrastructures thus preventing them from recidivating and being re-incarcerated."

In addition, the Nation of Islam is widely credited among legal experts with being the driving force and pioneering faith group whose legal fight won not only the right to practice Nation of Islam religion in American jails and prisons, but the "Black Muslim" litigation helped secure rights for inmates of all faiths to practice their religion while incarcerated. According to Claire A. Cripe in her article **"Religious Freedom In Prisons"**, we learn the following:

> "It is a matter of some interest to correctional administrators and to lawyers that the "correctional law revolution" can be traced to religious cases-specifically, to cases brought by Black Muslim prisoners in the early 1960's. ...Not all would agree, but there is considerable validity to the proposition that Black Muslim litigation was the fuse to this legal explosion. With the Black Muslims making demands for recognition and for religious activities in prisons, prison administrators, and then courts, from one end of the country to the other, had to face the practical and the first amendment issues."

**Support From The Holy Qur'an**-Surah 39:53 - Say: O My servants who have been prodigal regarding their souls, despair not of the mercy of Allah; surely Allah forgives sins altogether. He is indeed the Forgiving, the Merciful.

Surah 3:16 - Those who say: Our Lord, we believe, so forgive our sins and save us from the chastisement of the fire.

Surah 46:31 - O our people, accept the Inviter to Allah and believe in Him. He will forgive you some of your sins and protect you from a painful chastisement

**Support From The Bible-** "The Lord hears the needy and does not despise his captive people."-Psalms 69:33

"The Spirit of the Sovereign Lord is on me, because the Lord has anointed me to proclaim good news to the poor. He has sent me to bind up the brokenhearted, to proclaim freedom for the captives and release from darkness for the prisoners, to proclaim the year of the Lord's favor and the day of vengeance of our God, to comfort all who mourn, and provide for those who grieve in Zion—to bestow on them a crown of beauty instead of ashes, the oil of joy instead of mourning, and a garment of praise instead of a spirit of despair. They will be called oaks of righteousness, a planting of the Lord for the display of his splendor."-Isaiah 61:1-3

"Then He will also say to those on the left hand, 'Depart from Me, you cursed, into the everlasting fire prepared for the devil and his angels: for I was hungry and you gave Me no food; I was thirsty and you gave Me no drink; I was a stranger and you did not take Me in, naked and you did not clothe Me, sick and in prison and you did not visit Me.' "Then they also will answer Him, saying, 'Lord, when did we see You hungry or thirsty or a stranger or naked or sick or in prison, and did not minister to You?' Then He will answer them, saying, 'Assuredly, I say to you, inasmuch as you did not do it to one of the least of these, you did not do it to Me.' And these will go away into everlasting punishment, but the righteous into eternal life."-Matthew 25:41-45

"Suddenly, there was a massive earthquake, and the prison was shaken to its foundations. All the doors immediately flew open, and the chains of every prisoner fell off!"-Acts 16:26

"I, the LORD, have called you for a righteous purpose, and I will take hold of your hand. I will keep you and appoint you to be a covenant for the people and a light to the nations, to open the eyes of the blind, to bring prisoners out of the dungeon and those sitting in darkness out from the prison house. I am the LORD; that is My name! I will not yield My glory to another or My praise to idols. Behold, the former things have happened, and now I declare new things. Before they spring forth I proclaim them to you."-Isaiah 42:6-9

---

# 6. We want an immediate end to the police brutality and mob attacks against the so-called Negro throughout the United States. We believe that the Federal government should intercede to see that black men and women tried in white courts receive justice in accordance with the laws of the land--or allow us to build a new nation for ourselves, dedicated to justice, freedom and liberty.

**POINT NO. 6 Notes:** According to the Brookings Institute Report entitled **"A Crisis Within A Crisis: Police Killings Of Emerging Adults"** we learn the following:

> " The Washington Post found that police killings are a leading cause of death for young men in America, specifically young Black men. In 2017, Black emerging adults, 20 – 24 years old, were killed by police at more than triple the rate of white emerging adults. ...Since there is still no national database reporting use of force data by police, we've collected data drawn from news coverage about police killings to estimate the scale of police violence against emerging adults. What we found is genuinely alarming. Of the 6,577 reported police killings during that period, 20 percent were emerging adults, twice their representation in the general population. For emerging adults of color, the disparity is even worse. Of all Black people killed by police, Black emerging adults accounted for 31 percent, despite representing only 12 percent of the Black population and just one percent of the entire U.S. population. On average, Black emerging adults are five

times more likely to be killed by a police officer than a white emerging adult and nearly three times more likely than a Latinx emerging adult. Further, Latinx emerging adults are about two times more likely to be killed than white emerging adults. One of the underlying drivers of these disparities is overly aggressive policing in communities of color, which is seldom driven by actual evidence of wrongdoing. For example, stop-and-frisk encounters disproportionately impact communities of color, but data show that only three percent of the incidents rendered adequate evidence of a crime. This treatment by police often leads to an erosion of trust in law enforcement, including willingness to report crime, and belief in the legitimacy of the law more generally. Thus, these racially-biased tactics do not create safer, stronger communities but, instead, erode trust between the communities – particularly amongst young adults — and the police and ultimately result in unconscionable rates of victimization among Black and Latinx emerging adults by law enforcement."

Harvard Researchers have researched the impact of police killings of Black people on the mental health of Black people. In a May 13, 2021 article published by the Harvard Gazette entitled "**How unjust police killings damage the mental health of Black Americans**", we read:

"A first-ever study in 2018 found that a police killing of an unarmed African American triggered days of poor mental health for Black people living in that state over the following three months — a significant problem given there are about 1,000 police killings annually on average, with African Americans comprising a disproportionate 25 percent to 30 percent of those. The accumulation of painful days over the course of a year was comparable to the rate experienced by diabetics, according to the study's author, David R. Williams, Florence Sprague Norman and Laura Smart Norman Professor of Public Health and chair of the Department of Social and Behavioral Sciences at the Harvard T.H. Chan School of Public Health."

The Institute for Health Metrics and Evaluations article published on May 13, 2021 entitled "**The Lancet: More than half of police killings in USA are unreported and Black Americans are most**

**likely to experience fatal police violence" examines** a Lancet research study and notes:

> More than 55% of deaths from police violence in the USA from 1980-2018 were misclassified or unreported in official vital statistics reports according to a new study in The Lancet. (link is external) The highest rate of deaths from police violence occurred for Black Americans, who were estimated to be 3.5 times more likely to experience fatal police violence than white Americans. Researchers estimate that the US National Vital Statistics System (NVSS), the government system that collates all death certificates in the USA, failed to accurately classify and report more than 17,000 deaths as being caused by police violence during the 40-year study period.

**Support From The Holy Qur'an**-Surah 6: 165 And He it is Who has made you successors in the land and exalted some of you in rank above others, that He may try you by what He has given you. Surely thy Lord is Quick in requiting (evil), and He is surely the Forgiving, the Merciful.

Surah 17:70 - And surely, We have honoured the children of Adam, and We carry them in the land and the sea, and We provide them with good things, and We have made them to excel highly most of those whom We have created.

Surah 21: 105 - And certainly We wrote in the Book after the remainder that My righteous servants will inherit the land.

**Support From The Bible**- "I call heaven and earth as witnesses against you today that I have set before you life and death, blessing and cursing. Therefore, choose life, so that you and your descendants may live, 20and that you may love the LORD your God, obey Him, and hold fast to Him. For He is your life, and He will prolong your life in the land that the LORD swore to give to your fathers, to Abraham, Isaac, and Jacob."-Deuteronomy 30:19

---

7. As long as we are not allowed to establish a state or territory of our own, we demand not only equal justice under the laws of the United States, but equal employment

opportunities--NOW! We do not believe that after 400 years of free or nearly free labor, sweat and blood, which has helped America become rich and powerful, so many thousands of black people should have to subsist on relief or charity or live in poor houses.

**POINT NO. 7 Notes:** The December 5, 2019 article entitled **"African Americans Face Systematic Obstacles to Getting Good Jobs"** states:

> "African American workers regularly face higher unemployment rates than whites. There are several explanations for this. Blacks often face outright discrimination in the labor market.5 They also are less likely to attend and graduate from college, which stems from the fact that African Americans face greater financial barriers to getting a college education,6 ending up with more debt than white graduates and paying more for their loans.7 Yet even among college graduates, African Americans often face greater job instability and higher unemployment rates."

A March 25, 2022 article published by the Economic Policy Institute entitled **"Understanding black-white disparities in labor market outcomes requires models that account for persistent discrimination and unequal bargaining power"** states:

> "One of the most durable and defining features of the U.S. labor market is the 2-to-1 disparity in unemployment that exists between black and white workers. Attempts to explain the gap often cite observed average differences in human capital—particularly, education or skills—between black and white workers as a primary cause. But African Americans have made considerable gains in high school and college completion over the last four-and-a-half decades—both in absolute terms as well as relative to whites—and those gains have had virtually no effect on equalizing employment outcomes. Indeed, the significant racial disparities in unemployment that are observed at each level of education, across age cohorts, and among both men and women are the strongest evidence against the notion that

education or skills differentials are responsible for the black-white unemployment gap."

**Support From The Holy Qur'an**-Surah 42:42 - The way (of blame) is only against those who oppress men and revolt in the earth unjustly. For such there is a painful chastisement.

Surah 42:41 - And whoever defends himself after his being oppressed, these it is against whom there is no way (of blame).

Surah 22:60 - That (is so). And whoever retaliates with the like of that with which he is afflicted and he is oppressed, Allah will certainly help him. Surely Allah is Pardoning, Forgiving.

Surah 22:39 - Permission (to fight) is given to those on whom war is made, because they are oppressed. And surely Allah is Able to assist them —

**Support From The Bible**- "You have condemned and murdered the innocent one, who was not opposing you."-James 5:6

"For the Scripture says, "Do not muzzle an ox while it is treading out the grain," and, "The worker is worthy of his wages.""

-1Timothy 5:18

"There is neither Jew nor Greek, there is neither slave nor free, there is no male and female, for you are all one in Christ Jesus."

-Galatians 3:28

"So, David reigned over all Israel. And David administered justice and equity to all his people." -2Samuel 8:15

# 8. We want the government of the United States to exempt our people from ALL taxation as long as we are deprived of equal justice under the laws of the land.

**POINT NO. 8 Notes:** According to an April 22, 2021 CNN Business article written by Jeanne Sahadi entitled **"The US tax code can make things even harder for Black Americans"** we learn the following:

> "Racial and ethnic inequities exist in nearly every system of society. And when it comes to ways in which Americans typically build wealth, the US federal income tax code may be helping to increase those disparities. The code has been designed with the intention of being broadly progressive – meaning the less you make, the less you are taxed. Or put another way, those with the ability to pay more should be taxed more.
>
> At the same time, it also rewards certain economic and wealth building activities, such as home ownership, retirement savings and investing. But it is White Americans who disproportionately benefit from the tax breaks for those things, Emory University tax law professor Dorothy Brown told lawmakers on the Senate Finance Committee this week.
>
> And even when Black Americans engage in those same activities, they often don't benefit from the tax advantages, said Brown, who is also the author of The Whiteness of Wealth: How the Tax System Impoverishes Black Americans – and How We Can Fix It.
>
> That's why she believes the US tax code helps to perpetuate the racial wealth gap, in which the typical White family has eight times the wealth of the typical Black family, according to a 2019 Federal Reserve analysis."

In an April 1865 speech by Fredrick Douglass entitled "What The Black Man Wants" he stated:

> "It is said that we are ignorant; I admit it. But if we know enough to be hung, we know enough to vote. If the negro knows enough to pay taxes to support the government, he knows enough to vote; taxation and representation should go together. If he knows enough to shoulder a musket and fight for the flag, fight for the government, he knows enough to vote."

According to Mfflin Wistar Gibbs in his Letter to the Editor, published in THE LIBERATOR, July 3, 1857 edition we learn the following:

"Now, while we cannot understand how a "white" man can refuse to pay each and every tax for the support of government, under which he enjoys every privilege—from the right to rob a negro up to that of being Governor of the State—we can perceive and feel the flagrant injustice of compelling "colored men" to pay a special tax for the enjoyment of a special privilege, and then break their heads if they attempt to exercise it. We believe that every voter should pay poll-tax, or every male resident who has the privilege of becoming a voter; but regard it as low and despicable, the very quiescence of meanness, to compel colored men to pay it, situated as they are politically. However, if there is no redress, the great State of California may come around annually, and rob us of twenty or thirty dollars' worth of goods, as we will never willingly pay three dollars as poll-tax as long as we remain disfranchised, oath-denied, outlawed colored Americans"

**Support From The Holy Qur'an**-Surah 90:2 - And thou wilt be made free from obligation in this City

**Support From The Bible**- "Then Jesus told them, "Give to Caesar what is Caesar's, and to God what is God's." And they marveled at Him."-Mark 12:17

"Furthermore, the Israelites acted on Moses' word and asked the Egyptians for articles of silver and gold, and for clothing. 36And the LORD gave the people such favor in the sight of the Egyptians that they granted their request." -Exodus 12:35-36

---

9. We want equal education -- but separate schools up to 16 for boys and 18 for girls on the conditions that the girls be sent to women's' colleges and universities. We want all black children educated, taught and trained by their own teachers. Under such school system we believe we will make a better nation of people. The United States government

should provide free all necessary text books and equipment, schools and college buildings. The Muslim teachers shall be left free to teach and train their people in the way of righteousness, decency and self-respect.

**POINT NO. 9 Notes:** From the very important work The Mis-Education Of The Negro by Carter G. Woodson we learn:

"How we have arrived at the present state of affairs can be understood only by studying the forces effective in the development of Negro education since it was systematically undertaken immediately after Emancipation. To point out merely the defects as they appear today will be of little benefit to the present and future generations. These things must be viewed in their historic setting. The conditions of today have been determined by what has taken place in the past, and in a careful study of this history we may see more clearly the great theatre of events in which the Negro has played a part. We may understand better what his role has been and how well he has functioned in it.... How we have arrived at the present state of affairs can be understood only by studying the forces effective in the development of Negro education since it was systematically undertaken immediately after Emancipation. To point out merely the defects as they appear today will be of little benefit to the present and future generations. These things must be viewed in their historic setting. The conditions of today have been determined by what has taken place in the past, and in a careful study of this history we may see more clearly the great theatre of events in which the Negro has played a part. We may understand better what his role has been and how well he has functioned in it.... If you teach the Negro that he has accomplished as much good as any other race he will aspire to equality and justice without regard to race Such an effort would upset the program of the oppressor in Africa and America. Play up before the Negro, then, his crimes and shortcomings. Let him learn to admire the Hebrew, the Greek, the Latin and the Teuton. Lead the Negro to detest the man of African blood—to hate himself. The oppressor then may conquer exploit, oppress and even annihilate the Negro...With the truth hidden there will be little expression of thought to the contrary.... to handicap a student by teaching him that his black face is a curse and that his struggle to change his condition is hopeless is the worst sort of lynching. It kills one's aspirations and dooms him to vagabondage and crime. It is strange, then, that the friends of truth and the promoters of freedom have not risen up against the present propaganda in the schools and crushed it. This crusade is much more important than the anti-lynching movement, because there would be no lynching if it did not start in the schoolroom. Why not exploit, enslave, or exterminate a class that everybody is taught to regard as inferior?... In schools of theology Negroes are taught the interpretation of the Bible worked out by those who have justified segregation and winked at the economic debasement of the Negro sometimes almost to the point of starvation...In theology, literature, social science, and education, however, radical reconstruction is necessary. The old worn-out theories as to man's relation to God and his fellowman, the system of thought which has permitted one man to exploit, oppress, and exterminate another and still be regarded as righteous must be discarded for the new thought of men as brethren and the idea of God as the lover of all mankind...."

On the need for separate schools for Black children we cite W.E.B. Dubois who an article in 1935 entitled **"Does The Negro Need Separate Schools"** and noted:

"... race prejudice in the United States today is such that most Negroes cannot receive proper education in white institutions...... a separate Negro school where children are treated like human beings, trained by teachers of their own race, who know what it means to be black in the year of salvation 1935, is infinitely better than making our boys and girls doormats to be spit and trampled upon and lied to by ignorant social climbers, whose sole claim to superiority is ability to kick "niggers" when they are down. I say, too, that certain studies and discipline necessary to Negroes can seldom be found in white schools. To sum up this: theoretically, the Negro needs neither segregated schools nor mixed schools. What he needs is Education. What he must remember is that there is no magic, either in mixed schools or in segregated schools. A mixed school with poor and unsympathetic teachers, with hostile public opinion, and no teaching of truth concerning black folk, is bad. A segregated school with ignorant placeholders, inadequate equipment, poor salaries, and wretched housing, is equally bad."

Rachel Higson's May 2, 2016 article entitled **"Removing Slavery From Textbooks' states:**

"In McGraw-Hill's "World Geography" textbook, a caption, overlapping a map of the United States, points generally to South Carolina and reads: "The Atlantic Slave Trade between the 1500s and 1800s brought millions of workers from Africa to the southern United States to work on agricultural plantations." The page is titled: "Patterns of Immigration." There is no mention of the violent removal of Africans from their homes and families. The caption uses the verb "brought," a euphemism that atrociously misrepresents the inhumane and deadly transportation of Africans across the Atlantic. The caption does not even present the existence of slave owners or traders...It converts slavery's malicious pillage, cruel exploitation, and inhumane treatment of Africans into an opportunity for employment on plantations. This gross misrepresentation is followed by a passage on the next page, which validates the struggle of white indentured servants: "'an influx of English and other European peoples, many of whom came as indentured servants to work for little or no pay,' but made no mention of how Africans came to the country."

Higson's article helps us to see that a new and current trend inside of public schools is the robbing of students of developing any healthy sympathy and respect for the suffering endured by Black people in America that is the result of our enslavement and subjection to subsequent systems of oppression. This denial of compassion and sympathy for the Black people of America is the ultimate aim of removing slavery from textbooks. For at the same time Black and White children are being denied an opportunity to learn of what many historians have dubbed as the "Black Holocaust," there is ample space provided within K-12 curriculums to expose children to the "Jewish Holocaust."

**Support From The Holy Qur'an**-Surah 2:255- Allah — there is no god but He, the Ever-living, the Self-subsisting by Whom all subsist. Slumber overtakes Him not, nor sleep. To Him belongs whatever is in the heavens and whatever is in the earth. Who is he that can intercede with Him but by His permission? He knows what is before them and what is behind them. And they encompass nothing of His knowledge except what He pleases. His knowledge extends over the heavens and the earth, and the preservation of them both tires Him not. And He is the Most High, the Great.

Surah 3: 36 - And when she brought it forth, she said: My Lord, I have brought it forth a female — and Allah knew best what she brought forth — and the male is not like the female, and I have named it Mary, and I commend her and her offspring into Thy protection from the accursed devil.

Surah 3:79 - It is not meet for a mortal that Allah should give him the Book and the judgement and the prophethood, then he should say to men: Be my servants besides Allah's; but (he would say): Be worshippers of the Lord because you teach the Book and because you study (it);

Surah 7:169 - Then after them came an evil posterity who inherited the Book, taking the trail goods of this low life and saying: It will be forgiven us. And if the like good came to them, they would take it (too). Was not a promise taken from them in the Book that they would not speak anything about Allah but the truth? And they study what is in it. And the abode of the Hereafter is better for those who keep their duty. Do you not then understand?

Surah 20:52 - He said: The knowledge thereof is with my Lord in a book; my Lord neither errs nor forgets —

Surah 96: 1-5: Read in the name of thy Lord who creates — Creates man from a clot, Read and thy Lord is most Generous, Who taught by the pen, Taught man what he knew not.

**Support From The Bible-** "Train up a child in the way he should go; even when he is old he will not depart from it."-Proverbs 22:6

"You shall teach them to your children, talking of them when you are sitting in your house, and when you are walking by the way, and when you lie down, and when you rise." -Deuteronomy 12:19

"The fear of the Lord is the beginning of knowledge; fools despise wisdom and instruction."-Proverbs 1:7

---

# 10. We believe that intermarriage or race mixing should be prohibited. We want the religion Islam taught without hindrance or suppression.

---

**POINT NO. 10 Notes:** The Most Honorable Elijah Muhammad's call for the prohibition of race mixing is rooted within the strong support of scriptures found in the Bible and the Holy Qur'an (see below section of scriptures). However certain trends in demography add important support for his position in Point No. 10.

"For white civilization is today conterminous with the white race. . . . It will be swamped by the triumphant colored races, who will obliterate the white man by elimination or absorption. What has taken place in Central Asia, once a white and now a brown or yellow land, will take place in Australasia, Europe and America. Not today, not tomorrow; perhaps not for generations; but surely in the end. If the present drift be not changed, we whites are all ultimately doomed."
-T. Lothrop Stoddard, The Rising Tide of Color Against White World Supremacy

According to William A. Henry, III in an April 9, 1990 article inside Time Magazine entitled **"America's Changing Colors: What Will The U.S. Be Like When Whites Are No Longer The Majority"** we learn the following:

> "Someday soon, surely much sooner than most people who filled out their Census forms last week realize, white Americans will

become a minority group. Long before that day arrives, the presumption that the "typical" U.S. citizen is someone who traces his or her descent in a direct line to Europe will be part of the past."

In her timeless classic The Isis Papers written by Dr. Frances Cress Welsing, she introduces us to the concept of the "fear of white genetic annihilation." She states:

"The ultimate purpose of the system is to prevent white genetic annihilation on Earth-a planet in which the overwhelming majority of people are classified as non-white (black, brown, red and yellow) by white-skinned people. All of the non-white people are genetically dominant (in terms of skin coloration) compared to the genetically recessive white skinned people."

The strategic use of race mixing by the white power structure is a worthy study, particularly as it is juxtaposed against certain movements within that structure that stand against it. And despite which side of the race-mixing question any section of the white power structure is on, both views emerge out of a "fear of white genetic annihilation" that emerges from their study of the census data and other scientific studies. For further study one might consider the following books on this subject: "The Fall of The West, by Patrick Buchanan; The Rise and Fall of The Caucasian Race: A Political History by Bruce Baum; The Rising Tide of Color Against White World Supremacy by T. Lothrop Stoddard; and The End of White Christian America by Robert P. Jones

**Support From The Holy Qur'an**-Surah 4:1 - O people, keep your duty to your Lord, Who created you from a single being and created its mate of the same (kind), and spread from these two many men and women. And keep your duty to Allah, by Whom you demand one of another (your rights), and (to) the ties of relationship. Surely Allah is ever a Watcher over you.

Surah 5:57 – O you who believe, take not for friends those who take your religion as a mockery and a sport, from among those who were given the Book before you and the disbelievers; and keep your duty to Allah if you are believers.

Surah 24:3 The adulterer cannot have sexual relations with any but an adulteress or an idolatress, and the adulteress, none can have sexual relations with her but an adulterer or an idolater; and it is forbidden to believers.

Surah 49:13 - O mankind, surely We have created you from a male and a female, and made you tribes and families that you may know each other. Surely the noblest of you with Allah is the most dutiful of you. Surely Allah is Knowing, Aware.

Surah 60: 1 – O you who believe, take not My enemy and your enemy for friends. Would you offer them love, while they deny the Truth that has come to you, driving out the Messenger and yourselves because you believe in Allah, your Lord? If you have come forth to strive in My way and to seek My pleasure, would you love them in secret? And I know what you conceal and what you manifest. And whoever of you does this, he indeed strays from the straight path.

**Support From The Bible-** "Furthermore, you shall not intermarry with them; you shall not give your daughters to their sons, nor shall you take their daughters for your sons."-Deuteronomy 7:3

"So, Isaac called Jacob and blessed him and charged him, and said to him, "You shall not take a wife from the daughters of Canaan." -Genesis 28:1

"Shall we again break Your commandments and intermarry with the peoples who commit these abominations? Would You not be angry with us to the point of destruction, until there is no remnant nor any who escape?" -Ezra 9:14

"Do not be bound together with unbelievers; for what partnership have righteousness and lawlessness, or what fellowship has light with darkness?"-2Corinthians 6:14

# What The Muslims Believe

## 1. We believe in the One God Whose proper name is Allah.

**POINT NO.1 NOTES:** According to Biblical Scholar Lambert Dolphin:

> "EL: God ("mighty, strong, prominent") used 250 times in the OT. See Genesis 7:1, 28:3, 35:11; Numbers 23:22; Joshua 3:10; 2 Samuel 22:31, 32; Nehemiah 1:5, 9:32; Isaiah. 9:6; Ezekiel 10:5. El is linguistically equivalent to the Moslem "Allah,"

According to legendary Islamic defender Sheikh Ahmed Deedat of South Africa, who wrote the book **"What Is His Name",** the following is true of the name of Allah inside the Biblical text:

> "Please see page 28 of the book "What Is His Name". It is a photostatic reproduction of a page from the English Bible, edited by Rev. C. I. Scofield, D.D., with his Bible Commentary. This Doctor of Divinity is well respected among the Bible Scholars of the Christian world. He is backed in his "NEW AND IMPROVED EDITION" of this translation by a galaxy of eight other D.D.'s:
>
> Rev. Henry G. Weston, D.D., LL.D., President Crozer Theological Seminary.
> Rev. W. G. Moorehead, D.D., President Xenia (U.I.) Theological Seminary.
> Rev. James M. Gray, D.D., President Moody Bible Institute.
> Rev. Elmore Harris, D.D., President Toronto Bible Institute.
> Rev. William J. Erdman, D.D., Author "The Gospel of John," etc.
> Rev. Arthur T. Pierson, D.D., Author, Editor, Teacher, etc.
> Rev. William L. Pettingill, D.D., Author, Editor, Teacher.
> Arno C. Gaebelein, Author "Harmoney of Prophetic Word," etc.
>
> I have not listed the above luminaries to awe you. They have been unanimous in supporting Rev. Scofield in his "New and improved" commentary. Please note that in their comment No. 1 on page 28, they concur that - "Elohim, (sometimes El or Elah meaning

God)" and alternatively spelled "Alah" (line three, third word). All the eight D.D.'s above could not have been blind in dittoing the spelling "Alah" for God. How far were they from the Arabic word spelled - ALLAH - in English, I ask you dear reader? This is Allah's handiwork..."

According to the Encyclopedia Britannica's entry for the word **Allah**, it states:

"Allah, the one and only God in Islam. Etymologically, the name Allah is probably a contraction of the Arabic al-Ilāh, "the God." The name's origin can be traced to the earliest Semitic writings in which the word for god was il, el, or eloah, the latter two used in the Hebrew Bible (Old Testament). Allah is the standard Arabic word for God and is used by Arabic-speaking Christians and Jews as well as by Muslims."

**Support From The Holy Qur'an**-Surah 2:163 - And your God is one God; there is no God but He! He is the Beneficent, the Merciful.

Surah 16:51-Allah has commanded: "Do not take two gods; or He is but One God. So, fear Me alone.

Surah 17: 110 - Say: Call on Allah or call on the Beneficent. By whatever (name) you call on Him, He has the best names. And utter not thy prayer loudly nor be silent in it, and seek a way between these.

Surah 41:6 - Say, ʿO Prophet,ʾ "I am only a man like you, ʾbutʾ it has been revealed to me that your God is only One God. So, take the Straight Way towards Him, and seek His forgiveness. And woe to the polytheists

Surah 112 "Say He Allah is One. Allah is He on Whom all depend. He begets not, nor is He begotten. And none is like Him.

**Support From The Bible**- "One Lord, one faith, one baptism,"

-Ephesians 4:5

"Hear, O Israel: The Lord our God, the Lord is one."

-Deuteronomy 6:4

"Jesus answered, "The most important is, 'Hear, O Israel: The Lord our God, the Lord is one.'"-Mark 12:29

""Right, Teacher," the scribe replied. "You have stated correctly that God is One and there is no other but Him, and to love Him with all your heart and with all your understanding and with all your strength, and to love your neighbor as yourself, which is more important than all burnt offerings and sacrifices."

-Mark 12:32

"In the beginning God created the heavens and the earth."

-Genesis 1:1

Footnote: Elohim (sometimes "El" or "Elah"), English form "God," the first of the three primary names of Deity, is a uni-plural noun formed from "El" =strength, or the strong one, and "Alah", to swear, to bind oneself by an oath, so implying faithfulness. (1st Scofield Study Bible)

---

# 2. We believe in the Holy Quran and the Scriptures of all the Prophets of God.

---

**POINT NO. 2 NOTES:** According to religious scholar Bart D. Ehrman in his article, **"Is the Qur'an More Reliable than the New Testament?"** we learn:

> "The question is whether it simply isn't true that the Qur'an is more reliable than the New Testament. What the questioner almost always means by that is that the ancient manuscripts of the Qur'an tend to be amazingly similar to one another. Virtually identical up and down the line. Scribes kept it the way it was, without changing it. That's in contrast to the New Testament, where scribes changed it all the time, often in insignificant ways and sometimes in rather startling large ways, either by accident or on purpose..."

According to Dr. Maurice Bucaille, in his book **THE QUR'AN AND MODERN SCIENCE**, he states:

"A totally objective examination of it [the Qur'an] in the light of modern knowledge, leads us to recognize the agreement between the two, as has been already noted on repeated occasions. It makes us deem it quite unthinkable for a man of Muhammad's time to have been the author of such statements on account of the state of knowledge in his day. Such considerations are part of what gives the Qur'anic Revelation its unique place, and forces the impartial scientist to admit his inability to provide an explanation which calls solely upon materialistic reasoning."

According to great Black History scholar Edward Wilmot Blyden in his excellent book "Christianity, Islam and The Negro Race", the Holy Qur'an's beneficial impact on the Black man and woman can be seen by considering the role it plays within the lives of Africans. He notes:

"The Koran is almost always in their hand. It Seems to be their labour and their relaxation to pore over its pages. They love to read and recite it aloud for hours together. They seem to possess an enthusiastic appreciation of the rhythmical harmony in which it is written. But we cannot attribute its power over them altogether to the jingling sounds, word-plays, and refrains in which it abounds. These, it is true, please the ear and amuse the fancy, especially of the uncultivated. But there is something higher, of which these rhyming lines are the vehicle; something possessing a deeper power to rouse the imagination, mould the feelings, and generate action."

**Support From The Holy Qur'an**-Surah 2: 2 - This Book, there is no doubt in it, is a guide to those who keep their duty.

Surah 6: 82 And this is a Blessed Book We have revealed, verifying that which is before it, and that thou mayest warn the mother of the towns and those around her. And those who believe in the Hereafter believe in it, and they keep a watch over their prayers.

Surah 6: 155 - And this is a Book We have revealed, full of blessings; so, follow it and keep your duty that mercy may be shown to you.

Surah 13:1 And this is a Book We have revealed, full of blessings; so, follow it and keep your duty that mercy may be shown to you.

Surah 18:1 Praise be to Allah! Who revealed the Book to His servant, and allowed not therein any crookedness.

Surah 2: 136 - Say: We believe in Allah and (in) that which has been revealed to us, and (in) that which was revealed to Abraham, and Ishmael and Isaac and Jacob and the tribes, and (in) that which was given to Moses and Jesus, and (in) that which was given to the prophets from their Lord, we do not make any distinction between any of them and to Him do we submit

Surah 3:84- Say: We believe in Allah and that which is revealed to us, and that which was revealed to Abraham and Ishmael and Isaac and Jacob and the tribes, and that which was given to Moses and Jesus and to the prophets from their Lord; we make no distinction between any of them, and to Him we submit.

Surah 4: 150 - Those who disbelieve in Allah and His messengers and desire to make a distinction between Allah and His messengers and say: We believe in some and disbelieve in others; and desire to take a course in between--

Surah 4: 152 - And those who believe in Allah and His messengers and make no distinction between any of them, to them He will grant their rewards. And Allah is ever Forgiving, Merciful

Surah 29: 47 - And thus have We revealed the Book to thee. So those whom We have given the Book believe in it, and of these there are those who believe in it; and none deny Our messages except the disbelievers.


**Support From The Bible-** "All Scripture is inspired by God and is useful to teach us what is true and to make us realize what is wrong in our lives. It corrects us when we are wrong and teaches us to do what is right." -Timothy 3:16-17

"But he answered, "It is written, ""Man shall not live by bread alone, but by every word that comes from the mouth of God.""

-Matthew 4:4

"For the word of God is living and active, sharper than any two-edged sword, piercing to the division of soul and of spirit, of joints and of marrow, and discerning the thoughts and intentions of the heart."-Hebrews 4:12

# 3. We believe in the truth of the Bible, but we believe that it has been tampered with and must be reinterpreted so that mankind will not be snared by the falsehoods that have been added to it.

**POINT NO. 3 NOTES:** According to Biblical scholar Patricia Eddy in her excellent book **"Who Tampered With The Bible"**, the following is a part of the history of the Bible:

> "Most people realize that the NT reports about the words of Jesus were written by human beings attempting to capture the life and teachings of Jesus many years after his death. They also realize that in the process of hand recording and copying many scribal and translational errors were introduced. What is not generally understood, however, is that individual evangelists and sects actually altered the words and actions of Jesus to suit their own purposes."

According to History.com's article entitled "Why Bibles Given to Slaves Omitted Most of the Old Testament", tampering with the Bible was done in the history of Black suffering in the Western Hemisphere by slave masters and those who had a vested interest in the institution of chattel slavery and it being allowed to continue uninterrupted. The "Slave Bible" was found in 2018 as a "Bible mod" used by plantation owners to keep slaves docile and in a non-threatening subservient role. The History.com article states:

> "When slavery was legal, its proponents often justified it with the Bible; specifically, a verse that tells servants to obey their masters. The Slave Bible was actually titled Parts of the Holy Bible, selected for the use of the Negro Slaves, in the British West-India Islands. The first Slave Bible was published in 1807, three years after the Haitian Revolution ended. That revolution was the only slave revolt in history in which enslaved people successfully drove out their

European oppressors to formed a new nation, and it increased American and European paranoia that the people they oppressed would one day rise up against them. The Haitian Revolution could have been a motivation for publishing a Bible without the part where Moses tells the Pharoah to "Let my people go." Missionaries and planters may have thought that Christianity—at least, certain parts of it—would protect against revolutions by teaching enslaved people to respect their masters.

The Times of Israel's Ben Zehavi's article entitled, "19th-cent. Slave Bible that removed Exodus story to repress hope goes on display; Censored texts were used by missionaries in the Caribbean colonies to emotionally manipulate the forced laborers who built the British Empire" states:

"Missionaries were exhorted by farmers in the British West Indies (modern-day Jamaica, Barbados, and Antigua) to steer clear of any text with revolutionary implications. At stake was Britain's massive overseas empire, powered by millions of enslaved Africans forced to work on sugar plantations. In the Book of Revelation, for example, it's a story about the Overcomer," Pollinger said. "You have vivid language about God's presence coming to dwell again with his people and the end of darkness, the end of pain, and many of these different longings and hopes of what this prophetic restoration looks like. Dr. Seth Pollinger, curatorial director, Museum of the Bible, added, "A volume like this would have been used for manipulative and oppressive purposes,"

**Support From The Holy Qur'an**-Surah 5:46 - And We sent after them in their footsteps Jesus, son of Mary, verifying that which was before him of the Torah; and We gave him the Gospel containing guidance and light, and verifying that which was before it of the Torah, and a guidance and an admonition for the dutiful

Surah 5: 47 - And let the People of the Gospel judge by that which Allah has revealed in it. And whoever judges not by what Allah has revealed, those are the transgressors.

Surah 5: 66 - And if they had observed the Torah and the Gospel and that which is revealed to them from their Lord, they would certainly have eaten from above them and from beneath their feet. There is a party of them keeping to the moderate course, and most of them — evil is that which they do.

Surah 5: 68 - Say: O People of the Book, you follow no good till you observe the Torah and the Gospel and that which is revealed to you from your Lord. And surely that which has been revealed to thee from thy Lord will make many of them increase in inordinacy and disbelief: so, grieve not for the disbelieving people.

**Support From The Bible**- "And if any man shall take away from the words of the book of this prophecy, God shall take away his part out of the book of life, and out of the holy city, and from the things which are written in this book."-Revelations 22:18-19

"Every word of God proves true; he is a shield to those who take refuge in him. Do not add to his words, lest he rebuke you and you be found a liar."-Proverbs 30:5-6

"You shall not add to the word that I command you, nor take from it, that you may keep the commandments of the Lord your God that I command you."-Deuteronomy 4:2

---

# 4. We believe in Allah's Prophets and the Scriptures they brought to the people.

---

**POINT NO. 4 NOTES:** All of the prophets and sages who brought spiritual wisdom to the human family of the Earth are united in terms of the broad-based universal aspects of their teachings. Without a doubt, they each brought a specific message to their respective peoples and communities to address the moral, behavioral and spiritual ills of their day and time. However, they each taught principles and provided spiritual guidance that is good and applicable to people in every community and all times. The best example of the unity of the prophets can be seen in what is commonly referred to as the Golden Rule. A version of the Golden Rule is found in all of the great faith traditions as they are found all over the Earth. Consider the presentation of the Golden

Rule in world sacred traditions as printed in the book **"World Scripture: A Comparative Anthology of Sacred Texts"**:

**"Baha'ì:** "Blessed is who prefers his brother to himself" (Bahà'u'llàh tablets – 19th century).

**Buddhism**: "Whatever is disagreeable to yourself, do not do unto others" (The Buddha, Udana-Varga 5.18 – 6th century BC).

**Confucianism**: "Do not do to others what you do not want them to do to you" (Confucius, Analects 15.23 – 5th century BC).

**Christianity**: "You shall love your neighbour as yourself. On these two commandments depend all the Law and the Prophets." (Gospel of Matthew 22, 36-40 – 1st century CE).

**Judaism:** "What is hateful to you, do not do to your fellow-man. This is the entire Law, all the rest is commentary" (Talmud, Shabbat 3id – 16th century BC).

**Gandhi:** "To see the universal and all-pervading Spirit of Truth face to face, one must be able to love the meanest of all creation as oneself" (translated from: Il mio credo, il mio pensiero, Newton Compton, Rome 1992, page 70 – 20th century).

**Jainism:** "In happiness and sorrow, in joy and in pain, we should consider every creature as we consider ourselves" (Mahavira, 24th Tirthankara – 6th century BC).

**Judaism:** "Never do to anyone else anything that you would not want someone to do to you" (Tobias 4, 15 – 3rd century BC).

**Hinduism:** "This is the sum of duty. Do not unto others that which would cause you pain if done to you" (Mahabharata 5, 1517 – 15th century BC).

**Islam**: "None of you will believe until you love for your brother what you love for yourself" (Hadith 13, The Forty Hadith of Imam Nawawi – 7th century).

**Native Americans**: "Respect for every form of life is the foundation" (The Big Law of Peace– 16th century).

**Plato:** "I can do to others what I'd like them to do to me" (5th century BC).

**Yoruba wise saying (West Africa):** "If somebody stings a bird with a sharp stick, should be first try it on himself and realize how badly it hurts".

**Seneca:** "Treat your inferiors as you would be treated by your betters" (Letter 47 11 – 1st century).

**Shintoism:** "Be charitable to all beings, love is the representation of God" (approximately 500 CE: Ko-ji-ki Hachiman Kasuga – 8th century BC)

**Sikhism:** "I am a stranger to no one, and no one is a stranger to me. Indeed, I am a friend to all" (Guru Granth Sahib, religious scripture of Sikhism, p. 1299 – 15th century).

**Voltaire:** "Put yourself in the other person's shoes" (Letters on the English, n.42).

**Zoroastrianism**: "Do not do to others what is harmful for yourself" (Shayast-na-Shayast 13, 29 – between 18 and 15 century BC)."

**Support From The Holy Qur'an**-Surah 2:285 - The Messenger believes in what has been revealed to him from his Lord, and (so do) the believers. They all believe in Allah and His angels and His Books and His messengers. We make no difference between any of His messengers. And they say: We hear and obey; our Lord, Thy forgiveness (do we crave), and to Thee is the eventual course.

Surah 5: 15 - O People of the Book, indeed Our Messenger has come to you, making clear to you much of that which you concealed of the Book and passing over much. Indeed, there has come to you from Allah, a Light, and a clear Book.

**Support From The Bible-** "Your word is a lamp to my feet and a light to my path."-Psalms 19:105

"For the Lord God does nothing without revealing his secret to his servants the prophets."-Amos 3:7

"Do not think that I have come to abolish the Law or the Prophets. I have not come to abolish them, but to fulfill them."

-Matthew 5:17

"However, I admit that I worship the God of our ancestors as a follower of the Way, which they call a sect. I believe everything that is in accordance with the Law and that is written in the Prophets," -Acts 24:14

5. We believe in the resurrection of the dead -- not in physical resurrection but mental resurrection. We believe that the so-called Negroes are most in need of mental resurrection; therefore, they will be resurrected first.  Furthermore, we believe we are the people of God's choice as it has been written that God would choose the rejected and the despised. We can find no other persons fitting this description in these last days more than the so-called Negroes in America. We believe in the resurrection of the righteous.

**POINT NO. 5 NOTES:** The word Negro derives from the Latin Necro which means "dead".  The resurrection of the Negro being done by the Most Hon. Elijah Muhammad and the Hon. Min. Louis Farrakhan is the resurrection of the "mentally dead."  The American white man labeled the Black man of America, during the years of chattel slavery, as 3/5ths of a human.  In practical terms, this insulting and pejorative designation appears to reflect the wretched state and condition that the "peculiar institution" of American chattel slavery produced within the Black man and woman who were subjected to its evil.

The Most Hon. Elijah Muhammad stipulates that the true spiritual identity of the Black man and woman of America is the "chosen people of God", or as they are also dubbed in the Biblical texts "the Children of Israel."

Some important points that draw relevant parallels between the Biblical description of the Children of Israel and the history of Black people in America are as follows:

## Children of Israel in Bondage for 400 years:(Acts 7:6-7; Genesis 15:13-15)

"The Hon. Elijah Muhammad teaches that the most popular English slaver John Hawkins began bringing Africans as slaves to the Americas also in the year 1555. To date we are 461 years in bondage. "The transatlantic slave trade was, in many ways, still in its infancy during the 16th century, but thousands of captive Africans were already being loaded onto European ships and transported across the sea to Spanish America and Brazil every, year, especially after 1560. In this vein, an expedition under the command of John Lok reportedly returned to England with "certayne blacke slaves" in 1555." (Slaves and Englishmen: Human Bondage in the Early Modern Atlantic World by Michael Guasco p. 67")

## Children of Israel names were changed while in bondage (Daniel 1:7)

"We came to America with African and Islamic names, but our slave masters changed our names and gave us their names to identify us as their chattel property. "The slaves had been stripped of their status, their names, their families and friends, and their customs and culture. They were surrounded by fear, distrust, and sometimes hatred. No wonder it was commonplace for newly arrived slaves to try to run away or sink into a deep, sometimes suicidal depression. They stood naked to misery, not knowing what would happen to them." (Slavery In America by Dorothy and Carl Schneider p. 78)"

## Children of Israel oppressed through special laws and statutes (Psalms 94:20; James 5:6)

"Special laws known as the Slave Codes were written and executed to deprive Blacks in America of the right to read, marry, own property, testify in court, vote in elections, practice our native religion and constitute families. "Surely never before has mischief been framed by law with more diabolical ingenuity than in this infernal code. Your analysis of the slave laws is very able, and your exhibition of their practical application by the Southern Courts, evinces great and careful research." (Judge William Jay to Author William Goodell of the American Slave Code p.9)"

## Children of Israel corrupted and "robbed and spoiled" (Exodus 1:10; Isaiah 42:22; Daniel 5:2)

"Children of Israel corrupted and "robbed and spoiled" (Exodus 1:10; Isaiah 42:22; Daniel 5:2): Because of our strong birth rate, that far exceeds our slave masters and their children, Blacks have been poisoned, sterilized, aborted in the wombs of our mothers, infected with diseases, miseducated and blocked from all paths to freedom and independence. "Employers in the South had made a practice of supplying their black workers with cocaine (Grinspoon and Bakalar 1985:39). According to Ashley (1976:81), plantation owners had "discovered things went better with coke." Thus, they kept a steady supply on hand to increase productivity and keep workers content. Cocaine was also a cheap incentive to maintain control of workers. "A shrewd boss doling out one-quarter gram a day per man could keep sixteen workers happy and more productive for a full seven days on a single ounce" ("Coca and Cocaine in the United States" by Richard Harvey Brown, pg.1)"

**Support From The Holy Qur'an**-Surah 2:85 - Yet you it is who would slay your people and turn a party from among you out of their homes, backing each other up against them unlawfully and exceeding the limits. And if they should come to you as captives you would ransom them, whereas their turning out itself was unlawful for you. Do you then believe in a part of the Book and disbelieve in the other? What then is the reward of such among you as do this but disgrace in the life of this world, and on the day of Resurrection they shall be sent back to the most grievous chastisement. And Allah is not heedless of what you do.

Surah 2:113 - And the Jews say, The Christians follow nothing (good), and the Christians say, The Jews following nothing (good), while they recite the (same) Book. Even thus say those who have no knowledge, like what they say. So, Allah will judge between them on the day of Resurrection in that wherein they differ.

Surah 3:27 - Thou makest the night to pass into the day and Thou makest the day to pass into the night; and Thou bringest forth the living from the dead and Thou bringest forth the dead from the living; and Thou givest sustenance to whom Thou pleasest without measure.

Surah 22:5 - O people, if you are in doubt about the Resurrection, then surely, We created you from dust, then from a small life-germ, then from a clot, then from a lump of flesh, complete in make and incomplete, that We may make clear to you. And We cause what We please to remain in the wombs till an appointed time, then We bring you forth as babies, then that you may attain your maturity. And of you is he who is caused to die, and of you is he who is brought back to the worst part of life, so that after knowledge he knows nothing. And thou seest the earth barren, but when We send down thereon water, it stirs and swells and brings forth a beautiful (growth) of every kind.

Surah 22: 6 - That is because Allah, He is the Truth, and He gives life to the dead, and He is Possessor of power over all things

Surah 22:7 And the Hour is coming, there is no doubt about it, and Allah will raise up those who are in the graves.

Surah 36: 51 - And the trumpet is blown, when lo! from their graves they will hasten on to their Lord.

Surah 70: 43 - The day when they come forth from the graves in haste, as hastening on to a goal

**Support From The Bible-** "And many of those who sleep in the dust of the earth shall awake, some to everlasting life, and some to shame and everlasting contempt."-Daniel 12:2

"Therefore, let us move beyond the elementary teachings about Christ and be taken forward to maturity, not laying again the foundation of repentance from acts that lead to death, a and of faith in God, 2instruction about cleansing rites, b the laying on of hands, the resurrection of the dead, and eternal judgment. 3And God permitting, we will do so." -Hebrews 6:1-2

"Your dead shall live; their bodies shall rise. You who dwell in the dust, awake and sing for joy! For your dew is a dew of light, and the earth will give birth to the dead." -Isaiah 26:19

"Do not be amazed at this, for a time is coming when all who are in their graves will hear his voice and come out—those who have done what is good will rise to live, and those who have done what is evil will rise to be condemned." -John 5:29

"But he answered and said, I am not sent but unto the lost sheep of the house of Israel."-Matthew 15:24

"These twelve, Jesus sent forth, having instructed them, saying: "Do not go into the way of the Gentiles and do not enter into any city of the Samaritans. But go rather to those being the lost sheep of the house of Israel. And going on, proclaim, saying, 'The kingdom of the heavens has drawn near!' Heal the ailing, raise the dead, cleanse the lepers, a cast out demons! Freely you received; freely give."-Matthew 10:5-6

"The hand of the LORD was upon me, and He brought me out by His Spirit and set me down in the middle of the valley, and it was full of bones. He led me all around among them, and I saw a great many bones on the floor of the valley, and indeed, they were very dry. Then He asked me, "Son of man, can these bones come to life?" "O Lord GOD," I replied, "only You know." And He said to me, "Prophesy concerning these bones and tell them, 'Dry bones, hear the word of the LORD! 5This is what the Lord GOD says to these bones: I will cause breath to enter you, and you will come to life. 6I will attach tendons to you and make flesh grow upon you and cover you with skin. I will put breath within you so that you will come to life. Then you will know that I am the LORD.'"So I prophesied as I had been commanded. And as I prophesied, there was suddenly a noise, a rattling, and the bones came together, bone to bone. 8As I looked on, tendons appeared on them, flesh grew, and skin covered them; but there was no breath in them. Then He said to me, "Prophesy to the breath; prophesy, son of man, and tell the breath that this is what the Lord GOD says: Come from the four winds, O breath, and breathe into these slain, so that they may live!" So, I prophesied as He had commanded me, and the breath entered them, and they came to life and stood on their feet—a vast army. Then He said to me, "Son of man, these bones are the whole house of Israel. Look, they are saying, 'Our bones are dried up, and our hope has perished; we are cut off.' Therefore, prophesy and tell them that this is what the Lord GOD says: 'O My people, I will open your graves and bring you up from them, and I will bring you back to the land of Israel. 13Then you, My people, will know that I am the LORD, when I open your graves and bring you up from them. 14I will put My Spirit in you and you will live, and I will settle you in your own land. Then you will know that I, the LORD, have spoken, and I will do it, declares the LORD.'"-Ezekiel 37:1-12

# 6. We further believe in the judgment. We believe this first judgment will take place, as God revealed, in America.

**POINT NO. 6 NOTES:** That America is a powerful nation is without doubt. And that it is the beloved home of more than 300 million American citizens is also a reality. However, the idea being promoted by the Most Hon. Elijah Muhammad in Point No.6 shocks and stuns those who patriotism and love for America blinds them to the sins of America and just how far away from the standard of God, America has fallen.

In 1781 Thomas Jefferson wrote:

> "Indeed, I tremble for my country when I reflect that God is just: that his justice cannot sleep forever" ...

Ruth Graham, wife of America's legendary national evangelist Billy Graham read his book entitled **"World Aflame"** and exclaimed:

> "If God doesn't punish America, He'll have to apologize to Sodom and Gomorrah."

In **"The United States and Prophecy"** written by Edward Tracy, it states:

> "On what comfortable and convenient grounds can the U.S.A. claim immunity from divine judgement? "The nation that forgets God goes backward"-backward to defeat, backward to destruction. That we (U.S.A.) are going backward cannot be

denied? We are regressing spiritually, morally, legally, financially, governmentally, and that with alarming acceleration."

Famous Christian evangelist Herbert Armstrong wrote in his book, **"The United States and Britain in Prophecy":**

"Just as God has bestowed on us such material blessings as never before came to any nations, now to correct us so we may enjoy such blessings, He is going to bring upon our peoples such national disaster as has never before struck any nation! Many prophecies describe this!"

Rev. Dr. Martin L. King Jr., said in his **"Drum Major Instinct"** sermon, delivered on February 4, 1968:

"But God has a way of even putting nations in their place. The God that I worship has a way of saying, ... '[I]f you don't stop your reckless course, I'll rise up and break the backbone of your power.' And that can happen to America. Every now and then I go back and read Gibbons' Decline and Fall of the Roman Empire. And when I come and look at America, I say to myself, the parallels are frightening."

**Support From The Holy Qur'an**-Surah 6:62 - Then are they sent back to Allah, their Master, the True One. Now surely His is the judgment and He is Swiftest in taking account.

Surah 51: 6 - And the Judgment will surely come to pass

Surah 20:102- The day when the trumpet is blown; and We shall gather the guilty, blue-eyed, on that day,

Surah 22: 1-3 O people, keep your duty to your Lord; surely the shock of the Hour is a grievous thing. The day you see it, every woman giving suck will forget her suckling and every pregnant one will lay down her burden, and thou wilt see men as drunken, yet they will not be drunken, but the chastisement of Allah will be severe. And among men is he who disputes about Allah without knowledge, and follows every rebellious devil.

**Support From The Bible-** "After this I saw another angel descending from heaven with great authority, and the earth was illuminated by his glory. And he cried out in a mighty voice: "Fallen, fallen is Babylon the great! She has become a lair for demons and a haunt for every unclean spirit, every unclean bird, and every detestable beast. All the nations have drunk the wine of the passion of her immorality. The kings of the earth were immoral with her, and the merchants of the earth have grown wealthy from the extravagance of her luxury." Then I heard another voice from heaven say: "Come out of her, My people, so that you will not share in her sins or contract any of her plagues. For her sins are piled up to heaven, and God has remembered her iniquities. Give back to her as she has done to others; pay her back double for what she has done; mix her a double portion in her own cup. As much as she has glorified herself and lived in luxury, give her the same measure of torment and grief. In her heart she says, 'I sit as queen; I am not a widow and will never see grief.' Therefore, her plagues will come in one day—death and grief and famine—and she will be consumed by fire, for mighty is the Lord God who judges her."-Revelation 18:1-8

7. We believe this is the time in history for the separation of the so-called Negroes and the so-called white Americans. We believe the black man should be freed in name as well as in fact. By this, we mean that he should be freed from names imposed upon him by his former slave masters. Names which identified him as being the slave of the slave-master. We believe that if we are free indeed, we should go in our own people's names -- the black peoples of the earth.

**POINT NO. 7 NOTES:** Author Claire Suddath in her Time Magazine article written on February 21, 2011 about the peculiar continuation of Black people in America wearing the names of our former slave masters. Her article entitled **"How Did Washington Become The Blackest Name In America?"** states:

> "George Washington's name is inseparable from America, and not only from the nation's history. It identifies countless streets, buildings, mountains, bridges, monuments, cities — and people. In a puzzling twist, most of these people are black. The 2000 U.S. Census counted 163,036 people with the surname Washington. Ninety percent of them were African-American, a far higher black percentage than for any other common name."

On April 11, 1969 The Most Hon. Elijah Muhammad published an article inside the Muhammad Speaks newspaper entitled **"Why The Black Man Should Be Called By The Names Of God"**. In it he writes:

> "The Black man (so-called American Negro) is a member of the family and a direct descendant of the Creator Who made the Heavens and the Earth. Therefore, the son should be called by the Name of his Father and not called by the name of an alien.... It is only you, Black Brother, that by nature should be called by the Names of your God and Father, the Creator of the Heavens and the Earth."

**Support From The Holy Qur'an**-Surah 4: 75 - And what reason have you not to fight in the way of Allah, and of the weak among the men and the women and the children, who say: Our Lord, take us out of this town, whose people are oppressors, and grant us from Thee a friend, and grant us from Thee a helper!

Surah 7: 137 And We made the people who were deemed weak to inherit the eastern lands and the western ones which We had blessed. And the good word of thy Lord was fulfilled in the Children of Israel — because of their patience. And We destroyed what Pharaoh and his people had wrought and what they had built

Surah 7: 141 And when We delivered you from Pharaoh's people, who subjected you to severe torment, killing your sons and sparing your women. And therein was a great trial from your Lord

**Support From The Bible-** "And ye shall leave your name for a curse unto my chosen: for the Lord GOD shall slay thee, and call his servants by another name" — Isaiah 65:15

"The LORD will establish you as His holy people, just as He has sworn to you, if you keep the commandments of the LORD your God and walk in His ways. So, all the peoples of the earth will see that you are called by the name of the Lord, and they will be afraid of you."-Deuteronomy 28:9-10

"Then I looked, and behold, the Lamb was standing on Mount Zion, and with Him one hundred and forty-four thousand, having His name and the name of His Father written on their foreheads."

-Revelation 14:1

"Saying, Hurt not the earth, neither the sea, nor the trees, till we have sealed the servants of our God in their foreheads."- Rev. 7:3

---

8. We believe in justice for all whether in God or not. We believe as others that we are due equal justice as human beings. We believe in equality - as a nation -of equals. We do not believe that we are equal with our slave-masters in the status of Freed slaves. We recognize and respect American citizens as independent peoples, and we respect their laws which govern this nation.

---

**POINT NO. 8 NOTES:** The Honorable Minister Louis Farrakhan's excellent, and profound book, **A Torchlight For America** is a beautiful demonstration of the universality of the teachings of the Most Honorable Elijah Muhammad. In his powerful introduction we read the following:

"We believe that it is time for America to closely examine the Honorable Elijah Muhammad, his message and the people who have come to follow his teachings. As America prepares to make a change, she is seen searching for new solutions to her plethora of problems. Every aspect of American society is suffering. Her economy is faltering, her public schools are failing, maintaining the health of the American people has proven too costly, crime is rampant, her sense of morality seems to have been lost, and in general the whole future of the country has become a big question.

We would like to offer the words of the Honorable Elijah Muhammad, with ourselves as an example of what those words can produce, as a "torchlight" for America.

A torchlight is anything that serves to illuminate, enlighten or guide. It also means to love someone or something that does not necessarily reciprocate love. The bearer of the torchlight is a person who imparts knowledge, truth or inspiration to others.

This book is humbly submitted as a torchlight for guiding the country out from its present condition toward a more peaceful and productive society in which mutual respect governs the relations between the diverse members of America.

I hope that you receive this torchlight with open ears and an open heart, with the aim of discovering those truths that can lay the base for developing honest remedies for the condition of America."

**Support From The Holy Qur'an**-Surah 3: 108 - These are the messages of Allah which We recite to thee with truth. And Allah desires no injustice to (His) creatures.

Surah 4: 135 - O you who believe, be maintainers of justice, bearers of witness for Allah, even though it be against your own selves or (your) parents or near relatives — whether he be rich or poor, Allah has a better right over them both. So, follow not (your) low desires, lest you deviate. And if you distort or turn away from (truth), surely Allah is ever Aware of what you do.

Surah 5: 8 - O you who believe, be upright for Allah, bearers of witness with justice; and let not hatred of a people incite you not to act equitably. Be just; that is nearer to observance of duty. And keep your duty to Allah. Surely Allah is Aware of what you do.

Surah 16:90 - Surely Allah enjoins justice and the doing of good (to others) and the giving to the kindred, and He forbids indecency and evil and rebellion. He admonishes you that you may be mindful.

Surah 60: 8 - Allah forbids you not respecting those who fight you not for religion, nor drive you forth from your homes, that you show them kindness and deal with them justly. Surely Allah loves the doers of justice.

**Support From The Bible-** "So the last will be first, and the first will be last."-Matthew 20:16

"The LORD will make you the head and not the tail; you will only move upward and never downward, if you hear and carefully follow the commandments of the LORD your God, which I am giving you today."-Deuteronomy 28:13

"The stone which the builders refused is become the head stone of the corner. This is the LORD'S doing; it is marvelous in our eyes. This is the day which the LORD hath made; we will rejoice and be glad in it." -Psalms 118:22-24

---

9. We believe that the offer of integration is hypocritical and is made by those who are trying to deceive the black peoples into believing that their 400-year-old open enemies of freedom, justice, and equality are, all of a sudden, their friends. Furthermore, we believe that such deception is intended to prevent black people from realizing that the time in history has arrived for the separation from the whites of this nation. If the white people are truthful about their professed friendship toward the so-called Negro, they can prove it by dividing up America with their slaves. We do not believe that

America will ever be able to furnish enough jobs for her own millions of unemployed in addition to jobs for the 20,000,000-black people.

**POINT NO. 9 NOTES:** Tricks and deception have been the primary tools used to govern the "so-called Negroes" or Black people of America. The Most Honorable Elijah Muhammad in his various and illuminating writings and teachings discusses the use of "tricknology" by the white ruling class of America and the world. Consider the rise of the Civil Rights movement and its lack of a real "economic" thrust. Dr. Ridgely Abdul Mu'Min Muhammad discusses this in his insightful article entitled **"The NAACP and "Non-Economic Liberalism":**

"Non-economic liberalism" was the philosophy guiding the activities of the early NAACP (National Association for the Advancement of Colored People), which sought the social acceptance of Blacks instead of building our own business economy. The Honorable Elijah Muhammad warned Black people that Whites would never teach us "the science of business," so "noneconomic liberalism" was a philosophy developed by the longtime white Jewish president of the NAACP, Joel Spingarn, for Black people's social and political advancement without economic empowerment. This philosophy was in direct contrast to the economic and political empowerment goals of the Niagara Movement, which was supplanted by the NAACP. When historians write about the NAACP, they make you think that it was the direct outgrowth of the Niagara Movement, which was secretly started by 29 Black men, who stated in their 1905 Declaration of Principles that they "especially complain against the denial of equal opportunities to us in economic life; in the rural districts of the South this amounts to peonage and virtual slavery; all over the South it tends to crush labor and small business enterprises..." These Black men demonstrated that Black people in the South strove toward The Honorable Elijah Muhammad's brand of economic independence. In fact, by 1910 Black people had acquired over 16 million acres of land, mostly in the South, but Black landownership steadily declined after the advent of the NAACP, as this organization made the northern cities safer for Black people, thus facilitating the Great Migration(s) out of the South."

Author James Clingman writes in his **"A Case Against Non-Economic Liberalism"**:

> "A term made popular by the venerable Harold Cruse, noneconomic liberalism is a social strategy which focuses upon political empowerment without adequate attention to economic empowerment. The nascent NAACP, according to Dr. Khalid Tariq Al-Mansour, in his book, Betrayal by Any Other Name, wrote into its constitution a prohibition against owning land. Mansour goes on to describe a call by William English Walling, a white Southern journalist with liberal views on race, for the achievement of "absolute political and social equality" for Negroes. Sound familiar?
>
> Of course, we know the founding meeting of the NAACP was called by white citizens concerned about the so-called "Negro question," after the lynching of two Black men in Springfield, Illinois. No doubt some of them were sincere about wanting to help Black folks, just like some liberal whites today; but the lingering question then and now is, "How could (can) Black people be empowered politically and socially without being empowered economically?"
>
> The notion that Black people would achieve "equality" simply by participating in the political arena and through new social programming was, and still is, an absurdity that should have collapsed under its own weight decades ago. As Harold Cruse and others have pointed out many times, there is no power without economic power.
>
> Thus, for 100 years the NAACP has been self-constrained by an archaic, antiquated, outdated and, most of all, anti-empowering rule that keeps the largest Black organization landless. It's time to change our predicament."

According to ~ John Ehrlichman, Assistant to the President for Domestic Affairs under President Richard Nixon the "War on Drugs" was a ruse, an artifice of tricknology used to villainize Black people within the collective consciousness of the American people. He states:

"You want to know what this [war on drugs] was really all about? The Nixon campaign in 1968, and the Nixon White House after that, had two enemies: the antiwar left and black people. You understand what I'm saying? We knew we couldn't make it illegal to be either against the war or black, but by getting the public to associate the hippies with marijuana and blacks with heroin, and then criminalizing both heavily, we could disrupt those communities. We could arrest their leaders, raid their homes, break up their meetings, and vilify them night after night on the evening news. Did we know we were lying about the drugs? Of course, we did."

**Support From The Holy Qur'an**-Surah 4:120 - He promises them and excites vain desires in them. And the devil promises them only to deceive.

Surah 7:113-114 - And the enchanters came to Pharaoh, saying: We must surely have a reward if we prevail. He said: Yes, and you shall certainly be of those who are near (to me).

**Support From The Bible**-"Come, let us deal shrewdly with them, or they will increase even more; and if a war breaks out, they may join our enemies, fight against us, and leave the country."-Exodus 1:10

"They have taken crafty counsel against Your people, And consulted together against Your sheltered ones. They have said, "Come, and let us cut them off from being a nation, That the name of Israel may be remembered no more."-Psalms 83:3-4

"Then another king, who knew nothing of Joseph, arose over Egypt. He exploited our people and oppressed our fathers, forcing them to abandon their infants so they would die."-Acts 7:18-19

---

# 10. We believe that we who declared ourselves to be righteous Muslims should not participate in wars which take the lives of

humans. We do not believe this nation should force us to take part in such wars, for we have nothing to gain from it unless America agrees to give us the necessary territory wherein we may have something to fight for.

**POINT NO. 10 NOTES:** According to Gerald Horne's book **"Race War!: White Supremacy and the Japanese Attack on the British Empire"**, he states:

> "The U.S. government did not dismiss the efforts of black advocates of Tokyo as empty rhetoric. On the contrary, the government detained and placed many Negroes on trial in the fall of 1942 as Japan continued to rampage through Asia. Almost ninety were arrested, including Elijah Muhammad, leader of the group that was to become the Nation of Islam."

According to a June 8, 2016 Supreme Court Blog article entitled **"Muhammad Ali, conscientious objection, and the Supreme Court's struggle to understand "jihad" and "holy war": The story of Cassius Clay v. United States"** written by Marty Lederman we learn:

> "The Chief Justice assigned Justice Harlan to write the majority opinion, and one of Justice Harlan's law clerks began drafting it. Another of Harlan's clerks, Thomas Krattenmaker, who was himself busy at work on the majority opinion in another case involving draft protest was troubled by the Ali case, and he began to carefully review one of the canonical Nation of Islam texts that Ali had introduced as establishing the basis for his religious objection: Message to the Blackman in America, written by Elijah Muhammad, leader of the Nation of Islam. After reading Blackman and other Nation of Islam texts, Krattenmaker developed doubts about the nature of the so-called "holy war" in which Ali conceded he would be willing to participate.

Krattenmaker came to understand that the prospect of such a "holy war" was entirely abstract and hypothetical – contingent upon future events and a divine decree that were unlikely ever to occur. Ali's case thus appeared to be analogous to a 1955 case, Sicurella v. United States, involving a Jehovah's Witness, in which the government had introduced church texts depicting Witnesses as "extolling the ancient wars of the Israelites and ready to engage in a 'theocratic war' if Jehovah so commands them." "[G]ranting that the Jehovah's Witnesses will fight at Armageddon," the Court wrote in Sicurella, "we do not feel this is enough. . ... As to theocratic war, petitioner's willingness to fight on the orders of Jehovah is tempered by the fact that, so far as we know, their history records no such command since Biblical times and their theology does not appear to contemplate one in the future." Ali's willingness to fight in a war only if commanded to do so by God made his case analogous to Sicarella's, Krattenmaker reasoned: Ali was, as a practical matter, religiously opposed to fighting in any wars that might actually occur.

Krattenmaker conveyed his doubts about the proposed affirmance to his co-clerk, who agreed. The two of them then inveighed with Justice Harlan. Harlan was dubious at first, but agreed to read the pertinent excerpts from Message to the Blackman (or to listen to someone else read them, anyway: the Justice's eyesight was rapidly failing at the time). After doing so, Harlan concluded that Krattenmaker was right.

Harlan then began to draft an opinion that would result in reversal of Ali's conviction. ...Harlan's draft opinion included a fascinating, extended exegesis on the teachings of the Nation of Islam. According to those teachings, Harlan wrote, in the beginning all people were black, but the white race was later created at the instigation of an evil deity named Yakub, and was given 6000 years – a period that ended in 1914 – to rule the other races. The day of judgment of the ruling white race was expected to occur in the mid-1960s, and would consist of a battle of Armageddon, a physical war not between the races, but between Allah and the white race – a struggle in which Muslims would not participate physically – ending in Allah's destruction of the white race and the establishment of earthly paradise for Muslims.

"The Message teaches that Islam is the religion of peace," wrote Justice Harlan, "and that war-making is the habit of the race of devils created by Yakub."

But what about the Islamic notion of jihad, or "holy war"? Wouldn't Muslims within the Nation of Islam be willing to fight in such a battle?

To be sure, as Harlan acknowledged, Message to the Blackman in America did contain stray references to "Holy War." The text did not, however, offer much "substantive content with respect to Holy War," wrote Harlan; instead, it merely "reserve[d] the question of the appropriate course of conduct in the event divine marching orders are received."

**Support From The Holy Qur'an**-Surah 5:32 - For this reason, We prescribed for the Children of Israel that whoever kills a person, unless it be for manslaughter or for mischief in the land, it is as though he had killed all men. And whoever saves a life, it is as though he had saved the lives of all men. And certainly, Our messengers came to them with clear arguments, but even after that many of them commit excesses in the land.


**Support From The Bible**- "Blessed are the peacemakers: for they shall be called the children of God. Blessed are they which are persecuted for righteousness' sake: for theirs is the kingdom of heaven."-Matthew 5:9-10

"He will judge between the nations and will settle disputes for many peoples. They will beat their swords into plowshares and their spears into pruning hooks. Nation will not take up sword against nation, nor will they train for war anymore." -Isaiah 2:4

---

# 11. We believe our women should be respected and protected as the women of

# other nationalities are respected and protected.

**POINT NO. 11 NOTES:** According to the Most Hon. Elijah Muhammad in **"Instruction On The Law Of Women In Islam"**, he states:

> "The Following Are The Words of Allah ...The Dead Nation Must Rise for the time is at hand...Know that you are the Mother of Your Nation, and your Nation is no morally higher than you."

According to Author Bayyinah Jeffries in her book **"A Nation Can Rise No Higher Than Its Women"**:

> "On a national level, African American Muslim women in the original Nation of Islam participated in every stage of the community's development...women occupied roles like national directors of the University of Islam, deans, and supreme captains. Women also occupied local status positions like lieutenants, secretaries, and treasurers. As rank and file, women fundraised, took part in institution building, owned businesses, taught in Muslim school, directed girls' troops, and addressed their duties as wives and mothers."

Some of the history of the Nation of Islam's record of elevating women are excerpted here from our lecture entitled **"The Divine Rise Of Women"**:

> Brothers and Sisters, did you know...
> ...that the Great Mahdi, Master W. Fard Muhammad established a male free sanctuary for women called the Muslim Girls Training and General Civilization Class. No men are allowed in this class where women are trained along a curriculum of 7 core training units of righteous womanhood.
> ...that the first fight for our right to the freedom of our religion centered around the educational needs of a young girl named Sally Allah. This history signaled that the Nation of Islam would be willing to challenge any and all forces who interfered with the education of our children and the elevation of our women.

...that the Hon. Min. Louis Farrakhan chose to name the headquarters mosque of the Nation of Islam after a woman; Maryam or Mary the Mother of Jesus

...that Minister Farrakhan chose a woman; Student Minister Ava Muhammad to be his National Spokesperson and once appointed her as the Regional Minister in charge of a 5 state geographic region of mosques and study groups

...the leadership structure of the Muhammad's Mosques in the Nation of Islam is the most egalitarian in the world of religion. Of the 5 top leadership positions only 1 position -the Captain of the Fruit of Islam-has to be a male. All other positions, the mosque Minister, the secretary, the MGT Captain and the protocol Officer can be male or female.

...that during World War II the U.S. government arrested most of the male members of the Nation of Islam and put them into prison. During this time the Most Hon. Elijah Muhammad entrusted the Nation to his wife Mother Clara Muhammad and the women of the Nation.

The Hon. Min. Louis Farrakhan stated the following during his historic "**POWER At Last Forever**" message in Madison Square Garden in October of 1985:

"Now if you notice I have around me tonight sisters. I want to send a message to the entire world that the world is in the condition that it's in because the world disrespects women. The world is headed into hell because the world disrespects womanhood. Prophet Muhammad (PBUH) was the major contributor to the freeing of women. Unfortunately, traditions that are foreign to Islam have crept into Islam to push the woman out of that which almighty God intends for her. The oppression of Women in the world is a manifestation of the weakness of the societies of the earth. The HEM taught us that Allah is self-created. The Qur'an says he begets not nor was he begotten. Well if he was not begotten he's self-created. And if he's self-created and created himself out of the black womb of the darkness of space. Think about this now. He has so much respect for that womb, he kept going back into it creating sun and moon and stars and planets. Whenever a people disrespect the womb, they cut off their creative powers. When you disrespect woman, you disrespect that which absolutely shows you a part of the nature of God himself. This is why the oft repeated words of the Qur'an, Bismillah Ir-Rahman Ir-Rahim, you have Rahman and you have Rahim. You have the part coming out of the nature of God. Out of the love of the creator, he creates and does good for all his creatures. Then there is another part out of his love called Rahim or mercy, undeserved kindness, where he gives to you and you don't deserve anything.

A mother will love her child when it is wrong; she will love it and be kind to it when it doesn't Minister with Vanguard deserve it. This is part of her nature. When man denies woman, he denies a part of his own nature that gives him balance. This is why the world is messed up today! You have denied woman and you have denied the quality of mercy in your own self! So, I have sisters around me to say to the whole world; the woman must play an important part in the development of the nation or the nation will go to hell.

The woman must not be looked at brothers as an object of pleasure and something to bear babies with no intelligence. Any nation that has an uncultivated woman becomes an uncultivated nation. It is a foolish man who denies the mosque to the woman. The woman should be in the mosque because when she knows the Qur'an, studies the Qur'an, takes the Qur'an and internalizes it. She takes your children and she nurtures them in the Quran. But when you push her out and make her to feel like she's not wanted, that she's not as good as the man, then there's a dislike in her and she passes it on to the children. And so, the children go away from Allah rather than coming toward Allah. You mistreat your woman you mistreat yourself. You push your woman down you push yourself down. You pick your woman up; you and I go up.

Are you speaking about Black women? I am speaking about all women no matter what their color is. And let me say this, those who condemn me, who call me a bigot; who call me a racist; who call me a hater; who call me an anti-Semite; I want you to listen to me real carefully tonight. And if anything like that comes out of my mouth raise your hand and stop me, hear. But you'd only be raising your hand no matter what your color is and cheering me on. Because that is what they say I am; but tonight, you judge for yourself."

**Support From The Holy Qur'an**-Surah 4:19- O you who believe, it is not lawful for you to take women as heritage against (their) will. Nor should you straiten them by taking part of what you have given them unless they are guilty of manifest indecency. And treat them kindly. Then if you hate them, it may be that you dislike a thing while Allah has placed abundant good in it.

Surah 3:36 - So when she brought it forth, she said: My Lord, I have brought it forth a female — and Allah knew best what she brought forth — and the male is not like the female, and I have named it Mary, and I commend her and her offspring into Thy protection from the accursed devil.

Surah 33:59 - O Prophet, tell thy wives and thy daughters and the women of believers to let down upon them their over-garments. This is more proper, so that they may be known, and not be given trouble. And Allah is ever Forgiving, Merciful.

**Support From The Bible-** "Likewise, husbands, live with your wives in an understanding way, showing honor to the woman as the weaker vessel, since they are heirs with you of the grace of life, so that your prayers may not be hindered." -1Peter 3:7

"Thou shalt neither vex a stranger, nor oppress him: for ye were strangers in the land of Egypt. Ye shall not afflict any widow, or fatherless child. If thou afflict them in any wise, and they cry at all unto me, I will surely hear their cry; And my wrath shall wax hot, and I will kill you with the sword; and your wives shall be widows, and your children fatherless." -Exodus 22:21-24

"Yes, I ask you also, true companion, help these women, who have labored side by side with me in the gospel together with Clement and the rest of my fellow workers, whose names are in the book of life." -Philippians 4:3

"However, let each one of you love his wife as himself, and let the wife see that she respects her husband." -Ephesians 5:33

# 12. We believe that Allah (God) appeared in the Person of Master W. Fard Muhammad, July 1930 -- the long-awaited Messiah of the Christians and the Mahdi of the Muslims. We believe further and lastly that Allah is God and besides HIM there is no God and He will bring about a universal government of peace wherein we can live in peace together.

**POINT NO. 12 NOTES:** According to the Hon. Min. Louis Farrakhan Point No. 12 is the cardinal point of belief in the Nation of Islam.

There are many prophecies and expectations in sacred literature that describe certain eschatological ("end times") events. The most significant of the end time prophecies discuss the coming of God; the coming of the Messiah and the appearance of the Mahdi.

One of the most important is found in the Bible's Old Testament in the book of Ezekiel. Ezekiel 1:1 reads:

> "Now it came to pass in the thirtieth year, in the fourth month, in the fifth day of the month, as I was among the captives by the river of Chebar, that the heavens were opened, and I saw visions of God."

This verse highlights a vision of God experienced by the prophet Ezekiel. Visions and Dreams, particularly those of prophets or messengers are granted by Allah (God) to share with the prophet or messenger a glimpse or symbolic picture of some future occurrence or event. The Apostle Paul in the Bible famously exclaimed in 1 Corinthians 13:9-12 the following!:

> "For we know in part, and we prophesy in part. 10But when that which is perfect is come, then that which is in part shall be done away. 1When I was a child, I spake as a child, I understood as a child, I thought as a child: but when I became a man, I put away

childish things. For now, we see through a glass, darkly; but then face to face: now I know in part; but then shall I know even as also I am known."

Offering powerful insight into Ezekiel 1:1 is Nation of Islam scholar and spiritual giant, Minister Jabril Muhammad who wrote in his July 20, 2021 Final Call article entitled **"Prophecies in the Bible, prophecies in Ezekiel and teachings about The Wheel"** the following:

"The Bible has something to say of this plane appearing in the skies, on the 4th of July, "in the 30th year." Ezekiel opens with a prophecy of this terrifying plane. In Ezekiel, verse one, we read: "Now it came to pass in the thirtieth year, in the fourth month, in the fifth day of the month, as I was among the captives by the river of Chebar, that the heavens were opened, and I saw visions of God. The Messiah taught that these words refer to events of the 4th (and the immediate afterwards) in July 1930. The "fifth day" in the East, where this was written, is the fourth here in the West. Ezekiel was a type of, at least, a man and a servant of his today. He foresaw them among "the captives" who were a sign of Black people here in America today."

On December 14, 1957 the Most Hon. Elijah Muhammad wrote the following of the Great Mahdi:

"Allah, to whom be praised, came in the person of Master W. F. Muhammad, the Great Mahdi expected by the Muslims and the anti-Christs (the devils) under the names: Jesus Christ, Messiah, God, Lord, Jehovah, the last (Jehovah) and the Christ. These meanings are good and befitting as titles, but the meaning of His name "Mahdi," as mentioned in the Holy Quran Sharieff 22:54, is better. All of these names refer to Him. His name, FARD MUHAMMAD, is beautiful in its meaning. He must bring an end to war, and the only way to end war between man and man is to destroy the war-maker (the trouble-maker).

According to the history of the white race (devils), they are guilty of making trouble; causing war among the people and themselves ever since they have been on our planet Earth. So, the God of righteous has found them disagreeable to live with in peace and has decided to remove them from the face of the earth. God does not have to tell us that they are disagreeable to live with in peace; we already know it, for we are the victims of these trouble-makers. Allah will fight this war for the sake of His people (the black people), and especially for the American so-called Negroes. As I have said time and again, we, the so-called American Negroes, will be the lucky ones. We are Allah's choice to give life and we will be put on top of civilization.

Read your "poison book" (the Bible). What does your book say concerning the preparation of God against the devil? Take a look at Ezekiel's vision of it, 595 B.C. "Now it came to pass in the thirtieth year, in the fourth month, in the fifth day of the month, as I was among the captives by the river of Chebar, that the heavens were open and I saw visions of God. Now as I beheld the living creatures, behold one wheel upon the earth by the living creatures, with his four faces. As for their rings, they were so high that they were dreadful; and their rings were full of eyes around about them four." (Chapter 1:1, 2, 15, 18.)

It was on the fourth of July 1930, when the Great Mahdi, Allah, in person, made His appearance among us."

On July 20, 1957 the Most Hon. Elijah Muhammad wrote the following of the Mahdi:

"When the angels said: "O Mary, surely Allah gives you good news with a word from Him (of one) whose name is the Messiah, Jesus, Son of Mary, worthy of regards in this world and the hereafter."

NOTE: In the verse above, Jesus is called according to Arabic transliteration "Al-Masih, Isa and Ibn-Maryam," meaning in English, the Messi-ah, Son of Mary. "Masih," says the commentator on the language, means either one who travels much or one wiped over with some such thing as oil, the same word as the Aramaic "Messiah," which is said to mean, the anointed. If the name means one who travels much, it could not refer to Jesus of two thousand years ago who spent his life in the small state called Palestine.

One of the main things that one must learn is to distinguish between the history of Jesus two thousand years ago and the prophecy of the Jesus who is expected to come at the end of the world. What we have as a history of the birth of Jesus 2,000 years ago often proves to be that of the Great Mahdi, the Restorer of the Kingdom of Peace on Earth who came to America in 1930 under the name of Mr. W. D. Fard. Later, he admitted that he was Mr. Wallace Fard Muhammad, the one whom the world had been looking for to come for the past 2,000 years. According to the Holy Quran chapter and verse we have under discussion, the name Messiah, the meaning fits that of the Mahdi more than any other man.

The Mahdi is a world traveler. He told me that he had traveled the world over and that he had visited North America for 20 years before making himself known to us, his people, whom he came for. He had visit-ed the Isles of the Pacific, Japan and China, Canada, Alaska, the North Pole, India, Pakistan, all of the Near East and Africa. He had studied the wild life in the jungles of Africa and learned the language of the birds. He could speak 16 languages and could write 10 of them. He visited every inhabited place on the earth and had pictured and extracted the language of the people on Mars and had a knowledge of all life in the universe. He could recite by heart the histories of the world as far back as 150,000 years and knew the beginning and end of all things.

The names Christ, Jesus, Jehovah, God, Allah and many other good names, rightly are His names and He came to give divine names to the whole of the 17 million so-called Negroes, Jesus was made an example for the Jews (Holy Quran 43:59). Jesus and his mother were made as a sign (23:50)."

**Support From The Holy Qur'an**-Surah 2:210 - They wait for naught but that Allah should come to them in the shadows of the clouds with angels, and the matter has (already) been decided. And to Allah are (all) matters returned.

Surah 89:22 - And thy Lord comes with the angels, ranks on ranks

Surah 59:2 - He it is Who caused those who disbelieved of the People of the Book to go forth from their homes at the first banishment. You deemed not that they would go forth, while they thought that their fortresses would defend them against Allah. But Allah came to them from place they expected not and cast terror into their hearts — they demolished their houses with their own hands and the hands of the believers. So, take a lesson, O you who have eyes!

Surah 16:33 - Await they aught but that the angels should come to them or that thy Lord's command should come to pass. Thus, did those before them. And Allah wronged them not, but they wronged themselves

Surah 16:102-103: Say: The Holy Spirit has revealed it from thy Lord with truth, that it may establish those who believe, and as a guidance and good news for those who submit. And indeed, We know that they say: Only a mortal teaches him. The tongue of him whom they hint at is foreign, and this is clear Arabic language.

Surah 19:17 - So she screened herself from them. Then We sent to her Our spirit and it appeared to her as a well-made man.

**Support From The Bible**- "I will go down now and see whether they have done altogether according to the outcry against it that has come to Me; and if not, I will know.""-Genesis 18:21

"Then He said to Abram: "Know certainly that your descendants will be strangers in a land that is not theirs, and will serve them, and they will afflict them four hundred years. 14And also the nation whom they serve I will judge; afterward they shall come out with great possessions." -Genesis 15:13-14

"Now it came to pass in the thirtieth year, in the fourth month, on the fifth day of the month, as I was among the captives by the River Chebar, that the heavens were opened and I saw visions[a] of God."-Ezekiel 1:1

"For this we say unto you by the word of the Lord, that we which are alive and remain unto the coming of the Lord shall not prevent them which are asleep. 16For the Lord himself shall descend from heaven with a shout, with the voice of the archangel, and with the trump of God: and the dead in Christ shall rise first:"

-1Thessalonians 4:15-16

"For as the lightning cometh out of the east, and shineth even unto the west; so, shall also the coming of the Son of man be. 28For wheresoever the carcass is, there will the eagles be gathered together."-Matthew 24:27-28

"God came from Teman, and the Holy One from mount Paran. Selah. His glory covered the heavens, and the earth was full of his praise. And his brightness was as the light; he had horns coming out of his hand: and there was the hiding of his power. Before him went the pestilence, and burning coals went forth at his feet. He stood, and measured the earth: he beheld, and drove asunder the nations; and the everlasting mountains were scattered, the perpetual hills did bow: his ways are everlasting. I saw the tents of Cushan in affliction: and the curtains of the land of Midian did tremble." -Habbakuk 3:3-7

# Congress, Presidents & Founding Fathers Agree with Hon. Elijah Muhammad on Separation

**Most Hon. Elijah Muhammad-** "We must also realize that we, too, are taking part in the judgment, and we will be judged upon our acceptance of the Truth. We are today given a choice; all those who out of their own desire choose to remain with your and God's open enemy (white man), then let it written, let it be done. Those who separate from the devils (the Caucasian race) in this day will be among the chosen of God and will inherit the New World, the Kingdom of everlasting life, as we read in the Bible. As we further read in the Holy Qur'an, they will enter gardens beneath which rivers flow and where the greetings therein shall be "Peace!" **So, it comes to you as a warning of the time in which we now live, separation or death! It will mean death to both black and white to integrate; it will mean death to white America to refuse to give up the Negroes.**

–Hon. Elijah Muhammad, Separation or Death, Herald Dispatch

**Pres. Thomas Jefferson says Separation or Death-** "Deep rooted prejudices entertained by the whites; ten thousand recollections by the Blacks of the injuries they have sustained; new provocations; the real distinctions which nature has made; and many other circumstances, will divide us into parties, and produce convulsions, **which will probably never end but in the extermination of the one or the other race.**"

-Jefferson's Works, Vol. VIII, p.380, Notes on Virginia, written in 1782

"Nothing is more certainly in the book of fate than that these people are to be free; nor is it less certain that **the two races, equally free, cannot live in the same government**."

-Jefferson's Works, Vol.1 p.48, Autobiography written in 1821

**Thomas Hart Benton on divine nature of separation** - "It is a question of races, **involving consequences which go to the destruction of one or the other**. This was seen fifty years ago, and the wisdom of Virginia balked at it then...**It seems to be above human reason now. But there is a wisdom above human and to that we must look**. In the meantime, do not extend the evil."

-Thomas Hart Benton, Missouri Senator from 1821-1851

**Pres. Abraham Lincoln**- "Why should not the people of your race be colonized? Why should they not leave this country? This is, perhaps, the first question for consideration. You and we are a different race. To have between us a broader difference than exists between almost any other two races. Whether it is right or wrong, I need not discuss; but this physical difference is a great disadvantage to us both, as I think your race suffers greatly, many of them by living with us, while ours suffer from your presence. **In a word, we suffer on each side. If this is admitted, it shows a reason why we should be separated**. You, here, are freemen, I suppose. Perhaps you have long been free, or all your lives. **Your race is suffering, in my opinion, the greatest wrong inflicted on any people. But even when you cease to be slaves, you are yet far removed from being placed on an equality with the white race. You are still cut off from many of the advantages which are enjoyed by the other race. The aspiration of man is to enjoy equality with the best when free; but on this broad continent not a single man of your race is made the equal of ours**. Go where

**you are treated the best, and the ban is still upon you. I do not propose to discuss this, but to present it as a fact with which we have to deal.** I cannot alter it if I would. It is a fact about which we all think and feel alike. We look to our conditions owing to the existence of the races on this continent. I need not recount to you the effects upon white men growing out of the institution of slavery. I believe in its general evil effects upon the white race. See our present condition. The country is engaged in war. Our white men are cutting each other's throats, none knowing how far their frenzy may extend; and then consider what we know to be the truth. But for your race among us, there could not be a war, although many men engaged on either side do not care for you one way or the other. Nevertheless, I repeat, without the institution of slavery, and the colored race as a basis, the war could not have had an existence. **It is better for us both, therefore, to be separated. I know that there are free men among you who, even if they could better their condition, are not as much inclined to go out of the country as those who, being slaves, could obtain their freedom on this condition. I suppose one of the principal difficulties in the way of colonization is that the free colored man cannot see that his comfort would be advanced by it. You may believe you can live in Washington, or elsewhere in the United States, the remainder of your lives, perhaps more comfortably than you could in any foreign country. Hence you may come to the conclusion that you have nothing to do with the idea of going to a foreign country. This (I speak in no unkind sense) is an extremely selfish view of the case. But you ought to do something to help those who are not so fortunate as yourselves. . . . For the sake of your race you should sacrifice something of your present comfort, for the purpose of being as grand in that respect as the white people. It is a cheering thought throughout life that something can be done to ameliorate the condition of those who have been subject to the hard usages of the world.** It is difficult to make a man miserable while he feels that he is worthy of himself, and claims kindred with the great God who made him! In the American revolutionary war, sacrifices were made by men engaged in it, but they were cheered by the future. General Washington himself endured greater physical hardships than if he had remained a British subject; yet he was a happy man, because he was engaged in benefiting his race, and in doing something for the children of his neighbors, having none of his own."

—Abraham Lincoln, Address to a Deputation of Negroes, June, 1862

Post Master General, Montgomery Blair- **"All the early patriots of the South— Washington, Jefferson, Madison, Monroe, Jackson, Clay, and others—were the advocates of emancipation and colonization**. The patriots of the North concurred in the design. Is the faction now opposing it patriotic or philanthropic? Are they not rather, like Calhoun, working the Negro question to accomplish schemes of selfish ambition, and, after his method, making a balance of power party of a phalanx of deluded fanatics, keeping the Union and the public peace perpetually in danger, and seeking power in the government through its distractions? **The author of the Declaration of Independence and his associates declared equal rights impracticable in society constituted of masses of different races. De Tocqueville, the most profound writer of the Old World on American institutions, predicts the extermination of the blacks, if it is attempted to confer such rights on them in the United States**. It is obvious that an election would be a mockery in a community wherein there could be no other than black and white parties. In such communities, reason and experience show that one or the other race must be the dominant race, and that democracy is impossible. This is not less obvious to the Phillips school than it is to the Calhoun school, who concur in opposing the policy of Mr. Jefferson, adopted by the president, intended to effectuate the design of our fathers to establish popular government. They concur in pressing here the antagonism of races, and only differ in looking to different races to give them power. The result of this antagonism, so far as popular government is concerned, would be the same if either could succeed in their schemes; and you would scarcely have much preference between being governed by Jefferson Davis, as the leader of the Slave Power, and Wendell Phillips, as the - leader of the enfranchised blacks. But neither can succeed. Even the Calhoun scheme, matured through so many years of intrigue by men versed in public affairs, and attended with a temporary success, is a failure as a governing contrivance, though potent still to spread ruin widely through the land, and especially to desolate the homes of his deluded followers. The Phillips scheme is the dream of visionaries wholly unskilled in government, and will be a failure from the start. He may, in turn, make victims of the Negroes, as Calhoun has of their masters.

But I think not. They are not ambitions of ruling white men, and will, I believe, be contented to set up for themselves, in some neighboring and congenial clime, on the plan of Jefferson and Lincoln."

—Montgomery Blair-attorney and Postmaster General in Lincoln administration, Speech at Concord, N. H., June 17, 1863

**Sen. James Doolittle**- "I know it is said that the objection which is felt on the part of the white population of this country to living side by side in social and civil equality with the negro race is all a mere prejudice of caste. **But its foundations are laid deeper than mere prejudice. It is an instinct of our nature. Men may theorize on the condition of the two races living together, but the thing is impossible**; the instincts of both parties are against it."

—Senator James Rood Doolittle, of Wisconsin

**U.S. Rep. Samuel Sullivan Cox**- "**I lay down the propositions that the white and black races thrive best apart; that a commingling of these races is a detriment to both**; that it does not elevate the black, and it only depresses the white; that the history of this continent, especially in Hispano-America, shows that stable, civil order and government are impossible with such a population. . ..

Equality is a condition which is self-protective, wanting nothing, asking nothing, able to take care of itself. It is an absurdity to say that two races, so-dissimilar as black and white, of different origin, of unequal capacity, can succeed in the same society when placed in competition. There is no such example in history of the success of two separate races under such circumstances. Less than sixty years - ago, Ohio had thousands of an Indian population. She has now but thirty red men in her borders. **The Negro, with a difference of color indelible, has been freed under every variety of circumstances; but his freedom has, in most cases, as a matter of course, been only nominal. Prejudice stronger than all principles, though not always stronger than lust, has imperatively separated the whites from the blacks. In the school-house, the church, or the hospital, the black man must not seat himself beside the white; even in death and at the cemetery the line of distinction is drawn.**"

-S. S. Cox, U.S. Representative from Ohio and New York, U.S. Ambassador to Ottoman Empire, "Eight Years in Congress", p. 249, 250.

# The "No-Show Paradox":

## Can the Black Community get what it wants by not voting?

**The question of the day is what do Black people want and how do we get it?** It is safe to say that most in the Black electorate want to live in communities that are economically strong. We want safe neighborhoods free of violent crime. We want a healthy relationship with police that does not involve racial profiling and the resultant brutality and killing of Black men and women by law enforcement. We want good schools for our children where they can get an education that not only prepares them for a global economy but also roots them in the beautiful cultural heritage of their people.

The Most Honorable Elijah Muhammad answered this question in a brilliant and succinct way when he authored in 1963 the now famous document entitled **"What the Muslims Want."** Please don't be turned off by the term "Muslim." You have to understand that the Most Honorable Elijah Muhammad explained that the term "Muslim" simply means a *righteous person; one who is willing to submit their will in order to carry out the righteous will of the Creator (Allah/God).* And he taught that all Black people are righteous by nature; Muslim by nature. Thusly in his divinely inspired vernacular the terms **"Muslim"** and **"Black man and woman"** *(Black people, etc.)* are interchangeable. So **"What The Muslims Want"** is really **"What The Black Man and Woman Wants."**

This brilliant and all-encompassing list of righteous demands and wants originally appeared as the inside back cover of the Muhammad Speaks newspaper. Today it remains the inside back cover of the **Final Call newspaper**, published by the Honorable Minister Louis Farrakhan. And according to some of the founding members of the Black Panther Party, it was also the basis of the Panther Party's 10 Point program.

What may surprise most readers is that when we consider the collective wants and needs of the Black community in America we arrive at a startling conclusion. That conclusion is that **everything we want and desire as a collective mass or body of people can be achieved without voting** and with little to no involvement in electoral politics.

Certainly, this conclusion may anger traditionalists. But let's face the grim reality of our times. Barack Obama got 92% of the Black vote in his victory to become America's first Black president. His victory is by far the crowning achievement of all who say *"we've got to vote our way out of this."* For many years now, there have been Blacks holding office in every level of government; local, state and federal. And to have a Black president was a previously unbelievable feat. Yet despite this achievement, the Black community's needs and wants today are virtually identical as to what they were in 1963 when Mr. Muhammad penned his **"What the Muslims (Black People) Want."**

Again, consider that we have voted for judges, mayors, governors and even now for a Black president twice, yet we are still a community in need. **Poverty** is high among us; **disease** is prevalent among us; **blight** and **crime** are problems for us and we still have a **pitiful educational system** that we depend on to educated our children.

It is painfully clear and rather obvious at this point that *politics is not the answer.*

If electoral politics isn't the answer, then how do Black people get what we want?

## Ethnic Enclaves

The Most Honorable Elijah Muhammad was always telling his beloved Black people in America to *"hurry and unite on to your own kind."* He taught us that our own kind included all non-white peoples of the earth. Nowadays, America has received so many of *"our own kind"* as immigrants from their home countries and they have formed their own communities that exist within many major cities as carved out territories and neighborhoods.

The social conditions within immigrant communities in America are in stark contrast to those within the Black community. Scholars like to refer to immigrant communities as *"Ethnic Enclaves."* An ethnic enclave is defined as *"Usually urban areas, within which culturally distinct minority communities maintain ways of life largely separate from those of the generally larger communities that surround them"*

The most Hon. Elijah Muhammad encouraged his beloved Black people that we should have knowledge of self and kind. The practical application of acquiring such knowledge in today's world involves an examination and study of these ethnic enclaves that are in many areas made up of our Black, Brown, Red and Yellow brethren of the global Black diaspora.

As Minister Farrakhan has pointed out most recently in his profound analysis of the National Presidential Election, the major cities of America and their ethnic enclaves must become the new model for the disparate and dis-unified Black community-affectionately and pejoratively dubbed **"the hood."**

Chinatown, Koreatown, Little Haiti, Little Africa, Greek Town, and the more than 850 ethnic enclaves in America are examples of something that academics refer to as the **"No Show Paradox."** I am not a political scientist and most who read this will not be. So, I won't bore you with the complex mathematical and academic jargon related to the specifics of this concept within the academy. My usage of it in this article is to emphasize the larger general concept of the **"No Show Paradox"** which is essentially, as author Grant Hayden defines it in his work *Abstention: The Unexpected Power of Withholding Your Vote* that **"there are times when a voter is better off (in terms of achieving a desired outcome) by not voting rather than voting according to her preferences."**

As we have already pointed out, voting in National Elections does not change the reality of suffering, injustice and poverty in the Black community. In fact, the Black community has essentially become the victim of over usage of a failing strategy. This strategy termed by author Harold Cruse in his *Crisis of the Negro Intellectual* is that of "non-economic liberalism." The NAACP and other **white led Black groups** steered many leading Blacks under their influence to prioritize voting and electoral politics rather than the pooling and harnessing of economic wealth and capital as the primary means of achieving what the Black community wants and needs.

To a large extent the various immigrant groups throughout America have not been so victimized with such poisonous strategies and ideologies. They thrive in spite of being poorly represented in electoral politics. They are examples of the **"Do For Self"** mantra and philosophy of the Most Honorable Elijah Muhammad.

In one example, the *New American Leaders Project* is a part of an effort to increase the level of political participation among Asian and Hispanic immigrants. Their report entitled **States of Inclusion: New American Journeys to Elected Office** points out that Blacks make up 9% of all state legislators, Asians only 2% and Hispanics are 4% of the 7,388 total of state legislators. And even though state level elections have a potentially greater impact on the locales that they have created their enclaves inside of, the immigrant communities are clearly not emphasizing political participation as a way to live "the American dream."

As far as the 2012 National Election is concerned, the Pew Research Center points out that among eligible voters, Blacks voted at 67% while Asians voted at 47% and Hispanics at 48%. According to the philosophy of **non-economic liberalism**, such higher voter turnout by Blacks should mean that social conditions within the Black community would be far better than those within immigrant communities and enclaves. But we only need consider as an indicator the high rate of Black deaths at the hands of law enforcement to make the point that social conditions in the Black community make it an environment whereby most who live there are seeking the means of escape to someplace else.

## On Crime

Immigrant communities have less crime than the Black community. At the University of Texas in El Paso (UTEP), Professor Theodore Curry, Ph.D., is an associate professor of criminal justice who is leading a research project that is challenging popular beliefs about crime among immigrants. "Curry pointed out that there are interesting theories addressing this issue, which has blindsided criminologists and other experts. **One is that immigrant neighborhoods have lower crime rates because they are stronger communities of families that are more strongly connected to each other. In addition, immigrants tend to be working even though they may be poor, so they are invested in their community.**" Professor Curry's project is officially titled *Why are Immigrant Neighborhoods Low Crime Neighborhoods? Testing Immigrant Revitalization Theory and Cultural Explanations.* It is being funded by a grant from the National Science Foundation.

UTEP News in its coverage of this project shared an important perspective that further illustrates our overall thesis in this article. According to Jorge Luis Hernandez who is a research assistant working with Professor Curry, his experience growing up in an immigrant community was very positive. He said, "Growing up in an immigrant community, **I always detected a sense of togetherness where everybody had each other's backs and would help each other any way they can.**"

## On Economics

According to a CNN Money report prepared by Jose Pagliery entitled *On the Rise: Immigrant Entrepreneurs*, there is a strong **"Do For Self"** zeitgeist among foreign born workers and citizens. Pagliery writes, "Immigrants created 28% of all new firms last year. They were also **twice as likely to start a new business when compared to those born in the United States.** It's a notable shift. Nearly all new firms are small, and many are hiring new workers, seeking small business loans and shaking up established industries.

Pagliery continues by sharing words from Rob Fairlie who authored the Kaufman Foundation report entitled *Immigrant Entrepreneurs and Small Business Owners, and their Access to Financial Capital*, "the recession drove low-skilled workers into figuring out what to do...the same applies to Hispanics, who are creating new businesses at a faster clip than any other ethnic group. Hispanics make up more than half of the nation's 40 million foreign-born, and **they are starting businesses at a rate that exceeds even their population growth**.

That is a fascinating statistic. I wonder if there is any other ethnic group in America like the Hispanic community who are **starting businesses faster rate than they are making babies!** Wow!

This CNN Money article concludes with a strong reminder of some of the divine wisdom and sage advice offered to the Black man and woman of America by the Most Honorable Elijah Muhammad and the Honorable Minister Louis Farrakhan:

*"Javier Palomarez, president of the Hispanic chamber, links the rise of entrepreneurship to the **immigrant frame of mind.** "It's certainly a boot-strap mentality: 'I had the gumption to leave where I came from to get here. By God, I'm in the land of opportunity. These people need some good baked goods, so I'm opening a bakery."*

## On Education

Writer Lee Dye authored a report for ABC News entitled *Why Immigrants' Children Do Better in School* that plainly stated **"Children who immigrate to the United States with their** families are likely to outperform kids with a similar background who were born here. And when they grow up, their own children are also likely to do better than their peers."

Dye's report highlights and discusses the findings of a study performed by Johns Hopkins University. In preparation for Dye's article she interviewed sociologist Lingxin Hao, who serves as the lead author of the study. According to Dye, "Hao offered one theoretical explanation for why immigrant children do so much better than their peers: 'It's about family,' she said. 'The parents have an optimistic view of bringing up their children in the United States. One important motivation for immigrants is to improve their children's lives. The United States is the land of opportunity. If we work hard, we will get it."

Dye's report concludes, **"New immigrants tend to settle in communities that have many other residents from the same part of the world, thus buttressing the "cultural tools" that might otherwise diminish over time."** And according to lead research Hao, **"If you go to Chinatown you see bankers there, but you also see people washing dishes. There's many different people there. So even if your parents aren't highly educated, you have other role models in your community."**

## Nation of Islam Example

**Again, the strong economic activity and subsequent societal benefits within America's ethnic enclaves is what the Most Honorable Elijah Muhammad not only advocated and taught, but also demonstrated in his magnificent work of building the Nation of Islam in America.** His message of self-help, unity, pride, decency and righteous living can never be considered as empty platitudes and slogans. No, his weighty word and teaching produced 'a nation within a nation.' Consider how in 1974 His National Secretary read off from a report that outlined just some of the accomplishment of the Most Honorable Elijah Muhammad and his enthusiastic followers:

- Muhammad's Temples of Islam in more than 150 cities in North America, Bermuda, Jamaica and Belize.
- Muhammad Universities of Islam in 46 cities.
- Muhammad Speaks Newspaper and Printing Press, ( a multi-million dollar complex printing the international news weekly with a circulation of more than 850,000 copies).
- Cold and dry storage and warehouse facilities.
- Good Foods, Inc. (meat, produce and eggs).
- Chicago Lamb Packers
- A cross-country trucking system.
- "A fixed base Aviation Department" at the Gary Municipal Airport.
- A Cannery in Georgis.
- Fruit and Vegetable, poultry, and dairy farms in Georgia, Alabama, and Michigan (thousands of acrres of farmland)
- Shabazz Barber Shop and Cleaners
- Salaam Snack Shop.
- Your Supermarket and Fish House.
- Muslim Import Store
- Capitol Cleaners.
- Temple No. 2 Clothing Store and Office Building.
- National Clothing Factory.
- National Fez Factory.
- Guaranty Bank and Trust Company.
- Muhammad's Sales and Office Building (a $1.5 million structure being completed in Chicago).
- Shabazz Bakery and Coffee Shop.
- Shabazz Restaurant.
- Residential Homes
- More than 200 apartment units in Chicago alone.
- Muhammad's Fish Imports: Importation of millions of pounds of fish each month for rat least the next year from the unpollute waters around South America

The Most Honorable Elijah Muhammad, in similar fashion to the Jewish community and other economically powerful groups within America, gained quite a bit of political power based on the popularity of His movement among the masses and due in large part to His focus and emphasis on developing economic strength as a prerequisite to political involvement. Many have falsely accused Mr. Muhammad and Minister Farrakhan of being anti-voting. Nothing could be further from the truth. Instead, the Nation of Islam's position has always been to take care of first things first. So, since electoral politics **bends and submits to "moneyed interests,"** any people who want to gain privilege and power in the political realm would be wise to become a "moneyed interest." In other words, the Black man and woman should work first to make their vote matter by developing the ability to hold accountable all who would receive our vote. And this is only achieved through economic strength.

More evidence of Mr. Muhammad's wise and judicious use of the vote is seen in that he **waited some 33 years to lead the Nation of Islam into electoral politics**. His announcement that the Nation of Islam would take up an interest in the political realm was published in the March 18, 1963.

He understood as a close friend and scholar said to me that brother

> "voting DOES have great value to a people who know what they are doing. Jews, for instance, needed to build an infrastructure to move their plantation products to market—that means bridges, roads, docks, mail, courts, etc. to support their international business aims. THAT is why they needed that cadre of middleman operatives known as politicians. In other words, once economics are locked in, politics can grease the skids with permits, ordinances, regulations, laws, etc."

Because of the Most Honorable Elijah Muhammad's initial guidance in 1963, the Nation of Islam has supported Adam Clayton Powell, Julian Bond, Rev. Jesse Jackson, Cynthia McKinney, Barack Obama, Earl Hilliard and numerous other Black elected officials. And Minister Farrakhan has been a frequently sought-after speaker at events and functions where Black elected officials were convened.

## Blacks During Reconstruction

Thus, what emerges when we look at the Nation of Islam is not the common misuse of the Black vote. No, the Nation of Islam is a modern portrait of the wise strategic use of the Black vote much like the early Blacks during the Reconstruction Era.

> "Flourishing black towns, such as Langston in Oklahoma, Nicodemus in Kansas, Davis Bend in Mississippi, and Eatonville in Florida, sprang up across the nation. **In these communities, blacks could exercise authority over themselves and lead productive and successful lives, unhindered by white racism.** They owned farms (which they purchased), schools, stores, newspapers, and churches. **Blacks who lived in predominately white areas were often poorer than those who lived in black communities, as they received less pay than their white counterparts and worked at**

**inferior jobs.** Denied opportunities for advancement and self-empowerment, and alienated from mainstream society, poverty and crime became a way of life for many of these blacks." (Encyclopedia of Reconstruction Volume 1, page 443)

## Why Do People Vote?

After reviewing these and other indicators of the health and vibrancy of most immigrant communities in America, and how they don't emphasize voting as the solution to getting what they want as a people, I begin to ask myself the question, "Why do people vote if you really get nothing out of it?"

Some scholars and researchers have concluded that most people who vote are not voting to make their lives better. They are not voting to necessarily solve the problems of their communities. According to jurist and economist Richard Posner most people vote for entirely different reasons than what we have been led to believe.

In his short blog written in 2012 entitled The Paradox of Voting, Posner lists several reasons that people vote. Consider the following passage excerpted from his treatise on the subject:

"The paradox of voting in national elections is that, since a single vote is almost certain to have no effect on the outcome (in a Presidential election, it will merely add one digit to an eight-figure number), there seems to be no benefit from voting.

1. Some people vote because the political campaigns make it costly for them not to vote—one technique in "get out the vote" drives is pestering people to vote so that they will feel uncomfortable not voting.
2. Some vote because they think that it will encourage others to do so.
3. Some vote because they consider it a civic duty.
4. Some voting is purely expressive—a way of expressing strong feelings pro or con a candidate (or pro one and con his opponent); certainly, anger played a role in votes against Romney by members of groups that he or his party seemed to disrespect, and anger at Obama played a role in the large number of votes that Romney received. In this respect voting is like booing or cheering at an athletic event

or other entertainment. One person's applause at a concert is inaudible to the performers, yet people applaud, and not mainly I think because others in the audience would look askance at them if they did not.

5. And finally, people interested in politics like to vote to convince themselves and others that their interest is serious—they are willing to put their money (not money exactly, but the cost in time and bother of voting) where their mouth is.

No one thinks that applauding is irrational, even though like voting it has no instrumental value, and has some, though very slight, cost."

It is noticeable that Judge Posner **not once makes mention of voters voting to make a change in the social conditions of their communities**. Not once does he mention that voting leads to freedom, independence, and equality. **He doesn't even reference voting as a way to get justice, despite him himself serving as a judge, and knowing that many judges are elected!** And this is because as a member of the ruling class of whites in this country, he understands that community change is not a product of the electoral process. Community development and change is the product of groups of people coming together with a like mind and agreed upon goals and finding a way to live work and worship together. Such can be achieved in nearly all possible political scenarios in America.

## Conclusion

In my brief overview of the concept of the **No Show Paradox** and the healthy and powerful conditions of ethnic enclaves I have deepened my appreciation for what the Most Honorable Elijah Muhammad and Minister Farrakhan have been encouraging the Black man and woman of America to do for many years. Their advice and guidance have been that we **Do For Self** and that we work to unite as a people and make our own communities safe places to live. Their call has never been to alleviate from responsibility the United States Government. To the contrary, their call has been to give guidance to both the Black people of America and the American government. Black people must take charge of our own fate and destiny. The American government owes Black people land and territory since it was our ancestor's free labor that made America the wealthiest nation on earth. And at this date, both sides have failed in accepting the divine guidance of Mr. Muhammad and the man who the Aaron to his Moses, the Paul to his Jesus, the Ali to his Muhammad-Minister Louis Farrakhan. So, unfortunately, dire consequences have appeared to vex and place in peril the descendants of the former slaves and the descendants of the former masters.

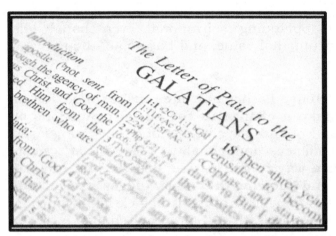

But while there is still a little time left before total and complete collapse of the American government and social order, the immigrant community model should be implemented and acted upon as we bid farewell to non-economic liberalism's over-emphasis on electoral politics. We have shown clearly in this short essay that when it comes to the major significant changes that need to be made in the Black community, participation in electoral politics is not necessary. We can get safe neighborhoods, clean streets, better schools and job creation by almost completely ignoring the political process. All we need is operational unity among the diverse elements within the Black community around common goals and objectives, utilizing our shared ancestry, shared suffering and shared abilities as the ties that bind us together. We have proven that the immigrant model of building community life among your own ethnicity or race is the superior approach and strategy for Blacks nationwide. We have discussed the instances where voting and participation in electoral politics is of value and that being as a tool for an already established economic engine to make use of. But in a capitalist economic system, and as has been declared by Minister Farrakhan, **"politics without economics is symbol without substance."** We have identified benefits that can be obtained by taking a deliberate "no-show" behavior at the ballot box when the choice is, as they are in today's national presidential election, a lose-lose proposition.

We end this essay on a spiritual note and reflection. As a student of the ministry class led by the Honorable Minister Louis Farrakhan, I can't help but consider the scriptures in this analysis. For when I look upon the seemingly unconcerned posture of the ethnic enclave and its members to any of the developments and trends in the political realm, I think about certain principles from the scriptures that are similarly impervious to any legal mandates or statutes. Consider the Bible in the Book of Galatians. In Galatians chapter 5 verses 22-23 we read the following:

**"But the fruit of the Spirit is love, joy, peace, patience, kindness, goodness, faithfulness, gentleness, and self-control. Against such things there is no Law."**

It is clear to me that what we witness on display within the immigrant communities/ethnic enclaves is the implementation of these spiritual principles that the Book of Galatians refers to as the *fruits of the spirit*. These fruit of the spirit of God, when carried out in a group or community setting, serve as laws that do more to regulate a society than any statue voted on or approved of by the U.S. Congress or state legislatures. So perhaps these insular, separate and interdependent societies where the members share a common ethnicity or race, a common language, a common history, a common suffering, a common goal and a common spirit have found a way to live above the law. They live among each other largely observing the highest of all possible laws, which are the universal laws of the Creator that are also the same principles that govern and regulate the natural world. In other words, by living by the laws of God, they never worry about the laws of man.

These model communities have found a way to live and take advantage of what America has to offer by living together in unity, love and mutual respect. And **against such there is no law.** I argue that my beloved Black people should do the same.

# The Brotherhood of The Most Hon. Elijah Muhammad & The Rev. Dr. Martin Luther King Jr.: 14 Important Facts of Hidden History

After the assassination of the Rev. Dr. Martin Luther King Jr, mainstream America has pounced to seized control of his legacy, with intentions to weaken his message and rob him of any revolutionary appeal. As a part of the white power structure's taking control of Dr. King's narrative and legacy has been the tendency to position Dr. King as the polar opposite or antithesis of men like the Most Hon. Elijah Muhammad. The mainstream narrative yarn spinners engage in reductionism when they distill King down to the idea of integration, in order to paint him as the much more acceptable alternative to Muhammad who is distilled down to the idea of separation. As we study the Muslim Program offered by the Most Hon. Elijah Muhammad, we find it necessary to highlight major points where the Most Hon. Elijah Muhammad and the Rev. Dr. Martin Luther King Jr. can be seen in the same light and as brothers who shared much more in common than is frequently acknowledged.

# 1. Both Dr. King and Messenger Muhammad are sons of the state of Georgia

Dr. King was born on January 15, 1929, in Atlanta, Georgia. The Hon. Elijah Muhammad was born October 7, 1897 in the community of Deep Step near Sandersville, GA. The state of Georgia is named for King George II of England. He is the grandfather of King George III, who was the King of England during the American War for Independence. Thus, the name of the state of Georgia is connected to a history of the struggle for freedom and independence. This is an intriguing anecdote of history to consider that in a state that shares the name of the king who oppressed the early colonists, 2 of the Black Nation's greatest freedom fighters were born to ultimately fight against the oppressive forces inside America.

*Chicago civil rights leader Al Raby (l) and Mrs. King accompany Dr. King as he and Muhammad exchange greetings.*

# 2. Both Dr. King and Messenger Muhammad are the sons of Baptist preachers

Dr. King was born the son of the Rev. Martin Luther King Sr. The Hon. Elijah Muhammad was born the son of the Rev. William Poole Sr.

# 3. Both Dr. King and Messenger Muhammad were viewed by J. Edgar Hoover of candidates for the position of "Black Messiah"

From a March 4, 1968 FBI document, we read: Prevent the RISE OF A "MESSIAH" who could unify, and electrify, the militant black nationalist movement. Malcolm X might have been such a "messiah;" he is the martyr of the movement today. Martin Luther King, Stokely Carmichael and Elijah Muhammed all aspire to this position. Elijah Muhammed is less of a threat because of his age. King could be a very real contender for this position should he abandon his supposed "obedience" to "white, liberal doctrines" (nonviolence) and embrace black nationalism. Carmichael has the necessary charisma to be a real threat in this way.

# 4. Both Dr. King and Messenger Muhammad were spied on by Jewish groups like the ADL

Henry Schwartzschild waited a long time to go public with his personal horror story about the Anti-Defamation League of B'nai B'rith. Today an employee of the American Civil Liberties Union (ACLU), he resigned from a high-ranking position in the ADL' s publicity office in the mid-1960s when he discovered, to his shock, that the ADL was spying on Rev. Martin Luther King, Jr. on behalf of J. Edgar Hoover and the FBI. It was not until the spring of 1993- nearly 30 years after he quit the ADL-that Schwartzschild came forward and told about the League's efforts against Dr. King. In an April 28, 1993 interview, Schwartzschild told San Francisco Weekly: "They [ADL] thought King was sort of a loose cannon. He was a Baptist preacher and nobody could be quite sure what he would do next. The ADL was very anxious about having an unguided missile out there."

-ADL Caught in Spy Scandal of the Decade by Jeffrey Steinberg

In 1942: A secret ADL of B'nai Brith file entitled "Temple of Islam Infiltration" states that a "Negro employed by us" prove "quite instrumental" in an FBI raid on the Chicago mosque resulting in 82 arrests.

In 1959 The American Jewish Committee sent Black spies from the Urban League to Mr. Muhammad's Newark, New Jersey, appearance.

-The Secret Relationship Between Blacks and Jews Vol.2

## 5. Both Dr. King and Messenger Muhammad took anti-war stances against the U.S. Government

*"Somehow this madness must cease. We must stop now. I speak as a child of God and brother to the suffering poor of Vietnam. I speak for those whose land is being laid waste, whose homes are being destroyed, whose culture is being subverted. I speak for the poor of America who are paying the double price of smashed hopes at home, and death and corruption in Vietnam. I speak as a citizen of the world, for the world as it stands aghast at the path we have taken. I speak as one who loves America, to the leaders of our own nation: The great initiative in this war is ours; the initiative to stop it must be ours.* A true revolution of values will lay hands on the world order and say of war, 'This way of settling differences is not just.' This business of burning human beings with napalm, of filling our nation's homes with orphans and widows, of injecting poisonous drugs of hate into the veins of peoples normally humane, of sending men home from dark and bloody battlefields physically handicapped and psychologically deranged, cannot be reconciled with wisdom, justice, and love. A nation that continues year after year to spend more money on military defense than on programs of social uplift is approaching spiritual death."

-A Time to Break Silence, Speech by Rev. Dr. Martin Luther King Jr. April 4, 1967

"In the year 1942-43, according to reports, there were nearly a hundred of my followers sentenced to prison terms of from 1 to 5 years for refusing to take part in the war between America, Japan and Germany because of our peaceful stand and the principle belief and practice in Islam, which is peace. The very dominant idea in Islam is the making of peace and not war; our refusing to go armed is our proof that we want peace. We felt that we had no right to take part in a war with nonbelievers of Islam who have always denied us justice and equal rights; and if we were going to be examples of peace and righteousness (as Allah has chosen us to be), we felt we had no right to join hands with the murderers of people or to help murder those who have done us no wrong."

-Message To The Blackman in America, by the Most Hon. Elijah Muhammad

## 6. Both Messenger Muhammad and Dr. King were arrested and imprisoned for their bold activism

**The Most Hon. Elijah Muhammad was arrested on May 8 and September 21, 1942. Dr. King Arrested April 12, 1963**

## 7. Both Messenger Muhammad and Dr. King believed in the power of developing Black economics and the use of economic withdrawal and boycotting of white businesses who refuse to give justice to Black consumers

"There is no need for us, millions through the country, spending our money for the joy and happiness of others. As a result, as soon as they throw us out of a job we are back at their doors begging for bread and soup. How many clothing shops do we operate in the country? Very few! Yet, all of us wear clothes. Who made our clothes for us? Who sold them to us? We have thousands of grocery stores, but what about our naked bodies? Should we not have more stores to sell our people clothes? Should we not sell our people everything they want or need? But no, we give all the money out of our pockets to the slave-master. We are satisfied in doing so. There are millions of us. We do not have enough factories to weave clothes for our people here in America. Think over that. Where is our shoe factory? Where are our cattle that we are skinning to make shoes for our people? These are small things, but we want equality with a nation that is doing these things."

-Message To The Blackman in America by the Most Hon. Elijah Muhammad

The other economic lever available to the Negro is as a consumer. As long ago as 1932, in his book Moral Man and Immoral Society, Reinhold Niebuhr pointed out that "boycotts against banks which discriminate against Negroes in quantity credit, against stores which refuse to employ Negroes while serving Negro trade, and against public service corporations which practice racial discrimination, would undoubtedly be crowned with some measure of success.... Along with requesting new job opportunities, we are now requesting that businesses with stores in the ghetto deposit the income for those establishments in Negro-owned banks, and that Negro-owned products be placed on the counters of all their stores. In this way we seek to stop the drain of resources out of the ghetto with nothing remaining there for its rehabilitation.

-Where Do We Go From Here, Dr. Martin Luther King Jr.

# 8. Both Messenger Muhammad and Dr. King condemned Christmas as a pagan holiday

Dr. King writes "It is well-nigh impossible to grasp Christianity through and through without knowledge of these cults. That there were striking similarities between the developing church and these religions cannot be denied. Even Christian apologist had to admit that fact. In Dr. King's discussion of the specific mystery religion known as Mithraism he documents that Mithra was believed to be the "genius of celestial light," one who "goes through the heaven with a team of white horses...he was the god of wide pastures and the giver of gifts. "What Dr. King documents is that the modern Christmas tradition of light decorations and Santa Claus with reindeer originates in an entirely different religion and has nothing at all to do with Jesus the Christ!

-King and Muhammad Agree Christmas is Rich Man's Pagan Holiday, Demetric Muhammad

So, you go out and spend your hard-earned money to worship with white people. They

force you under disguise and defraud you into worshipping the birthday of that

wicked old Nimrod on December. And if you knew the truth of him, you would not dare to worship it... Nimrod gets a great ovation on the 25th day of December; one of the most wicked leaders that ever lived....

The great false worship of December 25 is a lie. The worship of Jesus' birthday, which they claim is on the 25th of December, is one of the most open lies against the truth. And the authors of their religion, Christianity, know that they are wrong in trying to tell the world that that is the day Jesus was born on....

God taught me that the 25th day of December is the day of the birth of Nimrod, and that the scientists know that that is Nimrod's birthday. Nimrod was a leader, born as an opponent of Moses' teachings.

-Our Saviour Has Arrived, Most Hon. Elijah Muhammad

# 9. Both Messenger Muhammad and Dr. King met and developed a private friendship

"But of course, Dr. Martin Luther King and him (grew to) become secret friends. And I really think a lot that caused his killing – I think the government was in back of it, maybe not, but someone was in back of it – (there) was two things (to consider): 1) he spoke out against the war (Vietnam), and 2) he and the Messenger were pretty close. Because he (The Honorable Elijah Muhammad) told me that with the two of them working together, they could take it. So, you see there is a lot that the average person thinks they know that they don't know Brother."

-Min. Lucius Bey' Muhammad, 103-year-old Dean of the Ministers of the Most Hon. Elijah Muhammad, interview by Cedric Muhammad, 2004

## 10. Both Messenger Muhammad and Dr. King partnered to work on the problem of poverty in Chicago and America's inner-city.

# King, Muslims Join Forces In War On Slums

### Leaders Agree To Form Common Front After Historic Meeting

Dr. Martin Luther King, Jr., and Elijah Muhammad have agreed to form a "common front" in a war against slums.

Only three days before the start of an annual Black Muslim convention, Dr. King visited the home of the Muslim leader at 4847 S. Woodlawn, where the two agreed to cooperate in "slum and areas other than slums."

It was the first meeting between the two leaders.

A spokesman for King said both men agreed Negroes are "trapped in deplorable slums because of an evil system."

After the meeting, Dr. King told a reporter that he, as a Christian, had obvious religious

differences with Muhammad, "but there now appear to be some areas, slums and areas other than slums, in which our movements can cooperate."

King also emphasized he might not always agree with the Black Muslims in philosophy or tactics, stressing that his was a non-violent movement which favors racial integration.

The Black Muslims have long called for a separate state and separation of the races.

At the meeting, Dr. King cracked a joke about both of them being "Georgia Boys," since both were born there. Muhammad enjoyed the joke, a King aide said.

**Sons of Georgia become Brothers in the Struggle together pledging to work for the benefit of Blacks and the poor**

Economist and Nation of Islam researcher Bro. Cedric in an interview with the "Dean of Muhammad's Ministers" Minister Lucius Bey captured this from the esteemed and time-honored minister for the Most Honorable Elijah Muhammad. In an interview originally published on BlackElectorate.Com we note the following:

> Cedric Muhammad: "I wanted to know what you may have heard the Honorable Elijah Muhammad say about two men – Marcus Garvey and Dr. Martin Luther King."
>
> Minister Lucius Bey: "Well he said he (Marcus Garvey) was a forerunner. What he (referred to) were two (men) as forerunners. But of course, Dr. Martin Luther King and him (grew to) become secret friends. And I really think a lot that caused his killing – I think the government was in back of it, maybe not, but someone was in back of it – was two things : 1)he spoke out against the war (Vietnam), and 2) he and the Messenger were pretty close.
>
> Because he (The Honorable Elijah Muhammad) told me that with the two of them working together, they could take it.
>
> So you see there is a lot that the average person thinks they know that they don't know Brother."

# 11. Both Messenger Muhammad and Dr. King worked with youth street gangs

More than a hundred members of Chicago's most notorious street gangs convened in a downtown hotel on a June afternoon. The Black P. Stone Rangers, the Gangster Disciples, the Vice Lords -- all were represented. In the ornate glamor of a Sheraton ballroom -- "an atmosphere of carpeting and candelabra," one reporter called it -- gang heads sat alongside clerics and activists, lawyers and community organizers.

Martin Luther King, Jr. sat with them. His Southern Christian Leadership Conference had sponsored the meeting. The year was 1966. King and his allies in the Chicago community hoped to mobilize the gangs toward nonviolent direct action in service of the Chicago Freedom Movement. And they hoped to turn them away from the fratricidal violence that had recently begun tearing through the city's black neighborhoods, where gunfire had become a soundtrack to the daily lives of many residents. 395 people had been murdered the previous year -- many of them in gang wars, almost all of them with guns.

-MLK's Forgotten Plan to End Gun Violence in Chicago by Simon E. Balto

> ## Blackstone Rangers
>
> ### By Elijah Muhammad
>
> *Blackstone Rangers, do not let the "whitestone rangers" deceive you into killing your own Black brothers.*
>
> *You should first love to do good to yourself and kind. This is the great love and respect of self. Do not take up the practice of the slavemasters of our fathers which has affected our Nation in such a way that our people are helpless to try finding dignified unity of self.*
>
> *We, the Muslims, would like to make you the brothers of your Black people, of whom you are, by nature, the brothers. We are your friends and not your enemies. Make yourselves our friends and you will not have to depend on bribes to destroy yourselves and your kind.*
>
> *Write us and visit us in our meetings. Thank you for reading this.*

**Most Hon. Elijah Muhammad Fatherly Love**

# 12. Both Messenger Muhammad and Dr. King were targets of assassination

**Assassination attempt on Most Hon. Elijah Muhammad foiled, cover story of Muhammad Speaks August 18, 1967**

Demetric Muhammad-Page 131

# 13. Minister Farrakhan and the SCLC

Despite Dr. King's association with the NAACP, it was the SCLC-Southern Christian Leadership Conference- that was actually founded by Dr. King. In modern times the SCLC fell into near obsolescence until the Rev. Dr. Charles Steele became its president. Rev. Steele would later reveal that it was the Nation of Islam under the direct guidance of the Hon. Min. Louis Farrakhan that gave to Dr. King a gift of funding that allowed the SCLC to keep its door open and ultimately rebuild its coffers and associated activism on behalf of poor and impoverished communities throughout America.

According to Rev. Steele:

I looked at the Minister, I said, "Minister let me just be honest

**TO:** The Family of Dr. Martin Luther King

I extend my deepest sympathy and condolences on the loss of Dr. Martin Luther King. A great and courageous black man who died in the effort to get for his people that which belonged to them — **FREEDOM**

Signed

Elijah Muhammad

*Messenger of Allah*

April 12, 1968-Published Condolences from the Most Hon. Elijah Muhammad after Dr. King was assassinated

with you. I'm broke. SCLC is broke. We don't have no money. But if you just help me and loan me a few dollars. In terms of my plight of SCLC. I promise you that I will multiply it and I will pay you back."

And the Minister looked at me and he said "My brother, you got my attention." He said, "Just one thing that I want you to realize. I'm going to give you the money that you asked for because I know you mean well and you are going to do what is right to uplift the organization." He said, "You must realize you can't pay me back. You just go and be successful with Dr. King's organization and make it work for our people and I will be proud and I will commend the fact that you had enough motivation to come all the way to Chicago and to share with me your vision and your strategy. I encourage you to continue and this is what I will do to help you. But. I repeat you can't pay me back."

# 14. Minister Farrakhan as the heir to Dr. King's legacy

Former Chicago Tribune Editorial page editor Don Wycliff boldly declared that of all the national leaders in the Black community, it is Nation of Islam's Minister Louis Farrakhan who is the true heir of Dr. King's legacy of function as the most magnetic, most spiritually rooted and the most dynamic orator anywhere to be found in Black America.

According to Don Wycliff:

"Not since the death of Martin Luther King, Jr., in 1968, has black leadership spoken in a genuine, effective way to the souls of black folk. Not, that is, until October 16 and the Million Man March. The genius of the event—which is to say the genius of Louis Farrakhan, who conceived it--was to couch its purpose in religious terms: atonement, reconciliation, recommitment to God, women, family, and community. In so doing, he spoke to the souls of black folk in a way that not even Jesse Jackson had managed to in the twenty-seven years since Dr. King's death. In so doing, he transformed the Million Man March into an occasion for re-fusing a severed cord, for reconnecting with the hopeful, faith-filled religious tradition that King represented and that seemed to fall into decay after his murder."

# The Hard Sayings of Dr. King

In 1983 author F.F. Bruce penned the book entitled the Hard Sayings of Jesus. That book was devoted to the sayings of Jesus that lift him from the popular portrayal as a meek and mild self-sacrificial lamb-like figure to the more realistic revolutionary figure whose bold teachings challenged not only the common man and woman toward moral reforms, but also were like arrows from the bow of truth piercing the egos of the "puffed up" political powers of his day. As Mr. Muhammad and Dr. King were both looked at by J. Edgar Hoover's FBI as potential Black "messiahs" of their people, we also identify some of Dr. King's "hard sayings" that debunk the popular opinion of him as a "polyanna" type, "kum bah yah" singing, "go along to get along" leader.

## Fairness In America Is A Delusion

Dr. King asked, "Why does white America delude itself, and how does it rationalize the evil it retains?" He said white people's belief in the fairness of America "is a fantasy of self-deception and comfortable vanity.... There aren't enough white persons in our country who are willing to cherish democratic principles over privilege."

- "Where Do We Go From Here?" by Rev. Dr. Martin Luther King Jr

## White Liberal & White Conservative United

"White Americans left the Negro on the ground and in devastating numbers walked off with the aggressor. It appeared that the white segregationist and the ordinary white citizen had more in common with one another than either had with the Negro."

- "Where Do We Go From Here?" by Rev. Dr. Martin Luther King Jr.

## Integration Into Death

To his friend Harry Belafonte, he said: "I've come to the realization that I think we may be integrating into a burning house."

-Restoring Hope: Conversations on the Future of Black America By Cornel West, Kelvin Shawn Sealey

## Slumlords Exposed

King's critique of Jewish behavior in the ghetto was stinging: "We were living in a slum apartment owned by a Jew and a number of others, and we had to have a rent strike. We were paying $94 for four run-down, shabby rooms, and we would go out on our open housing marches on Gage Park and other places and we discovered that whites with five sanitary, nice, new rooms, apartments with five rooms, were paying only $78 a month. We were paying 20 percent tax. The Negro ends up paying a color tax, and this has happened in instances where Negroes actually confronted Jews as the landlord or the storekeeper."

-The Autobiography of Dr. Martin Luther King Jr. edited by Clayborne Carson

### Legal System Won't Protect Blacks

If you thought King had faith in the "political process": "Throughout our history, laws affirming Negro rights have consistently been circumvented by ingenious evasions which render them void in practice. Laws that affect the whole population—draft laws, income-tax laws, traffic laws—manage to work even though they may be unpopular: but laws passed for the Negro's benefit are so widely unenforced that it is a mockery to call them laws."

- "Where Do We Go From Here?" by Rev. Dr. Martin Luther King Jr.

### The System Must Be Changed Into A New One

King's systems analysis could only frighten the American elite: "The trouble is that we live in a failed system. Capitalism does not permit an even flow of economic resources. With this system, a small privileged few are rich beyond conscience and almost all others are doomed to be poor at some level.... That's the way the system works. And since we know that the system will not change the rules, we're going to have to change the system."

-My Song: A Memoir By Harry Belafonte, Michael Shnayerson

### The Practicality of Separation

Even Dr. Martin Luther King, Jr., conceded, "there are points at which I see the necessity for temporary separation as a temporary way-station to a truly integrated society."

-The Autobiography of Dr. Martin Luther King Jr. edited by Clayborne Carson

## White Man Created Darkness For Black Man

"If the soul is left in darkness, sins will be committed. The guilty one is not he who commits the sin but he who causes the darkness." "The policymakers of the White society have caused the darkness. They created discrimination. They created slums. They perpetuate unemployment, ignorance and poverty. It is incontestable and deplorable that Negroes have committed crimes, but they are derivative crimes. They are born of the greater crimes of the White society. When we ask Negroes to abide by the law, let us also declare that the White man does not abide by law in the ghettoes."

-Dr. Martin Luther King Jr.: The Crisis in America's Cities: An Analysis of Social Disorder and a Plan of Action Against Poverty, Discrimination and Racism in Urban America., 1967

## True Criminal Is The White Man

"When asking Negroes to abide by the law let us also declare that the white man does not abide by the law. Day in and day out he violates welfare laws to deprive the poor of their meager allotments. He flagrantly violates building codes and housing regulations. His police forces are the ultimate mockery of law. He violates laws on equal employment and education. The slums are the handiwork of a vicious system of the white society. Negroes live in them, but they do not make them any more than a prisoner makes a prison. And so, let us say forthrightly that, if the total slum violations of law by the white man over the years are calculated and compared with the lawbreaking of a few days of riots, the hardened criminal would handily be the white man. In using the term white man, I am seeking to describe in general terms the Negro's adversary."

-Rev. Dr. Martin Luther King, Jr. "A New Sense Of Direction", 1968

# POWER QUOTES:

# A Divine Prescription For Black America From The Most Hon. Elijah Muhammad

Select Themes of Quotes From Message To The Blackman In America by The Most Honorable Elijah Muhammad

**Unity**

page 25      Seek first the friendship of your own people and then the friendship of others (if there is any friendship in the others).

page 32 Let us refrain from doing evil to each other, and let us love each other as brothers, as we are the same flesh and blood.

page 43      I warn you to wake up and accept your own or go to the doom with other than your own. page 100 You must be reunited to your own Nation.

page 100 Accept your own! Stop destroying yourself trying to be other than your own kind and patterning after a doomed race of devils.

page 176 Unite and stop your extravagant spending, trying to live on the level with millionaires, and you will make a heaven for yourselves like other nations have done.

page 194 No. 2. Do not be too proud to meet together as leaders and teachers to discuss the solution of "How to stop this reckless down-hill fall of our people."

page 203 Join us (the Muslims) and our program for a united Black Nation, so that we may free ourselves from our oppressors with whom we cannot get along in peace.

page 220 But let us start first here in America where we are the victims of no freedom, justice and equality and we know the pains of being divided.... At present, we have hundreds of clubs and organizations; thousands of teachers; hundreds of educators, scholars, scientists, technicians, doctors, lawyers, judges, congressmen, ambassadors, professors, tradesmen of all kinds and engineers of most every kind. We have all kinds of religious believers, teachers, preachers by the thousands, agriculturists, herdsmen and cattlemen and fisherman and hundreds of hunters of wild game.

page 222 We must know self to gain self-respect. This will remove that old slave idea that the so-called Negroes cannot unite and build an independent nation on some of this good earth that we can call our own. Stop looking for others to help you in that in which you can help yourself.... Come and let us unite under the crescent and do something for ourselves in the way of supporting our own needs. Go after some of this earth for our nation of 22 million here in North America. If it cannot be had here, there is plenty of earth elsewhere.

page 226 There are probably many independent people who do not have among them many who have the "know how" of the American educated class of so-called Negroes. We have enough technicians, such as mathematicians, construction engineers, civil engineers, mechanical engineers, electrical engineers, physicists, chemists, educators, agriculturists, navigators and aeronauts, among the 22 million or more of us. You will find scholars or scientists whom we can use in every branch of government; then there are our own independent people outside of this country who would be glad to help us get going in a country or state for ourselves. We do not expect to build, nor do we desire to build a government patterned after the order of the white race. Naturally we would need help for the next 20 or 25 years. After that, we would be self- supporting! The spirit of "doing for self" is now fast coming into our people. They only need a new education of self and others.... We must accept the true religion (Islam) of Jesus and the Prophets before and after Him before we can be successful in doing anything.

**Separation**

page 36      Separation of the so-called Negroes from their slave-masters' children is a MUST. It is the only solution to our problem.

page 64      It is time for a separation of the two-black and white. Allah, God, is calling for a separation!

page 180-81 Separate ourselves from the slave-master.

page 184 Know from this day on that if you are a so-called Negro or red, or black or an Indian or any member of the aboriginal

Black Nation you are an un-American. Even though you may have been born in the United States of American you CANNOT be an American.

page 202 Since that is true, I am appealing to you to seek separation from such people on some of this earth that we can call our own, away from a people who openly show and tell you that they hate you and any or all good that may come to you.

page 234 We must be separated, whether we like it or not. I say we must be separated. I do not know why they want to hold on to us unless Allah is forcing them to do it so that he can get a better chance to punish them as he has wanted to do -- as he did Pharaoh.

page 234-35 Let us go back to our native land and people. Every Muslim can go. We, the Muslims, are the true owners of the heavens and the earth.... I give the white people credit. They do the best they can in some instances, but, at the same time, I cannot say that they are angels. They have jailed us and bound us up among them. They should take care of us, give us a chance. If not, they should let us go.

page 317 If you are going to prevent us from going to our own, or back where we came from, where you found us, then give us a place here to ourselves.

**Politics**

page 173 We must give good black politicians the total backing of our population.

page 199 Beware of the national elections, my black brothers and sisters. There is no salvation in them for you -- only false promises.

page 199 Do not follow those self-made leaders who are seeking only the praise of the people and have no good in mind for you and will lead you back into becoming more of a slave than ever.

page 218 Certainly there is power in voting if there is justice for the so-called Negroes. But the crooked political machine of America can always keep the once-slaves, free slaves.... We are a Nation in a nation! Why not use these 22 million people's powers for their eternal salvation instead of temporary enjoyment with the same wicked people who murder our people? (Let us build our own political machine.) Unite with me and with the help of Allah I will get you what you want. And I know what you want for I am your brother.

## History

page 36      Trace over the earth. Check back 5,000, 10,000 or 20,000 years ago. Look at history.  Who were those people? They were our people.

page 125 Study the history of how America treats the freedom, justice and equality which is supposed to be given to all citizens of America (of course, the Negroes are not citizens of America).

page 125-26 Study them and their history and dealings with people and you will without hesitation agree with me 100 per cent that these are the people meant by the Revelator who foresaw their future and end and wrote it while he and his followers were in exile from the Holy Land 6,600 years ago on the Island of Pelan in the Aegean Sea, where he grafted the present white race.

page 171 Educators should teach our people of the great history that was theirs before they were brought to America in shackles by slave-masters.

page 185 Read some of their books as to what was done against our slave parents by the fathers of these modern murderers of ours.

## Personal Habits & Hygiene

page 192 If you have only one suit of clothing, you should wash it and press it each night so that you can wear it the next day. If you are not able to have your hair trimmed at the barbershop, you should take turns and trim each other's hair. You must shave yourselves and look like men.

page 192 And our women should clean up. You do not have to have a dozen dresses. Just keep the one you have clean and pressed.

page 193 Let the entire nation sacrifice for three years. Confine ourselves to buy not more than three suits of clothes a year, never exceeding $65 in cost. Buy the minimum number of shoes, never paying over $16 a pair, as long as current prices for the above-mentioned merchandise remain the same. (Of course, inflation can run prices up until money has no value.)

page 193 We should cut down on waste in high-priced food. Eat pure and wholesome food without being extravagant. Let us cut our extravagances.

page 194 Let us be taught how to spend and save by those of us who desire to see us out of poverty and want.

page 197 Try and save your people from unnecessary high-price buying.

page 199 Look at TV only when you know there is something of importance to be seen; not for foolishness and sport.

page 199 Follow me and live. Reject me and die as people with the help of God and friend.

page 243 Let us examine our thoughts to see what we are actually thinking about and just what we would like to be. Let us present ourselves to the world as we really are. I do not think that God could have taken a better subject to teach us than the one He has: "Accept Your Own and Be Yourself."...Remember this, we are the aboriginals of the earth and are called the black people, and we are the Black Nation.

page 244 Let us take a look at some of what Allah has revealed to me on this subject.  Spiritually He says that your own self (referring to you) is a righteous Muslim. Physically, He says that we are the first and the last and that there were no people before us.

page 275 Be wise, my people, and shut our eyes to them -- do not look at them in such an indecent way. Clean your homes of white people's pictures – put your own on the walls.

page 321 And their training is on this basis, as being Muslims, to keep in practice, not just say it is their faith or belief. You must put into practice the principles of Islam that you believe in and serve as an example for others who would accept Islam....They take physical training and exercises in many ways to keep physically fit and healthy and to try to get away from many of the physical ailments that they have suffered long before coming into the knowledge of Islam....And trained into the knowledge of what the aims and purpose of Islam are, they are to clean up a people who are not clean, morally as well as spiritually, in America and to make them fit to become good members of the society.

## Business/Industry/Land

page 56     As a people, we must become producers and not remain consumers and employees. We must be able to extract raw materials from the earth and manufacture them into something useful for ourselves.

page 174 If there are six or eight Muslims with knowledge and experience of the grocery business -- pool your knowledge, open a grocery store -- and you work collectively and harmoniously, Allah will bless you with success.

page 174 If there are those with knowledge of dressmaking, merchandising, trades, maintenance -- pool such knowledge. Do not be ashamed to seek guidance and instructions from the brother or sister who has more experience, education and training than you have had. Accept his or her assistance.

page 176 I advised you to accept our 3 Year Economic Plan, which will work a miracle for you. page

193 Send your quarters every week to Muhammad's Mosque No. 2 in Chicago, Illinois. These quarters will be banked until we have a million dollars to begin building a banking system.

page 193 But try three years on an "Economic Savings Program" to fight against poverty among our people here in America.

page 193 Please respond and help yourself. Each and every one of you will be sent a receipt which will be recorded in our books for the Muslims' Three-Year Economic Program for the Black Nation in America.

page 196 Purchase real estate, buy farm and timberland. Convert the timber into lumber and build homes for yourselves as the white man is doing.

page 196 Get clay land. With marsh clay land and hill clay, you can make your own bricks. Bricks are inexpensive to make once you get your kiln built and tracks laid.

page 196 Build brick homes for your own people and sell them to your people at a very reasonable price.

page 197 Take your cotton to the mills and have it converted into lint. And take the lint to the textile mills and have it converted into cloth.

page 200 Put these millions of dollars to work buying farm land, since this is the basis of independence.

page 200 Raise cotton, corn, wheat, rye, rice, chicken, cattle, and sheep.

page 201 Turn your millions of dollars over to our National Three-Year Economic Savings Plan and I will show you how you can do all of these things overnight and be a happy people right here in America. ...I am appealing to you -- each and every one of the 22 million black people of America -- to send every penny, nickel, dime, dollar, hundreds of dollars and millions of dollars that you can spare to the Three-Year Economic Plan...

page 203 Spend only when it is a "must" and contribute -- all of you -- all you can to this Three- Year Economic Plan. ...First, we must stop being so foolish as to spend our few hard-earned dollars with the rich of this land.... Those of us who are wealthy or rich should help set up independent businesses which our people need and which could add wealth to our communities. With such cooperation our own businessmen could actually help lower prices and provide employment for the multitude of unemployed.

page 223 What we must understand today is the importance of acquiring land of our own. We are no longer a mere handful of people. We are a little better than 22 million in population and still increasing. We cannot forever continue to depend upon America to give us a job, send us to school, build our houses and sell us her food and give nothing in return.... In order to build a nation, you must first have some land. From our first generation of slaves to the present generation of our people, we have been unable to unite and acquire some land of our own due to the mental poisoning of our former slave-masters, who destroyed in us the desire to think and do for self and kind.

page 229 The poor slave.... He must now realize that he must work hard to be equal of other nations. He must also remember that justice and righteousness is his defense and wickedness his enemy and the downfall of his government and his people. He must learn to make friends and to protect himself against enemies. He must dig into the earth for her rich treasures. He must now seek the friendship of other nations to do business with them and trade product for product.

page 233 The best and most intelligent way is to give Caesar what is Caesar's and let us go for ourselves on some of this earth that we can call our own, just as did the white people. When Europe was overpopulated, they found expansion in the Western Hemisphere. If we want freedom, justice and equality, we must look for it among ourselves and our kind, not among the people who have destroyed and robbed us of even the knowledge of ourselves, themselves, our God and our religion.... Our population runs into billions, and the earth belongs to us. We are the original owners of the earth and will take it and rule it again. This is the time.

page 234-35 We have a Savior today. He is with me. He is able to feed you. He is able to clothe you. He is able to shelter you. I say to you who think that I am begging for some of these states, as I read in the papers, I am not begging for states. It is immaterial to me. If the white government of America does not want to give us anything, just let us go.... We will make a way. Our God will make a way for us....

**Violence**

page 197 Come follow me and I will show you how to do this without having to shed a drop of blood.

page 212 I have even warned my followers never to be the aggressors, as the religion of Islam teaches us that we cannot teach peace and then be the first to break peace with carnal weapons.

page 214 Therefore, we believe that to keep peace with the Christians, we must teach our children in their own schools although they may study the same textbooks.... Know that by nature the black people are for peace and know by nature that the white people are for war, bloodshed and are destroyers of high morals.

page 224 Please do not think that they can be conquered by brickbats, shotguns, a few arms or homemade bombs. It takes the forces of nature and the confusion of minds and thoughts, which are controlled by the power of Allah. Be wise and submit to Allah, who has the power to defend you and destroy your enemies who are too powerful for you.

page 225 I say to you my followers, fear not! If you are with me, Allah is with you, and the more they attack us, the more Allah is attacking and will attack them. The truth of Allah will be universally and permanently established.

page 234-35 I am not going to start a war with them to take land, because all of it belongs to us. I say to the government that if they cannot agree on giving us justice and agree on giving us a chance to make a living for ourselves as they are for themselves, with freedom, justice and equality as they have, then let us go.

page 315 We are not going to take part in any violence whatsoever. We're not going to do anything other than what we are doing. That is trying to deliver the truth to our people and teach them that they are supposed to be Muslims, and that means they are supposed to be righteous people and that we have shed all things that pertain to wickedness.... We have respect for them and their professions, and we try to treat them as we treat ourselves, for that matter. We know they are not believers as we are. We know that. But as long as they tolerate our faith, we tolerate theirs, and we treat them as brothers.

**Education**

page 2 Such teaching (a mystery God) that God is a mystery makes the prophets' teachings of God all false. There should be a law made and enforced upon such teachers until they have been removed from the public.

page 7 We must not take our enemies for our spiritual guides lest we regret it. Fly to Allah! Come, follow me. Although I may look insignificant to you, you will find salvation with us. The white race is excited and cannot think rightly for themselves.

page 32     Awake and know that Allah has revealed the truth. Stop believing in something coming to you after you are physically dead.

That is untrue, and no one can show any proof of such belief. Love yourself and your kind.

page 39 Get an education, but not an education that leaves us looking to the slave-master for a job. Accept your own, that which you have been dead to the knowledge of, now that God has come in your midst to resurrect you and put you in your place of authority.

page 44      The duty of the civilized man is to teach civilization to the un-civilized—the arts and sciences of civilized people and countries of advanced civilization.

page 54      One of the first and most important truths that must be established in this day is our identity.... First, you must be given the names of your forefathers, whose names are the most Holy and Righteous Names of Allah. Again, I repeat, that restoring to you your identity is one of the first and most important truths to be established by God, Himself.

page 57      We must educate ourselves and our children into the rich power of knowledge which has elevated every people who have sought and used it. We must give the benefit of our knowledge to the elevation of our own people.

**Prayer**

page 136 Remember: And the best way for remembrance of Allah (God) is through prayer.... Let us give praises to our God and submit ourselves to the Lord of the worlds and learn how to pray the right prayers in the right manner.

page 137 Come to success; prayer and obedience to Allah will bring you success.

page 139 We must study the words and the different positions taken by the Muslim in his daily prayer.

page 143 No one of you must say his prayers in a garment without covering the whole body.

page 143 Order your children to say the state prayers when they are seven years of age, and beat them if they do not do so when they are ten years old.

page 146 A Muslim must say his prayers. When we say that we are Muslims (those who have submitted to the will of Allah) and then we must give praises to the One to whom we have submitted, to do His will.

page 147 But we must remember we are taking an oath in this prayer, that we will not accept any god but Allah, in the words: "My prayers, my sacrifice, my life and death are all for Allah."

page 147 Let the Muslims and hypocrites who read this teaching taught in the above prayer know that we have taken an oath with our life to live for Allah and sacrifice everything we have for Allah and that we will even die for Allah!

page 147 ...study and learn the prayer above and recite it if you are believers as often as you can and know that you have fled to Allah and have taken refuge in Him against the accursed devils.

page 152 We, the lost-founds, should repeat the above prayer seven (7) times a day. For it sums up our greatest hindrance to freedom and self-independence. ["O Allah! I seek The refuge from anxiety and grief..."]

page 160 NOTE: The latter verse (Quran 2:286) is a prayer; let us recite it very often. ["On no soul doth Allah Place a burden greater than it can bear..."]

"O Allah, guide me among those whom Thou hast guided aright and preserve me among those whom Thou has preserved and befriended and bless me in whatever Thou doest; grant me and deliver me from the evils of what Thou has judged. Surely Thou judgest and none can judge against Thee and He whom Thou befriendest is not disgraced."

## Protect Our Women

page 59 You and I may go to Harvard, we may go to York of England, or go to Al Ahzar in Cairo and get degrees from all of these great seats of learning. But we will never be recognized until we recognize our women.

page 60     You cannot control or protect your women as long as you are in the white race's false religion called Christianity. This religion of theirs gives you no desire or power to resist them.

The only way and place to solve this problem is in the Religion of Islam.

page 127 The so-called Negroes should unite and put a stop to the destruction of their women by the serpent.

page 171 Stop allowing the white men to shake hands or speak to your women anytime or anywhere.

## Do For Self/Independence

page 168 You and I should fight to the death to be free to do what we want.

page 169 We must remember that we just cannot depend on the white race ever to do that which we can and should do for self.

page 170-71 We must stop relying upon the white man to care for us. We must become an independent people.

1.    Separate yourselves from the "slave-master."

2.    Pool your resources, education and qualifications for independence.

3.    Stop forcing yourselves into places where you are not wanted.

4.    Make your own neighborhood a decent place to live.

5.    Rid yourselves of the lust of wine and drink and learn to love self and your kind before loving others.

6.    Unite to create a future for yourself.

7.    Build your own homes, schools, hospitals, and factories.

8.    Do not seek to mix your blood through racial integration.

9.    Stop buying expensive cars, fine clothes and shoes before being able to live in a fine home.

10.    Spend your money among yourselves.

11.    Build an economic system among yourselves.

12.    Protect your women.

page 174 The believers in truth, Islam, must stop looking up to the white race for justice and take the following steps to correct this problem:

1.      Recognize the necessity for unity and group operation (activities).

2.      Pool your resources, physically as well as financially.

3.      Stop wanton criticisms of everything that is black-owned and black-operated.

4.      Keep in mind -- jealousy destroys from within.

5.      Observe the operations of the white man. He is successful. He makes no excuses for his failures. He works hard in a collective manner. You do the same.

Page 204 Teach and train the blacks to do something for self in the way of uniting and seeking a home on this earth that they can call their own!

page 207 They should accept their own (Islam) and try to do something for themselves as other nations are doing, on land they can call their own.

page 301 What must be done? You must start thinking and working in the way of independence, as other dependent nations had to do and are still doing, when once free of those who hold you in bondage. Get away from that childish way of thinking that the white man forever owes it to you to provide for you the necessities of life. Should you not be too proud of yourself in this modern time to be thinking in the way of dependence instead of independence?

# Powerful Words From Black Leaders In Harmony With The Muslim Program

## Martin Luther King, Jr.

I've come to the realization that I think we may be integrating into a burning house. —Martin Luther King, Jr., to Harry Belafonte

King ultimately found that integration "ended up as merely adding color to a still predominantly white power structure." He conceded, "there are points at which I see the necessity for temporary separation as a temporary way-station to a truly integrated society."

## Paul Robeson

"Partisan interests must be subordinated to Negro interests—by each of us. Somehow, we must find the way to set aside all that divides us and come together, Negroes all. Our unity will strengthen our friends and win many more to our side; and our unity will weaken our foes who already can see the handwriting on the wall."

## Rev. Ralph Abernathy:

[The] programs of the American Government in her dealings with the poor of all minority groups lead to genocide.... When we look at America from the perspective of the poor, we see only destruction and death, exploitation and oppression, yes, we see genocide. Those things which make America great for you are denied to us and the attempts of the Government to administer to our needs lead only to further destruction.

## Ralph Bunche

Bunche adopted Muhammad Ali's anti-war stance when his own son was drafted and sent off in 1969:

"As I began to think about the boy's departure, I became furious and outraged....Our one son...was being taken off to an utterly senseless, useless war, a war that could bring no good to anyone, that no one could possibly win....I felt like going out into the street and denouncing in the strongest terms at my command the war, all of those who got us into it and those who keep us in it and the establishment in general."

Bunche wrote an unpublished paper titled, "The Programs, Ideologies, Tactics, and Achievements of Negro Betterment and Interracial Organizations," in 1940 in which he argued that Blacks needed an economic program for upliftment. After rejecting both Garveyism and the Nation of Islam, Bunche eventually stated "Today's black power demand however, is stronger, more insistent and more widely based and therefore gives new strength to the development of black unity."


## John Lewis

"I think past history will testify to the fact that white liberals and the so-called affluent Negro leaders will not support all our demands. They will be forced to support some of them in order to maintain an image of themselves as liberal. But we must also recognize that their material comforts and congenial relations with the establishment are much more important to them than their concern for an oppressed people. And they will sell us down the river for the hundredth time in order to protect themselves."


## Whitney Young

"We need to unleash all of the great researchers who have been spending all their time studying black people—and making money—onto the subject of white people to find out what in the world is wrong with that Man that makes him so obsessed with feeling superior. Why does he have to have somebody to feel superior to? I'd like to study why he wants to bring up his children in those bland, sterile, antiseptic, gilded ghettos, giving sameness to each other, producing stagnation and uncreative people in a world that's become a neighborhood. Why does he want to teach his child to disrespect people because of their occupation or their race? I think there's a sickness here, and it ought to be studied by those same people who've been making their living revealing the pathologies of black people."

## W.E.B. Du Bois

"I thank God that most of the money that supports the National Association for the Advancement of Colored People comes from black hands; a still larger proportion must so come, and we must not only support but control this and similar organizations and hold them unwaveringly to our objects, our aims and our ideals."

## Fannie Lou Hamer

"They're these middle-class Negroes, the ones that never had it as hard as the grass roots people in Mississippi. They'll sell their parents for a few dollars. Sometimes I get so disgusted I feel like getting my gun after some of these school teachers and chicken-eatin' preachers."

## Julian Bond

"It makes it easier for us to be a mental nation, a nation within a nation. We're a nation separate and apart in our problems and have to be dealt with separate and apart. And we have to think of ourselves as different from the whole."

# Minister Farrakhan Interviews Professor Daniel Patrick Moynihan On The Subject of The Crisis of the Black Family

## A Talk with the Man Who Wrote the 'Moynihan Report'

**NOTE:** This historical series of articles comprise the published interview from 1967, wherein the Hon. Min. Louis Farrakhan posed a series of questions to the author of the legendary "Moynihan Report". Professor and former Senator Daniel Patrick Moynihan has become infamous in the history of the Black struggle for advising President Nixon to treat the Black community with "benign neglect". The Muslim Program of The Most Hon. Elijah Muhammad can be considered as especially necessary when contrasted against the lack of concern and compassion of the American federal government toward the masses of Black people.

### Muhammad Speaks, January 27, 1967

Professor Daniel Patrick Moynihan of Harvard University is aptly rated as perhaps the greatest and certainly the most provocative American sociologist. He is the author of the recent documentary study on the Negro family upon which it is reported President Johnson based much of his famous Howard University address and obtained from its ideas for some of his poverty programs. Dr. Moynihan recently consented to a series of interviews with Minister Louis Farrakhan of Muhammad's temple of Islam in New York, which covered a variety of facets of the Negro issue in America. At the conclusion of this exclusive series, Minister Farrakhan's own views of the interview will be printed.

QUESTION: What is your definition of a family?

ANSWER: What we normally think of as being a family is a situation in which one or two adults care for dependent minor children. With very few exceptions, the people in the past and present - representing the thousands of cultures, different races and religions - have thought of the family in terms of a husband, a wife and their children.

Now, it can mean a mother and her children without a husband. It can mean a husband without a mother or adopted children.

QUESTION: We notice that throughout the world, there is a move toward birth control. We have what is called a population explosion - and there is a great concern about this, about this situation. But some people feel that birth control is used to limit mainly the families of non-whites while at the same time developing pills or hormone shots to increase the fertility of whites. Since most of the experimentation on birth control methods is being practiced on non-whites. What is your opinion on this, and do you think it is a form of genocide?

ANSWER: I think it is always necessary to start out with the facts; I mean the present facts. You do know that the birth rate of Negro women in this country today is much higher than that of white women - about 35 percent higher. Although the birth rate for Negros is dropping, just as it is for whites since the pill became widely available, that differential is not closing. The non-white rate is still about 35 percent higher.

I don't think it is generally known, for example, that one baby in six in America today is a Negro baby - a much higher rate than we've had since the time of the signing of the American Constitution. When it was about one in five. It was about one in five in the 18th century. It dropped to about one in 10 - now it's back to one in six.

I have a very strong view on birth control. It is an individual decision. It's a moral decision. Persons of different religious views have different positions on the question - and that's their own business. It's a very private matter, of course.

I think I know what you mean and I sympathize very much with your concern. When the issue of birth control is used as a device to solve the problem of poverty by limiting the number of poor people who are born, I think we sometimes get awfully close to that in our thinking.

I don't think the persons who are talking this way have reasoned the whole thing for themselves. But that's awfully close to what they are saying and I think we better be pretty careful of that.

The problem of poverty is resolved by providing people with jobs and decent incomes - not seeing that they are not born.

**THERE ARE**, however, such things as families with more children than they want and more children than they need. We have surveys which suggest that Negro mothers would by and large, prefer to have fewer children than they do have.

That may not be the last word, but I would say to you that I think we should enable people to do what they want to do - but we certainly should be very careful about solving our social problems by trying to eliminate populations that seem to present social problems. I'm not sure we face up to that.

## PART 2: Min. Farrakhan Interviews Professor Moynihan
### Muhammad Speaks, February 3, 1967

QUESTION: In Fauquier County, Virginia, there is a clinic that seeks to get black women to have hysterectomy operations, (surgical removal of the uterus, where the baby is nourished and developed before birth). And on the West Coast, a Puerto Rican woman arrested in a house where police found marijuana was given the choice by the judge of being sterilized and having all charges dropped or going to jail.

We realize that many people may want to limit the size of their families for various reasons, but we don't think this should be done in a way to permanently prevent people from producing except in the cases of malfunctioning organs or terribly diseased organs. What is your thinking on this?

ANSWER: I completely agree with you. I think that experience in Virginia as I understand it is outrageous and criminal.

QUESTION: I read an article which noted that according to the Food and Drug Administration, the birth control pill has not been perfected, and there were certain effects that the pill sometimes over activated the thyroid gland glands, and it produced obesity in some of the women who took the pill, though it is still in the experimental stage, the Food and Drug Administration has not turned thumbs down on the pill. According to your knowledge, is this true?

ANSWER: My knowledge on this, I suspect, is no different from yours. I know what I read in the papers and I know enough about the papers not to believe everything I read in them. I am not a chemist nor biologist - and certainly not a medical doctor. But I understand this is an open issue and we should regard it as such. And I assume and I assume that any effort to interrupt normal bodily functions can produce unexpected complexities.

QUESTION: The Negro family in America never has realized its full potential because of the excessive death rate for many and various reasons. Poverty, want squalor, disease, fratricidal conflicts, and the tremendous infant mortality rate.

Black people represent 10.9 percent of the American population, but the infant mortality rate among black babies is twice that for whites. Further deaths occurring to black women in pregnancy are twice those occurring to white women.

What steps are being planned or taken to remedy these conditions in the black communities of America?

ANSWER: As far as I now can recall, the statistics you cite are entirely accurate. Nonetheless, those death rates have been dropping very sharply. The infant death rate has been rising a bit, but there was a great drop off.  Getting rid of some of the basic diseases a generation ago was the cause of this drop. It's also true just as you say that a great many legal families are not intact because the mother and father are not together or the father is dead.

Negro men tend to have jobs that are more dangerous. You work in construction, for instance, and you might get killed, you're likely to get killed a lot sooner than if you worked a white-collar job in an office.

However, remember a lot fewer people get killed today than they did in the past. Lots of them may get hurt but they don't die as easily. I think doctors are better at patching up people.

**HOWEVER**, you are correct to point out that an important element in the problem of the Negros family is the problem of health and mortality.

QUESTION: In the Moynihan Report, there were some facts highlighting the crime rate among Black people. The great rate of aggravated assaults and murder perpetrated mainly by blacks against blacks. What are your views on the basic causes of this situation and what is being done to correct the causes?

ANSWER: If I knew that, I would be a more important person than I am. We just don't have that information. However, we do know that children who grow up in troubled families and bad neighborhoods who see a lot of crime, but don't see many opportunities for themselves in the world. Children who aren't going on to school for years and years. These children get into trouble. They get into trouble whatever their race, whatever their religion, whatever their country they're in.

AND DON'T kid yourself, they get into trouble a lot more than the children who grow up in steady families and good neighborhoods and go to good schools. We like to say that those kids out in the suburbs have a lot of trouble and the police just don't record it. That's not so. We're just fooling ourselves if we think that so.

The chances for those young people in the slums to get through life without getting into trouble with the police are a lot worse than perhaps your family or my family.

QUESTION: There were recent reports that there is a growing crime rate in suburbia. Among the more well to do though they don't have the broken homes or the terrible environmental conditions of the ghetto youngster. What do you feel contributes to this growing crime rate? Is it affluence?

ANSWER: I have to say to you that we're doing some research on that subject at the Joint Center of urban studies, Harvard University, and we have not finished it, but we have a pretty clear idea where we're coming out.

If you double the number of teenagers in a neighborhood, you're going to double the number of crimes. That's fairly certain. There are an awful lot of teenagers alive these days-a lot more than there used to be-and there are going to be a lot more. Consequently, there is going to be a lot more crime. Our crime wave has just begun. However, the actual percentage of boys getting into trouble is about the same. And girls don't get into much trouble. We tell ourselves something that may be comforting, but its's misleading if we think that the suburbs have a crime problem because they don't. I think that's important to know because it means that if you give people a decent life to live, they don't bother each other. Now there's always going to be crime. You know, there's a devil in the world. But there are things we can avoid-things we avoid in the suburbs but not in the slums, and we should learn something from that.

## PART 3: Outlook of Harvard Professor Moynihan On Negro Family, Crime, the Viet Draft
### Muhammad Speaks, February 10, 1967

Question: You mentioned that girls are much less prone to get into trouble than boys. What are your thoughts on that?

Answer: There are many thoughts about it. I think one of the unmistakable forces of crime is the effort to demonstrate manhood, courage and strength to a group of trends and contemporaries. Girls don't have that challenge. A girl is not asked to prove that she's tougher than the local policeman. Further, there is no doubt that children raised in broken homes-where there is no strong male-have a harder time. Where there is no decent father who tells them how to behave; who shows them how a man behaves, it's not easy for the boys to know when they are turning into young men themselves and they tend to try to act the only way they hear a man can act: go out and punch a policeman in the nose. It is a very common phenomenon in the world and it's very common in America. I was just reading that the President's Commission on Crime in the District of Columbia made its report, confirming your feelings, Minister Farrakhan, about the very sharp increase in crime. And the report said something very interesting: "Only 36%-only 36% "of the sampled adult offenders came from homes where both natural parents resided together through the offenders' 20th year. Only 21% of narcotic addicts and offenders were raised with both their parents." In other words, 79% of the narcotic addicts and offenders came from broken homes. 74% of the criminals, generally. Now that doesn't try to prove anything, but how much do you have to prove before you know what you knew anyway-that a boy raised in a disorganized family is a disorganized, mixed-up kid?

Question; Turning to the military draft, I understand that 3 out of 5 whites are turned down for medical or various other reasons. We understand also that the physical rate of rejection of whites is higher than that of Blacks, though in Blacks the mental rate of rejection is higher than that of Whites. This is a complete reverse of things. We'd like to know what you've discovered on this matter.

Answer: I do not know and I believe that no one knows. We could find out if we'd pay more attention to the subject. However, for some reason or other, we've never been willing to look closely enough at this very important source of information on how we are doing in this country-namely, who gets rejected and who gets accepted in the army. You are absolutely right in your proportions. I believe your actual percentages may be a bit off. In 1965, among persons called up for selective service, 26% of whites were rejected on medical grounds and only 16% of Negroes. Now this could have 2 meanings. It could mean that Negroes are healthier than whites. I rather doubt that because I think there's a real correlation between health and poverty.

There is another explanation I suspect this is probably so but there is absolutely no evidence for it. I know something about the system. I've studied it. That is in the induction station doctors are in short supply.

THEY BRING everybody into the room and an Army Sergeant can give the mental test. Then the doctors give the medical. I think it may be that they give the mental test first - and if they fail it they just don't bother to give them the medical because they're going to be rejected anyway. It takes a long time to examine a person medically.

However, there could be some other reason entirely. One I never heard of. I wish the army would find out and tell us they could learn anything. If they just take the trouble.

QUESTION: There has been much talk in recent months on the percentage of blacks involved in the Vietnam War - the 22 percent of US soldiers in Vietnam are black, and that the casualties of blacks are greater or greater - ratio and proportion-wise - than whites.

In another report, I read that blacks are selected for some of the most dangerous missions. Then critics of the Vietnam conflict have said the draft system works unfairly against black Americans because of the deprivation and poverty of black people. The only hope for many black young persons is to join some branch of the armed services. I would like to hear your comments.

ANSWER: There are two conflicting and different set of numbers you have to have in your mind in order to understand this problem. I find it is very difficult for most people to get it straight for most people to get it straight.

The first fact is that by and large Negro Americans have been underrepresented in the armed forces for the past 15 years.

Remember, the armed forces are the largest employer in the United States. The training, the jobs and careers are valuable. Some people don't like them and many people do remember for every two persons drafted three persons volunteer. People's tastes differ. Some like it in the Marines, some like to be in the Navy, and that's their business. These jobs by and large are sought after. And by and large the process of selection has worked to exclude Negros from getting their equal share of the jobs.

**I DON'T KNOW** if there's any law saying that everybody is to get an equal share. But if you're 12 percent of an age group, Do you or don't you have 12 percent of the jobs? That's irrelevant? If you read this article in the **New Republic**, you will if you read this article in the New Republic, you will find me saying that in 1964, if Negros had their proportion in the armed forces, and then by that amount, that number, the number of Negro males unemployed was reduced, and the reverse process occurred for whites. The unemployment rates for Negros would have been lower than the rates for whites.

The second thing and a different subject entirely is that Negros tend to be in the army. They seem to like the army, but perhaps they have an easier time getting into it. I don't know.

**ONE OUT OF** every six army sergeants is a Negro. Negro stay in the armed forces more than whites do. 49percent of Negro enlisted men reenlist as against 15percent of whites. That means they like it or they think there's nothing better or they're good at it, or any number of other reasons. I can't tell you why people do what they do.

## PART 4: On Destruction of Black Youth
### Muhammad Speaks, February 17, 1967

Muhammad speaks at the conclusion of this interview with Dr. Daniel Patrick Moynihan, Minister Louis Farrakhan of Muhammad's mosque number seven in Harlem, to whom Professor Moynihan granted the interview will give his personal views on Dr. Moynihan statements discussing the Negro and the military against a backdrop of a question concerning the disproportionate rate of induction of black youths and their alarming Lee high death rate. In Vietnam. Dr. Moynihan, a pro administration sociologist said in last week's installment that the Negroes that have been under represented in the armed forces for the past 15 years he made the points that one of every one out of every six army sergeants is a Negro, and that 49percent of Negro enlisted men re-enlist. He continues this discussion in the following.

These men, Negros tend also to get into combat jobs. Now, that's not because they like to fight, or they liked the extra pay, or they liked the way the girls treat them when they come home. Or because they didn't have any choice. I don't know why this is true, but it is. They are infantry platoons, in paratroopers in these types of fighting jobs, and they are in there out of proportion to their proportion of the population.

**NOW THERE** are more Negroes in our infantry platoons. There are more Negroes who are sergeants than there would be if they had just had a normal share. and more of them are getting killed and more of them are getting wounded.

Now why is that so? Well, it would be a natural thing, if more of them are getting shot at, but also perhaps they are taking more risks. I don't know.

The problem is, how do you not get them mixed up? How do you not say well 22percent of the casualties or Negros therefore 22 percent of the people in the armed forces must be Negros? Well, that's not true. As a matter of fact, there are an awful lot of good jobs in the armed forces. It seems to me, of which, Negroes are not getting their share.

**BUT LET ME** say one other thing to you. It's a hard thing to say. But worse things have happened to the Negro people than to have a heavy share of casualties in Vietnam. They are not heavy casualties, as you know...

I think 5,000 American soldiers died last year. Well, that's terrible, but it's not 500,000.

**I ASKED** my students at Harvard to name the three largest buildings on the campus. They all blinked. could not remember and did know. I pointed out to them that these buildings are Memorial Hall, Memorial Chapel and Soldiers Field. All of these great buildings were erected to sons of Harvard who died in battle.

QUESTION: If you have a greater proportion of blacks carrying the burden of an unpopular war, don't you think the government's commitment to the blood of these black soldiers should be to improve the sickening conditions under which black people have to live in a continental United States?

ANSWER: Well, a government's commitment to justice ought to be total and continuous and not be dependent on anything else. But that's not the way the world is, is it? And that not being the way the world is? The grounds cited in your question seem entirely sound to me that the fact of Negros the Negros sacrifices in Vietnam ought to make it much more important that they should have social justice at home and they do not now have it.

QUESTION: Would you advocate that Negros get a greater percentage of the jobs in the army to bring them within their proportion of the population? Would you advocate the same type of representation in the government - especially in view of the fact that we have only 1 percent representation in the Congress as opposed to 11 percent of the United States population?

ANSWER: Well, it seems to me that people should get elected to Congress on whether they can do a good job, dash and I certainly think that in the armed forces there are Negro us being rejected, who probably could be used and probably ought to be used.

Let me be very frank with you. In 1965 in North Carolina and South Carolina, 82 percent of the young Negro boys called up for selective service were rejected. I think most of those country boys in particular, who don't know very much about the big world, haven't seen much, haven't had much education; haven't had much good medical care and things like that - probably would benefit from being in the Army.

Now, I don't want to sound like the army is the greatest thing in the world. Anybody who's been in it knows better, but it's not the worst. thing in the world either rejecting 82 percent in one state and 70 percent and another you can't tell me some of these boys wouldn't like to be in and we couldn't figure out a place for them.

And don't forget you get rights when you get into the armed forces. You get the GI Bill, and you get home insurance and you get buried in Arlington Cemetery. Not that it makes much difference to you where you get buried, but it might make a difference to your children someday.

QUESTION: Turning to the unemployment situation we have seen that there has been a rise in unemployment among Black people in the United States. At the same time, however, the unemployment rate for whites has dropped. Some scholars feel that by 1970 the rate of unemployment among black Americans will be five times as much as it is now. How do you view the cutback and Great Society programs and its impact upon the economics of an already poverty-stricken black man because of the escalation of the Vietnam conflict?

ANSWER: I don't have an answer to that, because several contradictory things seem to be happening. That we don't understand. Remember that the unemployment problem tends to be less of a problem during a military period than in a peacetime period. I hate to say this, but as long as we are at war in Asia, there are going to be plenty of jobs in America.

Now if there is a problem of unemployment for Negros it definitely seems to be concentrated among the young people. We just have not solved this condition and I don't know how we can solve it.

Something's gone wrong. The system's not working. The fact is, there are jobs around and people who want jobs don't have them. We're not fitting things together very well.

Let me tell you something. The unemployment rate for Negro teenage girls couldn't increase 5 percent Because it would reach 100 percent before it increased four times. That's how high it all is already. I just think that we are probably going to have to start thinking less in terms of these percentages, and more in terms of individual people.

We've got to start saying, for instance, that Pat Moynihan's boy, Timmy, has got to have a job. He's getting out of school now and who is going to hire him?

I'm going to spend a week in Germany, you will be interested to know that is exactly how persons leaving school in Germany are treated. I mean they just don't leave it to the labor market. Everybody's registered and they find a job for everyone.

It's not a question of working itself out somehow. They see that it does work out. They don't find you a job in terms of percentages of unemployed they find you a job in terms of Pat Moynihan says boy to me who was going to get him a job. And I think we can do that in this country too. If we put our minds to it.

## PART 5: Crisis Inside the Black Family
### Muhammad Speaks, February 24, 1967

Dr. Daniel Patrick Moynihan concludes the interview he granted Minister Louis Farrakhan of Muhammad's mosque number seven in Harlem on this page, in a four-part series, Professor Moynihan, one of the greats so sociologists of the world authority on the Negro family and head of the Joint Center for Urban Studies, Harvard University has discussed many of the issues which involve black Americans. Muslim Minister Louis gives his personal views on Dr. Moynihan statements next week.

QUESTION: I'm thinking about the unemployment picture where black people qualified for certain jobs but are denied those jobs on the basis of race. I'm thinking of the broken promises so many through the years made to black people by the government.

The Promised mule and 40 acres of land to emancipated black slaves never materialized. Black Americans never saw the promised improvement of their play after World Wars. One and two, and the Korean conflict. Then there were the promises of the Great Society, especially the anti-poverty program, which raised so many hopes - now have come. Will the cutbacks in this project and others will the cutbacks proved to be the final straw so to speak, that will break the camel's back and bring about a definite estrangement between black Americans and the government? How does this whole situation look to you?

ANSWER: I can't answer that, but I'll tell you this. I've been in government a lot of my life and I would like to urge anyone reading this interview to get what you can out of the government, but don't depend on it. The government tends to oversell itself. We tend to over promise. I mean, we over promised in the poverty war. We said that in five- or 10-years' time, there will be no poverty left. Well, that's nonsense. We should have known better, but we didn't.

But you're absolutely right. It seems to me that we have a situation in which Negro people - or the poor persons - can complain: We were promised something and now you are breaking your promise. As soon as you get a chance to have a war in Asia instead of a war on poverty, off you go. I don't have an answer to that. And as far as the consequences of the broken promises are concerned, you would be in a much better position to know that.

I think we are trifling with the confidence people have in the government. If we let the poverty program drop the way some people seem to want to do now I don't think the President does. I'm sure he does not. But there are people in Congress who talk that way. And there's always the newspapers which talk that way. Well, as I have said, This is no way for a grown-up country to behave.

We started this thing more than two years ago. We don't know whether or not it's working. And we won't know for 10 years or more. You've got to keep working until you begin to see whether it's paying off.

QUESTION: There is a question relative to the percentages found in your Moynihan Report. You said in our last talk that you had been surprised that some of these figures are much worse than you had anticipated. Which of the finger figures do you feel are worse than you anticipated?

ANSWER: Minister Farrakhan, let me say that the report was intended to do something very simple, but many things have been read into it that were not and are not there. The report simply meant to say that the

QUESTION:   of family stability is a good measure of how successful or unsuccessful social policies have been.

If more families are living together, that's a sign things are getting better. But if more families are breaking up, that's a sign things are getting worse. I think this is true of all people. We began picking up signs that for Negro families living in poverty, things must have been getting worse because it was clear that there were more broken families and more abandoned children and more women having to cope somehow with raising families without a father.

We wrote a report saying that if this is so perhaps things are not getting better. Maybe things are getting worse. They certainly aren't very good and we ought to do something about it. What to do is another question.

Since the time of this report, which was the spring of 1965. We've begun receiving new figures and a new census, mid-decade census has been taken. I have here for example, a very recent report from Cleveland. Compare the number of families in Negro areas headed by females in 1960.

I see that in Hough, a well-known section where there was trouble last year - 22.5 percent of the Negro families were headed by females in 1960 or 1966. This figure has risen in 1966 to 32.1 percent.

In West Central, the increase was to 35.9percent this is much too high. And the Negro unemployment in west central is 20percent. That's an outrage.

Now in Mount Pleasant, where the unemployment rate was only 6.8percent. And I say that's too high - the number of female heads of families was only 15.8 percent. You have a corresponding picture of unemployment and broken families with females at the head. I'm not going to say which one causes the other because I don't know.

Anyway, just as you say many of the things we are trying to measure in the report turned out as bad as we thought and perhaps worse.

One of the sad facts is that so many people in our country were unwilling to deal with the problems of family life because they didn't want to admit that the problem existed. So, the great opportunity we had was missed. We failed.

QUESTION: Do you find a relationship between unemployment and crime as well as between unemployment and broken homes?

ANSWER: The relationship between unemployment and crime is more complicated. It's not clear. It could be suggested that it may be possible in times of high on high employment when people have a lot of things like cameras.

## PART 6: Minister Farrakhan Views Statements Made by Dr. Moynihan in Interview
### Muhammad Speaks, March 3, 1967

### By Minister Louis Farrakhan

My convictions are confirmed that black people must follow the Supreme Counsel and guidance of messenger Elijah Muhammad or suffer the consequences.

If I learned anything from my interview with the renowned Dr. Manuel Daniel Patrick Moynihan, I learned that the United States government is at a complete loss in its attempt to solve the problems of 25 million black people.

With all the human physical and economic resources at the command of government. All her programs, supposedly designed to change. The sickening condition of black people in America, are meeting with dismal failure.

Millions of black people today have pinned their hopes of an end to their frustrations and poverty on the promises of government. However, in our interview, Dr. Moynihan warned that "black people should get what they can out of government, but don't depend on it. For in the end, it's only going to be of limited use to anyone, for government tends to oversell itself. Government tends to over promise."

For 35 years the Honorable Elijah Muhammad has warned us that in the final analysis, we would have to unite and depend on ourselves. Let us as intelligent black people face the facts.

1. The government has no real program for our intentions of ending poverty among us;

2. The government has no real program to aid in rebuilding black families;

3. The government has no solution to the high unemployment among blacks, for the government has no real program for effectively eliminating squalor and disease among blacks;

4. The government has no real program to reduce the high death rate, the high no solution to the high unemployment among blacks;

5. The government has no real program for effectively eliminating squalor and disease among blacks.

However, the government does have a program to cut down the birth rate of black babies, which according to Dr. Moynihan is 35 percent higher than the birth rate of whites by the use of a pill sanctioned by the Food and Drug Administration, which they cannot by their own admission, say is safe. The Honorable Elijah Muhammad has warned us repeatedly through Muhammad Speaks radio and personal appearances, appearances of the government's wicked intentions against the black people of America.

Dr. Moynihan said that the Moynihan Report was intended to do something very simple. His study revealed simply that where families are getting on well and there is family stability, there are less social problems. Dr. Moynihan said his hopes were to try to get some legislation passed that would give to poor families a government subsidy.

However, he said because so many people in our country were unwilling to deal with the problems of family life because they did not want to admit that the problem existed, the great opportunity which we had, was missed. So out of that great Congress and that great opportunity came nothing.

It is absolutely criminal in my opinion, that after the government forgot about the Health Education and Welfare of black people all these years now since America's welfare is threatened, and it looks like perennial to black man, due to mental incapacitation will escape the draft the government throws open the door so the armed forces to black people who by their standards are unfit for the draft, under the pretense that acquiring a reputation for military valor is of the oldest known routes to social justice.

# Free Blacks Considered "A Grievous Affliction"

**NOTE:** The Most Honorable Elijah Muhammad lists freedom and a "full and complete freedom" as point number 1 of <u>What The Muslims Want</u>. The excerpt below is offered to place some important historical context to the idea of freedom for the Black man and woman in America. This passage sheds light on just how freedom for the Black people of America has been viewed by powerful members of the white ruling class in America, particularly those who occupy high positions within the judicial system.

It is eye opening to consider that according to the judicial opinions and legislative acts in the period between the Revolutionary and Civil Wars, "free Negrodom" was deemed a twofold "grievous affliction." Free Blacks ostensibly presented a danger to the institution of slavery because they would entice slaves to run away and revolt. Jurists and legislators also characterized free Blacks as a class unworthy of envy, lazy and incapable of self-care, destined to live in a state of squalor and degeneracy far below the station of the slave, and fated to create a burden on society as a whole.

On the heels of the Revolutionary War, **lawyers openly stated that free Blacks were immoral and posed a danger to societal and economic interests**. Similar language appeared in the body of judicial opinions in the early 1800s, but these opinions merely quoted or paraphrased prefatory wording of legislative enactments. In 1834, John Catron, who sat on the Tennessee Supreme Court from 1824 to 1834 and the United States Supreme Court from 1837 to 1865, provided the judiciary's first full-throated endorsement of this position. Justice Catron wrote the opinion in Fisher's Negroes v. Dabbs, a case concerning the manumission of several slaves through a will.:

"The injustice of forcing our freed negroes on our sister states without their consent, when we are wholly unwilling to be afflicted with them ourselves, is so plain and direct a violation of moral duty as to inhibit this court from taking such a step. . ... Would it not be treating the non-slaveholding states unjustly to force our freed negroes upon them without their consent? [A]nd would it not be treating the slaveholding states cruelly? **We are ejecting this description of population, fearing it will excite rebellion among the slaves; or that the slaves will be rendered immoral to a degree of depravity inconsistent with the safety and interest of the White population. These are fearful evils**. But are they not more threatening to Virginia (just recovering from the fright of a negro rebellion), to the Carolinas, to Georgia, Alabama, Mississippi, and Louisiana than to us? Compared with the Whites, most of them have two slaves to our one; some of them almost ten to our one. Even Kentucky has a higher proportion than Tennessee. How can we then, as honest men, thrust our freed negroes on our neighbors of the south?

Suppose the non-slaveholding states northwest of the Ohio were willing to receive our freed negroes (a supposition, by the way, wholly untrue), would it be good policy in us to locate them on our borders, beside our great rivers, **forming wretched free negro colonies in constant intercourse with our slaves? . . . That such a population, inhabiting a country near us, would become a most dangerous receptacle to our runaway slaves, and a grievous affliction to the state where situated, as well as to ourselves, need only be stated to gain universal admission.**

**The time would soon come when the attempt to seize on the harbored slaves would produce war with such a people**, and serious collisions with the state within whose jurisdiction they resided. This it is our interest to avoid. . ... **[T]he black man is degraded by his color, and sinks into vice and worthlessness from want of motive to virtuous and elevated conduct. The black man in [free] states may have the power of volition. He may go and come when it pleaseth him, without a domestic master to control the actions of his person; but to be**

**politically free, to be the peer and equal of the White man, to enjoy the offices, trusts, and privileges our institutions confer on the White man, is hopeless now and ever**. . ... He is a reproach and a byword with the slave himself, who taunts his fellow slave by telling him "he is as worthless as a free negro." . ... **The free black man lives amongst us without motive and without hope. He seeks no avocation, is surrounded with necessities, is sunk in degradation; crime can sink him no deeper, and he commits it of course**. . ... In the non-slaveholding states the people are **less accustomed to the squalid and dis gusting wretchedness of the negro**, have less sympathy for him . . ... **Nothing can be more untrue than that the free negro is more respectable as a member of society in the non-slaveholding than the slaveholding states. In each he is a degraded outcast, and his fancied freedom a delusion.**"

Ohio Supreme Court Justice Nathaniel C. Reed stated in State v. Hoppess, 1848 the following disdain for Negro freedom:

**"The question is, if free what will you do with [Blacks?] No one scarcely would wish to confer upon [them] equal political rights, and none certainly would wish for social equality and the amalgamation of the races. So, if all were free, the presence of the negro among our people is a vast evil**. . ... **It is to be furthermore observed that ours is a government of white men. That our liberties were achieved, and our government formed by white men and for white men. The negro was not included or represented—the hope then was as it now is—that the whole race of negroes should at some future time be removed to a country of their own, to be subject to their own government and laws.**"

Excerpted from: "Without Representation, No Taxation: Free Blacks, Taxes, and Tax Exemptions Between the Revolutionary and Civil Wars" by Christopher J. Bryant

# The Characteristics of the Negro People

## By H.T. KEALING

**NOTE:** The Most Honorable Elijah Muhammad's call for separation might be considered as especially needful when we reflect upon the lasting impact of slavery upon the behavioral characteristics of the Black man and woman in America. H.T. Kealing, Hightower Theodore Kealing was pioneer in Texas for the development of schools for Black children and was a contemporary of Booker T. Washingon. In 1903, he wrote the essay below entitled, The Characteristics of The Negro People. It was published within the book entitled, The Negro Problem: A Series of Articles by Representative American Negroes of Today. The book included essays from: Booker T. Washington, W.E.B DuBois, Paul Lawrence Dunbar and Charles Chesnutt.

A frank statement of the virtues and failings of the race, indicating very clearly the evils which must be overcome, and the good which must be developed, if success is really to attend the effort to uplift them.

The characteristics of the Negro are of two kinds—**the INBORN and the INBRED**. As they reveal themselves to us, this distinction may not be seen, but it exists. Inborn qualities are ineradicable; they belong to the blood; they constitute individuality; they are independent, or nearly so, of time and habitat. Inbred qualities are acquired, and are the result of experience. They may be overcome by a reversal of the process which created them. The fundamental, or inborn, characteristics of the Negro may be found in the African, as well as the American, Negro; but the inbred characteristics of the latter belong to the American life alone.

There is but one human nature, made up of constituent elements the same in all men, and racial or national differences arise from the predominance of one or another element in this or that race. It is a question of proportion. The Negro is not a Caucasian, not a Chinese, not an Indian; though no psychological quality in the one is absent from the other. The same moral sense, called conscience; the same love of harmony in color or in sound; the same pleasure in acquiring knowledge; the same love of truth in word, or of fitness in relation; the same love of respect and

Page 174-Demetric Muhammad

approbation; the same vengeful or benevolent feelings; the same appetites, belong to all, but in varying proportions. They form the indicia to a people's mission, and are our best guides to God's purpose in creating us. They constitute the material to be worked on in educating a race, and suggest in every case where the stress of civilization or education should be applied in order to follow the lines of least resistance.

## INBORN CHARACTERISTICS RESULTING FROM GOD

But there are also certain manifestations, the result of training or neglect, which are not inborn. As they are inculcable, so they are eradicable; and it is only by a loose terminology that we apply the term characteristics to them without distinction between them nd the inherent traits. In considering the characteristics of the Negro people, therefore, we must not confuse the constitutional with the removable. Studied with sympathy and at first hand, the black man of America will be seen to possess certain predominant idiosyncrasies of which the following form a fair catalogue:

### Intensely Religious-Spiritual

He is intensely religious. True religion is based upon a belief in the supernatural, upon faith and feeling. A people deeply superstitious are apt to be deeply religious, for both rest upon a belief in a spiritual world. Superstition differs from religion in being the untrained and unenlightened gropings of the human soul after the mysteries of the higher life; while the latter, more or less enlightened, "feels after God, if haply," it may find Him. The Negro gives abundant evidence of both phases. The absolute inability of the master, in the days of slavery, while successfully vetoing all other kinds of convocation, to stop the Negro's church meetings, as well as the almost phenomenal influence and growth of his churches since; and his constant referring of every event, adverse or favorable, to the personal ministrations of the Creator, are things unique and persistent. And the master class reposed more faith in their slaves' religion ofttimes than they did in their own. Doubtless much of the reverential feeling that pervades the American home to-day, above that of all other nations, is the result of the Negro mammy's devotion and loyalty to God.

## Imaginative

He is imaginative. This is not evinced so much in creative directions as in poetical, musical, combinatory, inventional and what, if coupled with learning, we call literary imagination. Negro eloquence is proverbial. The crudest sermon of the most unlettered slave abounded in tropes and glowing tongue pictures of apocalyptic visions all his own; and, indeed, the poetic quality of his mind is seen in all his natural efforts when the self-consciousness of education does not stand guard. The staid religious muse of Phillis Wheatley and the rollicking, somewhat jibing, verse of Dunbar show it equally, unpremeditated and spontaneous.

I have heard by the hour some ordinary old uneducated Negro tell those inimitable animal stories, brought to literary existence in "Uncle Remus," with such quaint humor, delicious conceit and masterly delineation of plot, character and incident that nothing but the conventional rating of Aesop's Fables could put them in the same class. Then, there are more Negro inventors than the world supposes. This faculty is impossible without a well-ordered imagination held in leash by a good memory and large perception.

## Affectionate

He is affectionate and without vindictiveness. He does not nurse even great wrongs. Mercurial as he is, often furiously angry and frequently in murderous mood, he comes nearer not letting the sun go down upon his anger than any other man I know. Like Brutus, he may be compared to the flint which,

"Much enforced, shows a hasty spark, And straight is cold again."

His affection is not less towards the Caucasian than to his own race. It is not saying too much to remark that the soul of the Negro yearns for the white man's good will and respect; and the old ties of love that subsisted in so many instances in the days of slavery still survive where the ex-slave still lives. The touching case of a Negro Bishop who returned to the State in which he had been a slave, and rode twenty miles to see and alleviate the financial distress of his former master is an exception to numerous other similar cases only in the prominence of the Negro concerned. I know of another case of a man whose tongue seems dipped in hyssop when he begins to tell of the wrongs of his race, and who will not allow anyone to say in his presence that any good came out of slavery, even incidentally; yet he supports the widowed and aged wife of his former master. And, surely, if these two instances are not sufficient to establish the general proposition, none will gainsay the patience, vigilance, loyalty and helpfulness of the Negro slave during the Civil War, and of his good old wife who nursed white children at her breast at a time when all ties save those of affection were ruptured, and when no protection but devoted hearts watched over the "great house," whose head and master was at the front, fighting to perpetuate slavery. Was it stupidity on the Negro's part? Not at all. He was well informed as to the occurrences of the times. A freemasonry kept him posted as well as the whites were themselves on the course of the war and the issue of each battle. Was it fear that kept him at the old home? Not that, either. Many thousands did cross the line to freedom; many other thousands (200,000) fought in the ranks for freedom, but none of them—those who went and those who stayed— those who fought and those who worked, —betrayed a trust, outraged a female, or rebelled against a duty. It was love, the natural wellings of affectionate natures.

## Endurance

He has great endurance, both dispositional and physical. So true is the first that his patience has been the marvel of the world; and, indeed, many, regarding this trait manifested in such an unusual degree, doubted the Negro's courage, till the splendid record of the '60's and the equal, but more recent, record of the '90's, wrote forbearance as the real explanation of an endurance seemingly so at variance with manly spirit.

Of his physical powers, his whole record as a laborer at killing tasks in the most trying climate in America speaks so eloquently that nothing but the statistics of cotton, corn, rice, sugar, railroad ties and felled forests can add to the praise of this burden-bearer of the nation. The census tables here are more romantic and thrilling than figures of rhetoric.

## Courageous

He is courageous. His page in the war record of this country is without blot or blemish. His commanders unite in pronouncing him admirable for courage in the field, commendable for obedience in camp. That he should exhibit such excellent fighting qualities as a soldier, and yet exercise the forbearance that characterizes him as a citizen, is remarkable.

## Cheerful

He is cheerful. His ivories are as famous as his songs. That the South is "sunny" is largely due to the brightness his rollicking laugh and unfailing good nature bring to it. Though the mudsill of the labor world, he whistles as he hoes, and no dark broodings or whispered conspirings mar the cheerful acceptance of the load he bears. Against the rubber bumper of his good cheer things that have crushed and maddened others rebound without damage. When one hears the quaint jubilee songs, set to minor cadence, he might suppose them the expressions of a melancholy people. They are not to be so interpreted. Rather are they the expression of an experience, not a nature. Like the subdued voice of a caged bird, these songs are the coinage of an occasion, and not the free note of nature. The slave sang of griefs he was not allowed to discuss, hence his songs. This cheerfulness has enabled the Negro to live and increase under circumstances which, in all other instances, have decimated, if not exterminated, inferior peoples. His plasticity to moulding forces and his resiliency against crushing ones come from a Thalian philosophy, unconscious and unstudied, that extracts Epicurean delights from funeral meats.

The above traits are inborn and fundamental, belonging to the race everywhere, in Africa as well as America. Strict correctness requires, however, that attention be called to the fact that there are tribal differences among African Negroes that amount almost to the national variations of Europe; and these are reflected in American Negroes, who are the descendants of these different tribes. There is as much difference between the Mandingo and the Hottentot, both black, as between the Italian and the German, both white; or between the Bushman and the Zulu, both black, as between the Russian and the Englishman, both white. Scientific exactness, therefore, would require a closer analysis of racial characteristics than an article of this length could give; but, speaking in a large way, it may be said that in whatever outward conformity may come to the race in America by reason of training or contact, these traits will lie at the base, the very warp and woof of his soul texture.

"The Europeans, to procure slaves there in Africa, create and perpetuate a state of constant warfare. Those regions are poisoned by their strong liquors, by every species of debauchery, of rapacity, cruelty and seduction. Is there a single vice(sin) which is not daily renewed in that country? ...

Yes, I repeat it; there is not a vice, not a species of wickedness, of which Europe is not guilty towards Negroes, of which she has not shown them the example. Avenging God! Suspend thy thunder; exhaust thy compassion, in giving her time and courage to repair, if possible, these horrors and atrocities."

Bishop Henri Gregoire

## INBRED CHARACTERISTICS RESULTING FROM SLAVERY

If, now, we turn to consider his inbred traits, those the result of experience, conditions and environments, we find that they exist mainly as deficiencies and deformities. These have been superimposed upon the native soul endowment. Slavery has been called the Negro's great schoolmaster, because it took him a savage and released him civilized; took him a heathen and released him a Christian; took him an idler and released him a laborer. Undoubtedly it did these things superficially, but one great defect is to be charged against this school—it did not teach him the meaning of home, purity and providence. To do this is the burden of freedom.

The emancipated Negro struggles up to-day against many obstacles, the entailment of a brutal slavery. Leaving out of consideration the many who have already emerged, let us apply our thoughts to the great body of submerged people in the congested districts of city and country who present a real problem, and who must be helped to higher things. We note some of the heritages under which they stagger up into full development:

## Shiftlessness

He had no need to devise and plan in bondage. There was no need for an enterprising spirit; consequently, he is lacking in leadership and self-reliance. He is inclined to stay in ruts, and applies himself listlessly to a task, feeling that the directive agency should come from without.

## Incontinence

It is not to the point to say that others are, too. Undoubtedly, example has as much to do with this laxity as neglect. We simply record the fact. A slave's value was increased by his prolificacy. Begetting children for the auction block could hardly sanctify family ties. It was not nearly so necessary for a slave to know his father as his owner. Added to the promiscuity encouraged and often forced among this class, was the dreadful license which cast lustful Caucasian eyes upon "likely" Negro women.

## Indolence

Most men are, especially in a warm climate: but the Negro acquired more than the natural share, because to him as a bondman laziness was great gain, for he had no pecuniary interest in his own labor. Hence, holidays were more to be desired than whole labor days, and he learned to do as little as he might, be excused as often as he could, and hail Saturday as the oasis in a desert week. He hails it yet. The labor efficiency of the Negro has greatly increased since the emancipation, for self-interest is a factor now. In 1865, each Negro produced two-thirds of a bale of cotton; now he produces an average of one whole bale to the man. But there is still woeful waste of productive energy. A calculation showing the comparative productive capacity, man for man, between the Northern[B] and Southern laborer would be very interesting.

## Improvidence and extravagance

He will drop the most important job to go on an excursion or parade with his lodge. He spends large sums on expensive clothing and luxuries, while going without things necessary to a real home. He will cheerfully eat fat bacon and "pone" corn-bread all the week[C] in order to indulge in unlimited soda-water, melon and fish at the end. In the cities he is oftener seen dealing with the pawn-broker than the banker. His house, when furnished at all, is better furnished that that of a white man of equal earning power, but it is on the installment plan. He is loath to buy a house, because he has no taste for responsibility nor faith in himself to manage large concerns; but organs, pianos, clocks, sewing-machines and parlor suits, on time, have no terrors for him. This is because he has been accustomed to think in small numbers. He does not regard the Scotchman's "mickle," because he does not stop to consider that the end is a "muckle." He has amassed, at full valuation, nearly a billion dollars' worth of property, despite this, but this is about one-half of what proper providence would have shown.

## Untidiness

Travel through the South and you will be struck with the general misfit and dilapidated appearance of things. Palings are missing from the fences, gates sag on single hinges, houses are unpainted, window panes are broken, yards unkempt and the appearance of a squalor greater than the real is seen on every side. The inside of the house meets the suggestions of the outside. This is a projection of the slave's "quarters" into freedom. The cabin of the slave was, at best, a place to eat and sleep in; there was no thought of the esthetic in such places. A quilt on a plank was a luxury to the tired farm-hand, and paint was nothing to the poor, sun-scorched fellow who sought the house for shade rather than beauty. Habits of personal cleanliness were not inculcated, and even now it is the exception to find a modern bath-room in a Southern home.

## Dishonesty

This is the logic, if not the training, of slavery. It is easy for the unrequited toiler in another's field to justify reprisal; hence there arose among the Negroes an amended Commandment which added to "Thou shalt not steal" the clause, "except thou be stolen from." It was no great fault, then, according to this code, to purloin a pig, a sheep, a chicken, or a few potatoes from a master who took all from the slave.

## Untruthfulness

This is seen more in innocent and childish exaggeration than in vicious distortion. It is the vice of untutored minds to run to gossip and make miracles of the matter-of-fact. The Negro also tells falsehoods from excess of good nature. He promises to do a piece of work on a certain day, because it is so much easier and pleasanter to say Yes, and stay away, than it is to say No.

## Business Unreliability

He does not meet a promise in the way and at the time promised. Not being accustomed to business, he has small conception of the place the promise has in the business world. It is only recently he has begun to deal with banks. He,

who has no credit, sees[D] no loss of it in a protested note, especially if he intends to pay it some time. That chain which links one man's obligation to another man's solvency he has not considered. He is really as good and safe a debt-payer when he owes a white man as the latter can have, but the methods of the modern bank, placing a time limit on debts, is his detestation. He much prefers the laissez-faire of the Southern plantation store.

## Lack of Initiative

It was the policy of slavery to crush out the combining instinct, and it was well done; for, outside of churches and secret societies, the Negro has done little to increase the social efficiency which can combine many men into an organic whole, subject to the corporate will and direction. He has, however, made some hopeful beginnings.

## Suspicion of his own race

He was taught to watch other Negroes and tell all that they did. This was slavery's native detective force to discover incipient insurrection. Each slave learned to distrust his fellow. And added to this is the knowledge one Negro has that no other has had half sufficient experience in business to be a wise counsellor, or a safe steward of another man's funds. Almost all Negroes who have acquired wealth have entrusted its management to white men.

**"The Aptitude of the Negro To Disobey Orders Coming From Himself"**

The Negro in Western civilization, because of his environments that force upon him a complete inferiority, is the most stubborn individual to discipline within the race. He has but little, if any, respect for internal racial authority. He cannot be depended upon to carry out an order given by a superior of his own race. If the superior attempts, in his presence, to enforce the order he is undermined and accused of "putting on airs." If the order is entrusted to a lieutenant, he, in turn, changes the order to suit himself and endeavors to constitute himself the superior individual.

In my experience, as head of the largest serious Negro organization in the world, I have found that to every hundred orders given to be executed for the absolute good of the organization and the race, not two percent of them have been carried out in their entirety. This lack of obedience to orders and discipline checkmates the real, worthwhile progress of the race. This accounts for the Negro's lack of racial nationalistic ideal. The only cure for him is his removal to an atmosphere entirely of his own, where he would be forced under rigid civil and other discipline to respect himself and his own racial authority.
—Marcus M. Garvey

## Ignorance

The causes of his ignorance all know. That he has thrown off one-half of it in forty years is a wonderful showing; but a great incubus remains in the other half, and it demands the nation's attention. What the census calls literacy is often very shallow. The cause of this shallowness lies, in part, in the poor character and short duration of Southern schools; in the poverty that snatches the child from school prematurely to work for bread; in the multitude of mushroom colleges and get-smart-quick universities scattered over the South, and in the glamour of a professional education that entices poorly prepared students into special work.

Add to this, too, the commercialism of the age which regards each day in school as a day out of the market. Boys and girls by scores learn the mechanical parts of type-writing and stenography without the basal culture which gives these callings their greatest efficiency. They copy a manuscript, Chinese-like, mistakes and all; they take you phonetically in sense as well as sound, having no reserve to draw upon to interpret a learned allusion or unusual phrase. Thus, while prejudice makes it hard to secure a place, auto-deficiency loses many a one that is secured.

We have discussed the leading characteristics of the Negro, his inborn excellencies and inbred defects, candidly and as they are to be seen in the great mass whose place determines the status of the race as a whole. It would, however, be to small purpose if we did not ask what can be done to develop the innate good and correct the bad in a race so puissant and numerous? This mass is not inert; it has great reactionary force, modifying and influencing all about it. The Negro's excellences have entered into American character and life already; so, have his weaknesses. He has brought cheer, love, emotion and religion in saving measure to the land. He has given it wealth by his brawn and liberty by his blood. His self-respect, even in abasement, has kept him struggling upward; his confidence in his own future has infected his friends and kept him from nursing despondency or planning anarchy. But he has laid, and does lay, burdens upon the land, too: his ignorance, his low average of morality, his low standards of home, his lack of enterprise, his lack of self-reliance—these must be cured.

Evidently, he is to be "solved" by educational processes. Everyone of his inborn traits must be respected and developed to proper proportion. Excesses and excrescences must not be carelessly dealt with, for they mark the fertility of a soil that raises rank weeds because no gardener has tilled it. His religion must become "ethics touched with feeling"—not a paroxysm, but a principle. His imagination must be given a rudder to guide its sails; and the first fruits of its proper exercise, as seen in a Dunbar, a Chesnutt, a Coleridge-Taylor and a Tanner, must be pedestaled along the Appian Way over which others are to march. His affection must be met with larger love; his patience rewarded with privilege; his courage called to defend the rights of others rather than redress his own wrongs. Thus, shall he supplement from within the best efforts of good men without.

To cure the evils entailed upon him by an unhappy past, he must be educated to work with skill, with self-direction, in combination and unremittingly. Industrial education with constant application, is the slogan of his rise from racial pauperism to productive manliness. Not that exceptional minds should not have exceptional opportunities (and they already exist); but that the great majority of awkward and unskilled ones, who must work somehow, somewhere, all the time, shall have their opportunities for training in industrial schools near them and with courses consonant with the lives they are to lead. Let the ninety and nine who must work, either with trained or fumbling hands, have a chance. Train the Negro to accept and carry responsibility by putting it upon him. Train him, more than any schools are now doing, in morals—to speak the truth, to keep a promise, to touch only his own property, to trust the trustworthy among his own race, to risk something in business, to strike out in new lines of endeavor, to buy houses and make homes, to regard beauty as well as utility, to save rather than display. In short, let us subordinate mere knowledge to the work of invigorating the will, energizing productive effort and clarifying moral vision. Let us make safe men rather than vociferous mountebanks; let us put deftness in daily labor above sleight-of-hand tricks, and common sense, well trained, above classical smatterings, which awe the multitude but butter no parsnips.

If we do this, America will have enriched her blood, ennobled her record and shown the world how to deal with its Dark Races without reproach.

# A Complete Glossary Of The Muslim Program

## able

ADJECTIVE: having the necessary power, resources, skill, time, opportunity, etc., to do something; qualified, competent, or authorized to do some specific act; capable; competent; talented

## about

PREPOSITION: relating to; concerning; on the subject of; near or close to (in space or time); on every side; all around; here and there; in all directions; in circumference; around the outside; near;

ADVERB: approximately; near in number, time, degree, etc.; nearby; here and there; from place to place; in no particular direction; all around; on every side

## accept

VERB (transitive): to take or receive (something offered); receive with approval or favor; to agree or consent to; accede to; to respond or answer affirmatively to; to undertake the responsibility, duties, honors, etc., of; to receive or admit formally, to accommodate or reconcile oneself to; receive as to meaning; understand, regard as true or sound; believe; to regard as normal, suitable, or usual; to acknowledge, by signature, as calling for payment, and thus to agree to pay, as a draft; to receive as an adequate performance of the duty with which an officer or a committee has been charged; receive for further action; to receive or contain (something attached, inserted, etc.); to receive (a transplanted organ or tissue) without adverse reaction

## accordance

NOUN: conformity; agreement; accord (esp. in the phrase in accordance with); the act of granting; bestowal

## added

ADJECTIVE: having more of a particular quality; containing more of a particular ingredient;

**addition**

NOUN: the act, process, or result of adding; a person or thing that is added or acquired; a mathematical operation in which the sum of two numbers or quantities is calculated.

**after**

PREPOSITION: following in time; in succession to; following; behind; in pursuit or search of; concerning; considering; next in excellence or importance to; in imitation of; in the manner of; in accordance with or in conformity to; with a name derived from;

**against**

PREPOSITION: opposed to; in conflict or disagreement with; standing or leaning beside or in front of; coming in contact with; in contrast to; having an adverse or unfavorable effect on; as a protection from or means of defense from the adverse effects of; in exchange for or in return for;

**agrees**

VERB: to be of the same opinion; concur; to give assent; consent; to come to terms (about); arrive at a settlement (on); to be similar or consistent; harmonize; correspond;

**all**

DETERMINER: the whole quantity or amount of; totality of; every one of a class; as pronoun; functioning as sing or plural; in combination with a noun used as a modifier); the greatest possible, in all earnestness, any whatever; adverb: apiece; each, completely; noun; (preceded by my, your, his, etc.) (one's) complete effort or interest; totality or whole

**Allah**

NOUN: Allah, the one and only God in Islam. The name's origin can be traced to the earliest Semitic writings in which the word for god was "il", "el", or "eloah", the latter two used in the Hebrew Bible (Old Testament). Allah is the standard Arabic word for God and is used by Arabic-speaking Christians and Jews as well as by Muslims. The association of the word specifically with Islam comes from the special status of Arabic as the language of Islam's holy scripture, the Qur'ān: since the Qur'ān in its original language is considered to be the literal word of God, it is believed that God described himself in the Arabic language as Allāh. The Arabic word thus holds special significance for Muslims, regardless of their native tongue, because the Arabic word was spoken by God himself.

**allow**

VERB (transitive): to permit (to do something); let; to set aside to let enter or stay; to acknowledge or concede; to let have; grant

**allowed**

ADJECTIVE: Physics involving a change in quantum numbers, permitted by the selection rules

**along**

PREPOSITION: over or for the length of, esp. in a more or less horizontal plane

ADVERB: continuing over the length of some specified thing; in accompaniment; together with some specified person or people; forward; to a more advanced state

**America**

NOUN: short for the United States of America; also called: the Americas the American continent, including North, South, and Central America

**American**

ADJECTIVE: of or relating to the United States of America, its inhabitants, or their form of English; of or relating to the American continent; noun; a native or citizen of the US; a native or inhabitant of any country of North, Central, or South America; the English language as spoken or written in the United States

**an**

DETERMINER: a form of the indefinite article used before an initial vowel sound; conjunction;

**and**

CONJUNCTION: along with; in addition to; as a consequence; afterwards; (preceded by good or nice) (intensifier) plus; used to join identical words or phrases to give emphasis or indicate repetition or continuity; noun: (usually plural) an additional matter or problem

**answer**

NOUN: a reply, either spoken or written, as to a question, request, letter, or article; a reaction or response in the form of an action; a solution, esp. of a mathematical problem; law -a party's written reply to his or her opponent's interrogatories; the respondent's written reply to the petition; a musical phrase that follows the subject of a fugue, reproducing it a fifth higher or a fourth lower;

TRANSITIVE VERB: to reply or respond (to) by word or action; to reply correctly to; solve or attempt to solve

INTRANSITIVE VERB: respond or react (to a stimulus, command, etc.)

**appeared**

VERB (intransitive): to come into sight or view; to seem or look; to be plain or clear, as after further evidence, etc.; to develop or come into being; to become publicly available; be published

**applied**

ADJECTIVE: related to or put to practical use

**are**

VERB: the plural form of the present tense (indicative mood) of the verb 'be' and the singular form used with 'you'

**area**

NOUN: any flat, curved, or irregular expanse of a surface; the extent of a two-dimensional surface enclosed within a specified boundary or geometric figure; the two-dimensional extent of the surface of a solid, or of some part thereof, esp. one bounded by a closed curve; a section, portion, or part; region; district; a geographical division of administrative responsibility; a part or section, as of a building, town, etc., having some specified function or characteristic

**arrived**

INTRANSITIVE VERB: to come to a certain place during or after a journey; reach a destination; (followed by at) to agree upon; reach to arrive at a decision; to occur eventually; informal (of a baby) to be born; informal to attain success or gain recognition

**as**

CONJUNCTION: (often preceded by just) when; at the time that; in the way that; that which; what; (of) which fact, event, etc. (referring to the previous statement); to become wise, as we all know, is not easy; see as it were adverb, conjunction: used correlatively before an adjective or adverb and before a noun phrase or a clause to indicate identity of extent, amount, etc. used with this sense after a noun phrase introduce by the same; preposition: in the role of; being

**asked**

VERB: (often followed by about) to put a question (to); request an answer (from);

TRANSITIVE VERB: to inquire about; direct or put (a question); (may take a clause as object or an infinitive; often followed by for) to make a request or demand; to demand or expect (esp. in the phrases ask a lot of, ask too much of)

**attacks**

VERB: to launch a physical assault (against) with or without weapons; begin hostilities (with);

INTRANSITIVE VERB: to take the initiative in a game, sport, etc....

TRANSITIVE VERB: to direct hostile words or writings at; criticize or abuse vehemently; to turn one's mind or energies vigorously to (a job, problem, etc.); to begin to injure or affect adversely; corrode, corrupt, or infect; noun: the act or an instance of attacking; strong criticism or abuse; an unjustified attack on someone's reputation; an offensive move in a game, sport, etc.; commencement of a task, etc.; any sudden and usually severe manifestation of a disease or disorder

**be**

VERB: to have presence in the realm of perceived reality; exist, live, (used in the perfect or past perfect tenses only); to pay a visit; go; to take place; occur; used as a linking verb between the subject of a sentence and its noun or adjective complement or complementing phrase. In this case be expresses the relationship of either essential or incidental equivalence or identity or specifies an essential or incidental attribute). It is also used with an adverbial complement to indicate a relationship of location in space or time; (takes a present participle); forms the progressive present tense

## become

VERB: to come to be; develop or grow into; (followed by of; usually used in a question); to fall to or be the lot (of); happen (to); (transitive) (of clothes, etc.) to enhance the appearance of (someone); suit; (transitive); to be appropriate; befit

## been

VERB: the past participle of be

## being

VERB: the state or fact of existing; existence; essential nature; self; something that exists or is thought to exist, esp. something that cannot be assigned to any category; a person; human being; (in the philosophy of Aristotle) actuality

## believe

TRANSITIVE VERB (transitive; may take a clause as object); to accept (a statement, supposition, or opinion) as true; to accept the statement or opinion of (a person) as true; to be convinced of the truth or existence (of);

INTRANSITIVE VERB: to have religious faith; (when transitive, takes a clause as object); to think, assume, or suppose

## believers

NOUN: if you are a great believer in something, you think that it is good, right, or useful; a believer is someone who is sure that God exists or that their religion is true.

## believing

ADJECTIVE: form of 'believe'

## besides

PREPOSITION: apart from; even considering; sentence connector- anyway; moreover; adverb, as well

**best**

ADJECTIVE; the superlative of good; most excellent of a particular group; category, etc.; most suitable; advantageous, desirable, attractive, etc.

ADVERB: the superlative of well; in a manner surpassing all others; most excellently, advantageously, attractively, etc.; (in combination) in or to the greatest degree or extent; most noun; (often preceded by at); the most excellent; pleasing, or skilled quality or condition; the most effective effort of which a person or group is capable; a winning majority; also: all the best

**better**

ADJECTIVE: the comparative of good; more excellent than other members of a particular group; category, etc.; more suitable, advantageous; attractive, etc.; improved in health; fully recovered in health

ADVERB: the comparative of well; in a more excellent manner; more advantageously; attractively, etc.; in or to a greater degree or extent; more

NOUN: (usually plural) a person who is superior; esp. in social standing or ability

VERB: to make or become better; (transitive) to improve upon; surpass

**between**

PREPOSITION: at a point or in a region intermediate to two other points in space; times, degrees, etc.; in combination; confined or restricted to between you and me; indicating a reciprocal relation or comparison; indicating two or more alternatives a choice between going now and staying all night;

ADVERB: also "in between", between one specified thing and another; two houses with a garage between

**Bible**

NOUN: the sacred book of Christianity; Old Testament and New Testament: some Roman Catholic versions also include all or part of the Apocrypha; a copy or particular edition of the Scriptures

**black**

ADJECTIVE: opposite to white; of the color of coal or pitch see also color; designating or of any of the dark-skinned traditional inhabitants of sub-Saharan Africa, Australia, or Melanesia or their descendants in other parts of the world; by, for, or about black people as a group; specif., in the U.S., by, for, or about black Americans

**blood**

NOUN: a reddish fluid in vertebrates that is pumped by the heart through the arteries and veins; supplies tissues with nutrients, oxygen, etc., and removes waste products. It consists of a fluid (blood plasma) containing cells (erythrocytes, leucocytes, and platelets); a similar fluid in such invertebrates as annelids and arthropods; bloodshed, esp. when resulting in murder; the guilt or responsibility for killing or injuring (esp. in the phrase have blood on one's hands or head); life itself; lifeblood; relationship through being of the same family, race, or kind; kinship

TRANSITIVE VERB: hunting to cause (young hounds) to taste the blood of a freshly killed quarry and so become keen to hunt: hunting to smear the cheeks or forehead of (a person) with the blood of the kill as an initiation in hunting; to initiate (a person) to an activity or organization, esp. by real-life experience

**books**

NOUN: a record of the transactions of a business or society; to keep the books; on the books; to close the books; to cook the books; "book"-a number of printed or written pages bound together along one edge and usually protected by thick paper or stiff pasteboard covers

**both**

NOUN: determiner, the two; two considered together;

PRONOUN: both

CONJUNCTION (COORDINATING): used preceding words, phrases, or clauses joined by and, used to emphasize that not just one; but also, the other of the joined elements is included both she and her sister enjoyed the play; both new and exciting

**boys**

NOUN: military personnel, esp. combat soldiers; a male child; lad; youth; a man regarded as immature or inexperienced; usually derogatory when used to refer to (esp. in former colonial territories) a Black person or native male servant of any age; an exclamation of surprise, pleasure, contempt, etc.

**bring**

VERB: to carry, convey, or take (something or someone) to a designated place or person; bring that book to me; to cause to happen or occur to (oneself or another); to cause to happen as a consequence; to cause to come to mind; to cause to be in a certain state, position, etc.

**brought**

VERB: the past tense and past participle of bring

**brutality**

NOUN: the condition or quality of being brutal; a brutal or savage act, treatment, etc.; brutal means of or belonging to beasts; very harsh or rigorous; savage; cruel; inhuman

**build**

VERB: to make, construct, or form by joining parts or materials; to build a house; to be a builder by profession; to order the building of; (followed by on or upon) to base; found; to establish and develop

**buildings**

NOUN: a structure with a roof and walls, such as a house, school, store, or factory;

**but**

CONJUNCTION (coordinating): contrary to expectation; in contrast; on the contrary; (usually used after a negative) other than

CONJUNCTION (subordinating): usually used after a negative; without it happening or being the case that; (followed by that) except that; archaic, if not; unless, sentence connector; informal, used to introduce an exclamation

PREPOSITION: except; save; but for

ADVERB: just; merely; only; Scottish, Australian and New Zealand informal, though; however; all but

NOUN: an objection (esp. in the phrase ifs and buts)

**by**

PREPOSITION: used to indicate the agent after a passive verb; used to indicate the person responsible for a creative work; via; through; followed by a gerund to indicate a means used; besides, next to; near

ADVERB: near, away; aside, passing a point near something; past. (Scottish) past; over and done with, (Scottish) aside; behind one

NOUN: a variant spelling of bye; by the by

**can**

AUXILIARY VERB: know(s) how to; am, are, or is able to; am, are, or is likely or at all likely to; have or has the moral or legal right to; Informal-am, are, or is permitted to; may

**cannot**

VERB: an auxiliary verb expressing incapacity, inability, withholding permission, etc.; can not

**charity**

NOUN: the giving of help, money, food, etc., to those in need; (as modifier); a charity show; an institution or organization set up to provide help, money, etc., to those in need; (as modifier) charity funds; the help, money, etc., given to the people in need; alms, a kindly and lenient attitude towards people; love of one's fellow people

**children**

NOUN: the plural of 'child'

**choice**

NOUN: the act or an instance of choosing or selecting; the opportunity or power of choosing; a person or thing chosen or that may be chosen; an alternative action or possibility; a supply from which to select

ADJECTIVE: of superior quality; excellent; carefully chosen, appropriate; vulgar or rude, choice language

**choose**

VERB: chooses, choosing, chose or chosen; to select (a person, thing, course of action, etc.) from a number of alternatives; (transitive; takes a clause as object or an infinitive); to consider it desirable or proper; to like; please; cannot choose but; nothing to choose between

**Christians**

NOUN: a person who believes in and followed Jesus Christ; a member of a Christian Church or denomination; informal, a person who possesses Christian virtues, esp. practical ones

ADJECTIVE: of, relating to, or derived from Jesus Christ, his teachings, example, or his followers (sometimes not capital); exhibiting kindness or goodness

**citizens**

NOUN: a native registered or naturalized member of a state, nation, or other political community; an inhabitant of a city or town; a native or inhabitant of any place; a civilian, as opposed to a soldier, public official, etc.

**civilized**

ADJECTIVE: having a high state of culture and social development: cultured; polite; a civilized discussion

**class**

NOUN: a collection or division of people or things sharing a common characteristic, attribute, quality, or property; a group of persons sharing a similar social position and certain economic, political, and cultural characteristics; (in Marxist theory) a group of persons sharing the same relationship to the means of production; the pattern of divisions that exist within a society on the basis of rank, economic status, etc.; (as modifier); a group of pupils or students who are taught and study together; a meeting of a group of students for tuition

VERB: to have or assign a place within a group, grade, or class

**college**

NOUN: an institution of higher education; part of a university; a school or an institution providing specialized courses or teaching; the building or buildings in which a college is housed; an organized body of persons with specific rights and duties

**Colleges**

NOUN: plural of college

**color**

NOUN: the sensation resulting from stimulation of the retina of the eye by light waves of certain lengths; the property of reflecting light of a particular wavelength: the distinct colors of the spectrum are red, orange, yellow, green, blue, indigo, and violet, each of these shading into the next; the primary colors of the spectrum are red, green, and blue, the light beams of which variously combined can produce any of the colors; any coloring matter; dye; pigment; paint: the primary colors of paints, pigments, etc. are red, yellow, and blue, which, when mixed in various ways, produce the secondary colors (green, orange, purple, etc.): black, white, and gray are often called colors ( achromatic colors), although black is caused by the complete absorption of light rays, white by the reflection of all the rays that produce color, and gray by an imperfect absorption of all these rays; any color other than black, white, or gray; chromatic color: color is distinguished by the qualities of hue (as red, brown, yellow, etc.), lightness (for pigmented surfaces) or brightness (for light itself), and saturation (the degree of intensity of a hue); color of the face; esp., a healthy rosiness or a blush; the color of a person's skin

VERB (transitive): to give color to; impregnate or cover with color, as with paint, stain, or dye; to change the color of; to give a pleasing, convincing, or reasonable appearance to; make plausible; to alter or influence to some degree, as by distortion or exaggeration

VERB (intransitive): to become colored; to change color, as ripening fruit; to blush or flush; to engage in the child's pastime of drawing or coloring pictures with wax crayons, etc.

**complete**

ADJECTIVE: having every necessary part or element; entire; ended; finished;(prenominal) thorough; absolute, perfect in quality or kind; (of a logical system) constituted such that a contradiction arises on the addition of any proposition that cannot be deduced from the axioms of the system

VERB (transitive): to make whole or perfect; to end; finish (intransitive); (in land law) to pay any outstanding balance on a contract for the conveyance of land in exchange for the title deeds, so that the ownership of the land changes hands; American football (transitive);(of a quarterback) to make (a forward pass) successfully

**condition**

NOUN: a particular state of being or existence; situation with respect to circumstances; the human condition, something that limits or restricts something else; a qualification. (plural); external or existing circumstances; state of health or physical fitness, esp. good health (esp. in the phrases in condition, out of condition); an ailment or physical disability

VERB: (mainly tr); psychology; to alter the response of (a person or animal) to a particular stimulus or situation; to establish a conditioned response in (a person or animal); to put into a fit condition or state; to improve the condition of (one's hair) by use of special cosmetics; to accustom or inure; to subject to a condition

**conflict**

NOUN: a struggle or clash between opposing forces; battle; a state of opposition between ideas, interests, etc.; disagreement or controversy; a clash, as between two appointments made for the same time; psychology, opposition between two simultaneous but incompatible wishes or drives, sometimes leading to a state of emotional tension and thought to be responsible for neuroses

VERB (intransitive): to come into opposition; clash; to fight

**continent**

NOUN: one of the earth's large land masses (Asia, Australia, Africa, Europe, North and South America, and Antarctica); any of the seven large areas into which the earth is conventionally divided (Asia, Africa, Europe, North and South America, Oceania, and Antarctica); that part of the earth's crust that rises above the oceans and is composed of sialic rocks. Including the continental shelves, the continents occupy 30 per cent of the earth's surface; mainland as opposed to islands; a continuous extent of land

## contributions

NOUN: the act of contributing; something contributed, such as money or ideas; an article, story, etc., contributed to a newspaper or other publication; insurance; a portion of the total liability incumbent on each of two or more companies for a risk with respect to which all of them have issued policies; archaic; a levy, esp. towards the cost of a war

## courts

NOUN: a place where justice is administered; a judicial tribunal duly constituted for the hearing and determination of cases; a session of a judicial assembly; an area open to the sky and mostly or entirely surrounded by buildings, walls, etc.

## creed

NOUN: any system, doctrine, or formula of religious belief, as of a denomination; any system or codification of belief or of opinion; a concise, formal statement of the essential articles of Christian belief, such as the Apostles' Creed or the Nicene Creed, any statement or system of beliefs or principles

## days

ADVERB: a period of time; era; age; 'day'- the period of light between sunrise and sunset; the 24-hour period (mean solar day) that it takes the earth to rotate once on its axis with respect to the sun: the civil or legal day is from midnight to midnight, the astronomical day from noon to noon; the time that it takes any celestial body to revolve once on its axis

## dead

ADJECTIVE: no longer alive

NOUN: the dead; not endowed with life; inanimate; no longer in use, valid, effective, or relevant; unresponsive or unaware; insensible; lacking in freshness, interest, or vitality; a period during which coldness, darkness, or some other quality associated with death is at its most intense

ADVERB: (intensifier) dead easy; stop dead; dead level; dead on

**Death**

NOUN: the permanent end of all functions of life in an organism or some of its cellular components; a murder or killing; termination or destruction; a state of affairs or an experience considered as terrible as death

**deceive**

VERB (transitive): to mislead by deliberate misrepresentation or lies; to delude (oneself); to be unfaithful to (one's sexual partner); archaic, to disappoint

**decency**

NOUN: conformity to the prevailing standards of propriety, morality, modesty, etc.; the quality of being decent

**deception**

NOUN: the act of deceiving or the state of being deceived; something that deceives; trick

**declare**

VERB: (mainly transitive); (may take a clause as object) to make clearly known or announce officially; to declare one's interests; to state officially that (a person, fact, etc.) is as specified; (may take a clause as object) to state emphatically; assert; to show, reveal, or manifest; (intransitive; often followed by for or against) to make known one's choice or opinion

**dedicated**

ADJECTIVE: devoted to a particular purpose or cause; assigned or allocated to a particular project, function, etc.; computing, designed to fulfil one function

**demand**

VERB: (tr; may take a clause as object or an infinitive); to request peremptorily or urgently; to require or need as just, urgent, etc.; to claim as a right; exact; his parents demanded obedience of him; law, to make a formal legal claim to (property, esp. realty)

NOUN: an urgent or peremptory requirement or request; something that requires special effort or sacrifice; the act of demanding something or the thing demanded; an insistent question or query

**deprived**

ADJECTIVE: lacking adequate food, shelter, education, etc.

**descendants**

NOUN: a person, animal, or plant when described as descended from an individual, race, species, etc.; something that derives or is descended from an earlier form

Adjective: a variant spelling of descendent

**Description**

NOUN: a statement or account that describes; representation in words; the act, process, or technique of describing; sort, kind, or variety; reptiles of every description; geometry, the act of drawing a line or figure, such as an arc; philosophy; a noun phrase containing a predicate that may replace a name as the subject of a sentence

**despised**

VERB (transitive): to look down on with contempt; scorn

**dividing**

ADJECTIVE: serving to divide

**do**

VERB (transitive): to execute; effect; perform (an act, action, etc.); to carry out; fulfill; to bring to completion; finish; to bring about; cause; produce; to exert (efforts, etc.); to have or take (a meal); to deal with as is required; attend to; to have as one's work or occupation; work at or on; to work out; solve; to produce or appear in (a play, etc.); to play the role of ( Informal) to imitate, or behave characteristically as; to write or publish (a book), compose (a musical score), etc.; to cover (distance); to move along at a speed of; to visit as a sightseer; tour; to translate; to give; render; to suit; be convenient to

VERB (intransitive): to act in a specified way; behave; to be active; work; to finish; to get along; fare; to be adequate or suitable; serve the purpose; to take place; go on; (Chiefly British, Informal) used as a substitute verb after a modal auxiliary or a form of have in a perfect tense

VERB (auxiliary): used to give emphasis, or as a legal convention; used to ask a question; used to serve as part of a negative command or statement; used to serve as a substitute verb; used to form inverted constructions after some adverbs

**due**

ADJECTIVE: immediately payable; owed as a debt, irrespective of any date for payment; requisite; fitting; proper; (prenominal)adequate or sufficient; enough; expected or appointed to be present or arrive

NOUN: something that is owed, required, or due; give a person his or her due

ADVERB: directly or exactly; straight

**earth**

NOUN: Earth or the Earth is the planet on which we live. People usually say Earth when they are referring to the planet as part of the universe, and the Earth when they are talking about the planet as the place where we live; the inhabitants of this planet; the dry surface of this planet as distinguished from sea or sky; land; ground; worldly or temporal matters as opposed to the concerns of the spirit

**educated**

NOUN: the act or process of acquiring knowledge, esp. systematically during childhood and adolescence; the knowledge or training acquired by this process; the act or process of imparting knowledge, esp. at a school, college, or university; the theory of teaching and learning; a particular kind of instruction or training

ADJECTIVE: having an education, esp. a good one; displaying culture, taste, and knowledge; cultivated; (prenominal) based on experience or information (esp. in the phrase an educated guess)

**education**

NOUN: the act or process of acquiring knowledge, esp. systematically during childhood and adolescence; the knowledge or training acquired by this process; the act or process of imparting knowledge, esp. at a school, college, or university; the theory of teaching and learning; a particular kind of instruction or training

## Elijah

NOUN The name Elijah is a very special name. It is a Hebrew name that means literally "Yahweh is God." Elijah is considered to be one of the many theophoric names found in the Bible as well as other sacred texts. Theophoric names, or theophories, refer to an ancient practice of embedding the name of a god or a deity, inside of a person's proper or given name.

## elsewhere

ADVERB: in or to another place; somewhere else

## employment

NOUN: the act of employing or state of being employed; the work or occupation in which a person is employed; the purpose for which something is used

## end

NOUN: the extremity of the length of something, such as a road, line, etc.; the surface at either extremity of a three-dimensional object; the extreme extent, limit, or degree of something; the most distant place or time that can be imagined; the time at which something is concluded

VERB: (transitive): to bring or come to a finish; conclude; to die or cause to die; to surpass; outdo; end it all

## enemies

NOUN: a person hostile or opposed to a policy, cause, person, or group, esp. one who actively tries to do damage; opponent; an armed adversary; opposing military force (as modifier) enemy aircraft; a hostile nation or people, (as modifier), an enemy alien; something that harms or opposes; adversary

## enough

DETERMINER: sufficient to answer a need, demand, supposition, or requirement; adequate

PRONOUN: enough is now known; that's enough!

ADVERB: so as to be adequate or sufficient; as much as necessary; (not used with a negative); very or quite; rather, (intensifier) adequately; tolerably

## equal

ADJECTIVE: (often followed by to or with) identical in size, quantity, degree, intensity, etc.; the same (as); having identical privileges, rights, status, etc.; having uniform effect or application; evenly balanced or proportioned; (usually followed by to); having the necessary or adequate strength, ability, means, etc. (for)

NOUN: a person or thing equal to another, esp. in merit, ability, etc.

VERB: equals, equaling, equaled, US equals, equaling or equaled; to be equal to; correspond to; match; (intransitive; usually followed by out); (transitive) to make, perform, or do something equal to; (transitive) archaic; to make equal

## equality

NOUN: the state of being equal; (mathematics) a statement, usually an equation, indicating that quantities or expressions on either side of an equal sign are equal in value

## equals

ADJECTIVE: (often followed by to or with) identical in size, quantity, degree, intensity, etc.; the same (as); having identical privileges, rights, status, etc.; having uniform effect or application; equal opportunities; evenly balanced or proportioned; (usually followed by to); having the necessary or adequate strength, ability, means, etc. (for)

NOUN: a person or thing equal to another, esp. in merit, ability, etc.

VERB (transitive): to be equal to; correspond to; match; (intransitive; usually followed by out); to become equal or level; (transitive) to make, perform, or do something equal to; to equal the world record; (transitive) archaic, to make equal

## equipment

NOUN: an act or instance of equipping; the items so provided; a set of tools, devices, kit, etc., assembled for a specific purpose, such as a soldier's kit and weapons

## establish

VERB: to make secure or permanent in a certain place, condition, job, etc.; to establish one's usefulness; to create or set up (an organization, etc.) on or as if on a permanent basis; to prove correct or free from doubt; validate; to establish a fact; to cause (a principle, theory, etc.) to be widely or permanently accepted; to give (a Church) the status of a national institution

## ever

ADVERB: at any time; by any chance; in any case; at all times; always; in any possible way or manner

## every

DETERMINER: each one (of the class specified), without exception; (not used with a negative), the greatest or best possible; each: used before a noun phrase to indicate the recurrent, intermittent, or serial nature of a thing

## example

NOUN: a specimen or instance that is typical of the group or set of which it forms part; sample, a person, action, thing, etc., that is worthy of imitation; pattern, a precedent, illustration of a principle, or model; a punishment or the recipient of a punishment serving or intended to serve as a warning

VERB: to present an example of; exemplify

## exempt

VERB: to release from an obligation, liability, tax, etc.; excuse; to exempt a soldier from drill

ADJECTIVE: (sometimes postpositive) freed from or not subject to an obligation, liability, tax, etc.; excused; obsolete; set apart; remote

NOUN: a person who is exempt from an obligation, tax, etc.

## experienced

ADJECTIVE: having become skillful or knowledgeable from extensive contact or participation or observation

**fact**

NOUN: an event or thing known to have happened or existed; a truth verifiable from experience or observation; a piece of information; law (often plural); an actual event, happening, etc., as distinguished from its legal consequences; philosophy, a proposition that may be either true or false, as contrasted with an evaluative statement

**falsehoods**

NOUN: the quality of being untrue; an untrue statement; lie, the act of deceiving or lying

**Fard**

NOUN: According to the Most Hon. Elijah Muhammad: "The Great Mahdi have taken FARD as a name for Himself corresponding with the time of His coming-which is in the early days (or years) of the seventh thousand year. The early morning being the first part of the seventh thousand years, and the year under the name Millennium (which Christians say means the 1,000 years Christ will reign on the Earth.) This is the 1,000 years in which it will take to restore peace and honor, after the removal of peace breakers. This time also includes the birth of a new nation from the mentally dead. However, the Name FARD fits the context. FARD is a name many of the scholars have said is not one of the 99 attributes but still it is a Name that is Self-Independent, and One which means that the Believers are obligated to obey. We can see clearly why He took this Name (FARD) for Himself."; According to The Concise Oxford Dictionary of World religions: "One who, in Islam, is filled with the realization of truth and illumination on his own." Duties in Islam are sometimes categorized as being "Fard Ayn" or "Fard Kifaya". In Islamic law Fard Ayn, refers to legal obligations that must be performed by each individual Muslim, including prayer, charity, fasting, and pilgrimage. Individual obligation is contrasted with communal obligation (fard al-kifayah). Fard Kifaya defines a communal obligation in Muslim legal doctrine. In juxtaposition to fard al-ayn, fard al-kifayah is a legal obligation that must be discharged by the Muslim community as a whole, such as military struggle; if enough members in the Muslim community discharge the obligation, the remaining Muslims are freed from the responsibility before God. However, if a communal obligation is not sufficiently discharged, then every individual Muslim must act to address the deficiency. In recent Islamic literature, this terminology is used to discuss social responsibility, such as feeding the hungry, commanding good, and forbidding evil.

## federal

ADJECTIVE: of or relating to a form of government or a country in which power is divided between one central and several regional governments; of or relating to a treaty between provinces, states, etc., that establishes a political unit in which power is so divided; of or relating to the central government of a federation; of or relating to any union or association of parties or groups that retain some autonomy

NOUN: a supporter of federal union or federation

## fertile

ADJECTIVE: capable of producing offspring; (of land) having nutrients capable of sustaining an abundant growth of plants; (of farm animals) capable of breeding stock; in biology: capable of undergoing growth and development; (of plants) capable of producing gametes, spores, seeds, or fruits; producing many offspring; prolific; highly productive; rich; abundant

## fight

VERB: to oppose or struggle against (an enemy) in battle; to oppose or struggle against (a person, thing, cause, etc.) in any manner; (transitive) to engage in or carry on (a battle, contest, etc.); (when intransitive often followed by for); to uphold or maintain (a cause, ideal, etc.) by fighting or struggling; to fight for freedom; (transitive); to make or achieve (a way) by fighting

## find

VERB: to meet with or discover by chance; to discover or obtain, esp. by search or effort; to find happiness; (may take a clause as object); to become aware of; realize; (may take a clause as object) to regard as being; consider; to look for and point out (something to be criticized)

NOUN: a person, thing, etc., that is found, esp. a valuable or fortunate discovery

**first**

ADJECTIVE: before all others; earliest, best, or foremost

NOUN: preceding all others in numbering or counting order; the ordinal number of one. Often written: 1st rated, graded, or ranked above all other levels; denoting the lowest forward ratio of a gearbox in a motor vehicle; music, denoting the highest part assigned to one of the voice parts in a chorus or one of the sections of an orchestra

NOUN: the beginning; outset; education, mainly in British use: an honors degree of the highest class; something which has not occurred before, the lowest forward ratio of a gearbox in a motor vehicle; low gear

**fitting**

ADJECTIVE: appropriate or proper; suitable

NOUN: an accessory or part; an electrical fitting: (plural) furnishings or accessories in a building; work carried out by a fitter; the act of trying on clothes so that they can be adjusted to fit

**for**

PREPOSITION: intended to reach; directed or belonging to; to the advantage of; in the direction of; over a span of (time or distance); the river ran for six miles; in favor of; in support of; those for the proposal

CONJUNCTION (coordinating): for the following reason; because; seeing that

**force**

NOUN: strength or energy; might; power; exertion or the use of exertion against a person or thing that resists; coercion; physics, a dynamic influence that changes a body from a state of rest to one of motion or changes its rate of motion; a static influence that produces an elastic strain in a body or system or bears weight; Symbol: F, in physics: any operating influence that produces or tends to produce a change in a physical quantity; intellectual, social, political, or moral influence or strength

VERB: to compel or cause (a person, group, etc.) to do something through effort, superior strength, etc.; coerce; to acquire, secure, or produce through effort, superior strength, etc.; to propel or drive despite resistance; to break down or open (a lock, safe, door, etc.); to impose or inflict; to cause (plants or farm animals) to grow or fatten artificially at an increased rate; to strain or exert to the utmost

**forced**

ADJECTIVE: done because of force; compulsory; false or unnatural; due to an emergency or necessity; physics, caused by an external agency

**former**

ADJECTIVE (prenominal): belonging to or occurring in an earlier time; having been at a previous time; denoting the first or first mentioned of two; near the beginning

**free**

ADJECTIVE: able to act at will; not under compulsion or restraint; having personal rights or liberty; not enslaved or confined

NOUN: land of the free; (often postpositive; and followed by from) not subject (to) or restricted (by some regulation, constraint, etc.); exempt; (of a country, etc.) autonomous or independent; exempt from external direction or restriction; not forced or induced

ADVERB: in a free manner; freely; without charge or cost

VERB: (sometimes followed by up); to set at liberty; release; to remove obstructions, attachments, or impediments from; disengage; (often followed by of or from); to relieve or rid (of obstacles, pain, etc.)

**freed**

ADJECTIVE: not under the control of some other person or some arbitrary power; able to act or think without compulsion or arbitrary restriction; having liberty; independent; characterized by or resulting from liberty; having, or existing under, a government that does not impose arbitrary restrictions on the right to speak, assemble, petition, vote, etc.; having civil and political liberty, not under control of a foreign government; able to move in any direction; not held, as in chains, etc.; not kept from motion; loose, not held or confined by a court, the police, etc.; acquitted; not held or burdened by obligations, debts, discomforts, etc.; unhindered; unhampered; at liberty; allowed; free to leave at any time; not confined to the usual rules or patterns; not limited by convention or tradition; not literal; not exact; not held or confined by prejudice or bias; not restricted by anything except its own limitations or nature; not busy or not in use; available for other work, use, etc.; readily done or made; spontaneous; not constrained or stilted; easy and graceful; generous; liberal; lavish; profuse; copious; frank; straightforward; too frank or familiar in speech, action, etc.; forward; indecorous; with no charge or cost; gratis; not liable to (trade restrictions, etc.); exempt from certain impositions, as taxes or duties; clear of obstructions; open and unimpeded; open to all; esp., without restrictions as to trade; not in contact or connection; not fastened; not united; not combined; free oxygen; not opposed

ADVERB: without cost or payment in a free manner; without obstruction, burden, obligation, etc. (Nautical)with a favorable wind

VERB (transitive): to make free; to release from bondage or arbitrary power, authority, obligation, etc.; to clear of obstruction, entanglement, etc.; disengage

**freedom**

NOUN: personal liberty, as from slavery, bondage, serfdom, etc.; liberation or deliverance, as from confinement or bondage; the quality or state of being free, esp. to enjoy political and civil liberties; (usually followed by from); the state of being without something unpleasant or bad; exemption or immunity; the right or privilege of unrestricted use or access

**frequently**

ADVERB: often; many times; at short intervals

**friends**

ADJECTIVE: of or having to do with Friends, or Quakers

**friendship**

NOUN: the state of being friends; attachment between friends; friendly feeling or attitude; friendliness

**from**

PREPOSITION: used to indicate the original location, situation, etc.; in a period of time starting at; used to indicate the distance between two things or places; used to indicate a lower amount; showing the model of

**full**

ADJECTIVE: holding or containing as much as possible; filled to capacity or near capacity; abundant in supply, quantity, number, etc.; having consumed enough food or drink; (esp. of the face or figure) rounded or plump; not thin; (prenominal) with no part lacking; complete

ADVERB: completely; entirely; (in combination) full-grown, full-fledged; exactly; directly; right; the boxer was hit full in the stomach; very; extremely (esp. in the phrase full well)

NOUN: the greatest degree, extent, etc.; British, a ridge of sand or shingle along a seashore; in full;

VERB: needlework to gather or tuck; (of the moon) to be fully illuminated

**furnish**

VERB: to provide (a house, room, etc.) with furniture, carpets, etc.; to equip with what is necessary; fit out; to give; supply

**further**

ADVERB: in addition; furthermore; to a greater degree or extent; to or at a more advanced point; to or at a greater distance in time or space; farther

ADJECTIVE; additional; more; more distant or remote in time or space; farther

VERB: to assist the progress of; promote

**furthermore**

ADVERB: in addition; moreover

**gain**

VERB: to acquire (something desirable); obtain; to win in competition; gain the victory; to increase, improve, or advance; to earn (a wage, living, etc.); (intransitive; usually followed by on or upon)

NOUN: something won, acquired, earned, etc.; profit; advantage; an increase in size, amount, etc.; the act of gaining; attainment; acquisition; Also called: amplification electronics; the ratio of the output signal of an amplifier to the input signal, usually measured in decibels

**get**

VERB: to come into possession of; receive or earn; to bring or fetch; to contract or be affected by; to capture or seize; (also intransitive); to become or cause to become or act as specified

NOUN: rare; the act of begetting; rare, something begotten; offspring

**girls**

NOUN: a female child from birth to young womanhood; a young unmarried woman; lass; maid; informal, a sweetheart or girlfriend; a woman of any age; an informal word for daughter

**give**

VERB: to present or deliver voluntarily (something that is one's own) to the permanent possession of another or others; (often followed by for) to transfer (something that is one's own, esp. money) to the possession of another as part of an exchange; to place in the temporary possession of another; (when intransitive, followed by of); to grant, provide, or bestow; to administer; to give a reprimand

NOUN: a tendency to yield under pressure; resilience

**giving**

ADJECTIVE: affectionate and generous where one's feelings are concerned

**go**

VERB: to move or proceed, esp. to or from a point or in a certain direction: (tr; takes an infinitive, often with to omitted or replaced by and) to proceed towards a particular person or place with some specified intention or purpose; to depart; to start, as in a race: often used in commands

NOUN: the act of going; informal, an attempt or try; an attempt at stopping a person suspected of a crime; an attack, esp. verbal; a turn

ADJECTIVE: (postpositive) informal; functioning properly and ready for action: esp. used in astronautics

**god**

NOUN: a supernatural being, who is worshipped as the controller of some part of the universe or some aspect of life in the world or is the personification of some force; an image, idol, or symbolic representation of such a deity; any person or thing to which excessive attention is given; a man who has qualities regarded as making him superior to other men; (in plural), the gallery of a theatre

**govern**

VERB: to direct and control the actions, affairs, policies, functions, etc. of (a political unit, organization, nation, etc.); rule; to exercise restraint over; regulate or direct; to govern one's temper; to be a predominant influence on (something); decide or determine (something); to control the speed of (an engine, machine, etc.) using a governor; to control the rate of flow of (a fluid) by using an automatic valve

**government**

NOUN: the exercise of political authority over the actions, affairs, etc. of a political unit, people, etc., as well as the performance of certain functions for this unit or body; the action of governing; political rule and administration; the system or form by which a community, etc. is ruled; tyrannical government; the executive policy-making body of a political unit, community, etc.; ministry or administration; (capital when of a specific country) the British Government; the state and its administration; (as modifier) a government agency; regulation; direction

**grandparents**

NOUN: the father or mother of either of one's parents

**has**

VERB: (used with he, she, it, or a singular noun) a form of the present tense (indicative mood) of have

**have**

VERB: to be in material possession of; own; to possess as a characteristic quality or attribute; to receive, take, or obtain; to hold or entertain in the mind; to possess a knowledge or understanding of

NOUN: (usually plural) a person or group of people in possession of wealth, security, etc.

**he**

PRONOUN (subjective): refers to a male person or animal; refers to an indefinite antecedent such as one, whoever, or anybody; refers to a person or animal of unknown or unspecified sex

NOUN: a male person or animal (in combination); he-goat

**held**

VERB: the past tense and past participle of hold

**helped**

VERB (transitive): to assist or aid (someone to do something), esp. by sharing the work, cost, or burden of something; to alleviate the burden of (someone else) by giving assistance; to assist (a person) to go in a specified direction; to promote or contribute to; to help the relief operations; to cause improvement in (a situation, person, etc.)

NOUN: the act of helping, or being helped, or a person or thing that helps; a helping; a person hired for a job; employee, esp. a farm worker or domestic servant; several employees collectively; a means of remedy; exclamation; used to ask for assistance

**her**

PRONOUN (objective): refers to a female person or animal; refers to things personified as feminine or traditionally to ships and nations

DETERMINER: of, belonging to, or associated with her

**him**

PRONOUN: refers to a male person or animal; mainly US a dialect word for himself

**hindrance**

NOUN: an obstruction or snag; impediment; the act of hindering; prevention

**his**

DETERMINER: of, belonging to, or associated with him

PRONOUN: his is on the left; his and hers; of his

**history**

NOUN: a record or account, often chronological in approach, of past events, developments, etc.; (as modifier); all that is preserved or remembered of the past, esp. in written form; the discipline of recording and interpreting past events involving human beings; past events, esp. when considered as an aggregate; an event in the past, esp. one that has been forgotten or reduced in importance

**holy**

ADJECTIVE: of, relating to, or associated with God or a deity; sacred; endowed or invested with extreme purity or sublimity; devout, godly, or virtuous

**honorable**

ADJECTIVE: worthy of being honored; of, or having a position of, high rank or worth; used as a title of courtesy for certain officials and for the children of certain British peers; noble; illustrious; of good reputation; respectable; having or showing a sense of right and wrong; characterized by honesty and integrity; upright; bringing honor to the owner or doer; doing honor; accompanied with marks of respect

**houses**

NOUN: a building used as a home; dwelling, (as modifier) house dog; a building used for some specific purpose; (in combination) a schoolhouse; (often capital) a family line including ancestors and relatives, esp. a noble one; a commercial company; firm

**human**

ADJECTIVE: of, characterizing, or relating to people; human nature; consisting of people; the human race; a human chain; having the attributes of people as opposed to animals, divine beings, or machines; human failings; kind or considerate; natural

Noun: a human being; person

**hypocritical**

ADJECTIVE: If you accuse someone of being hypocritical, you mean that they pretend to have qualities, beliefs, or feelings that they do not really have. 'hypocrite'(noun): a person who pretends to be what he or she is not; one who pretends to be better than is really so, or to be pious, virtuous, etc. without really being so

**identified**

VERB: identify; to prove or recognize as being a certain person or thing; determine the identity of; to consider as the same or equivalent; to consider (oneself) as similar to another, (intransitive; often followed by as); to declare oneself to be a member of a particular group; to identify as a communist; to determine the taxonomic classification of

**if**

CONJUNCTION (subordinating): in case that, or on condition that; used to introduce an indirect question. In this sense, if approaches the meaning of whether; even though; used to introduce expressions of desire, with only; used to introduce exclamations of surprise, dismay, etc.; as if

NOUN: an uncertainty or doubt; the big if is whether our plan will work at all; a condition or stipulation

**immediate**

ADJECTIVE: (usually prenominal) taking place or accomplished without delay; closest or most direct in effect or relationship the immediate cause of his downfall; having no intervening medium;

direct in effect; contiguous in space, time, or relationship; present; current

**imposed**

VERB: (usually followed by on or upon): to establish as something to be obeyed or complied with; enforce; to impose a tax on the people; to force (oneself, one's presence, etc.) on another or others; obtrude; to take advantage, as of a person or quality; to impose on someone's kindness; printing, to arrange (pages) so that after printing and folding the pages will be in the correct order; (transitive), to pass off deceptively; foist

**in**

PREPOSITION: inside; within; at a place where there is; indicating a state, situation, or condition; before or when (a period of time) has elapsed; using (a language, etc.) as a means of communication

ADVERB: (particle)in or into a particular place; inwards or indoors; so as to achieve office, power, or authority; so as to enclose; (in certain games) so as to take one's turn or one's team's turn at a certain aspect of the play; taking one's innings

**indeed**

ADVERB: sentence connector; certainly, actually,

ADVERB (intensifier): or rather; what is more; exclamation, an expression of doubt, surprise, etc.

**independent**

ADJECTIVE: free from control in action, judgment, etc.; autonomous; not dependent on anything else for function, validity, etc.; separate; not reliant on the support, esp. financial support, of others; capable of acting for oneself or on one's own; a very independent little child; providing a large unearned sum towards one's support (esp. in the phrases independent income, independent means)

NOUN: an independent person or thing; a person who is not affiliated to or who acts independently of a political party

**innumerable**

ADJECTIVE: so many as to be uncountable; extremely numerous

**integration**

NOUN: the act of combining or adding parts to make a unified whole; the act of amalgamating an ethnic or religious group with an existing community; the combination of previously racially segregated social facilities into a non-segregated system; psychology, organization into a unified pattern, esp. of different aspects of the personality into a hierarchical system of functions; the assimilation of nutritive material by the body during the process of anabolism

**intended**

ADJECTIVE: planned or future

NOUN: informal, a person whom one is to marry; fiancé or fiancée

**intercede**

VERB (intransitive): (often followed by in); to come between parties or act as mediator or advocate; to intercede in the strike; Roman history, (of a tribune or other magistrate) to interpose a veto

**intermarriage**

NOUN: marriage between persons of different clans, tribes, races, religions, castes, etc.; marriage between closely related persons

**into**

PREPOSITION: to the interior or inner parts of; to the middle or midst of so as to be surrounded by; against; up against; used to indicate the result of a transformation or change; (mathematics)used to indicate a dividend

**is**

VERB: (used with he, she, it, and with singular nouns) a form of the present tense (indicative mood) of 'be'

**Islam**

NOUN: Islam is the nature of Allah (God) and the nature of the original people. Islam means "surrendering to and obeying" Allah (God).

**it**

PRONOUN: (subjective or objective) refers to a nonhuman, animal, plant, or inanimate thing, or sometimes to a small baby; refers to an unspecified or implied antecedent or to a previous or understood clause, phrase, etc.; used to represent human life or experience either in totality or in respect of the present situation; used as a formal subject (or object), referring to a following clause, phrase, or word; used in the nominative as the formal grammatical subject of impersonal verbs. When it functions absolutely in such sentences, not referring to any previous or following clause or phrase, the context is nearly always a description of the environment or of some physical sensation

**jobs**

NOUN: an individual piece of work or task; an occupation; post of employment; an object worked on or a result produced from working; a duty or responsibility; informal, a difficult task or problem

VERB: to work by the piece or at casual jobs; to make a private profit out of (a public office, etc.); (intransitive; usually followed by in); to buy and sell (goods or services) as a middleman; British, to buy and sell stocks and shares as a stockjobber

**judgment**

NOUN: the faculty of being able to make critical distinctions and achieve a balanced viewpoint; discernment; the decision or verdict pronounced by a court of law; an obligation arising as a result of such a decision or verdict, such as a debt; the document recording such a decision or verdict; the formal decision of one or more judges at a contest or competition; a particular decision or opinion formed in a case in dispute or doubt; an estimation

**Judgment**

NOUN: the estimate by God of the ultimate worthiness or unworthiness of the individual (the Particular Judgment) or of all humankind (the General Judgment or Last Judgment); God's subsequent decision determining the final destinies of all individuals

**July**

NOUN: according to the Gregorian Calendar, the seventh month of the year, consisting of 31 days, under the Julian Calendar the month of April was the first month of the year, making July the fourth month of the year in the historical period of time when the Julian Calendar was used.

### justice

NOUN: the quality or fact of being just; in ethics: the principle of fairness that like cases should be treated alike; a particular distribution of benefits and burdens fairly in accordance with a particular conception of what are to count as like cases; the principle that punishment should be proportionate to the offence; the administration of law according to prescribed and accepted principles; conformity to the law; legal validity; title of a judge of the Supreme Court

### justifies

VERB: (often passive) to prove or see to be just or valid; vindicate; to show to be reasonable; warrant or substantiate; to declare or show to be free from blame or guilt; absolve; law, to show good reason in court for (some action taken) to show adequate grounds for doing (that with which a person is charged); (also intransitive) printing, computing; to adjust the spaces between words in (a line of type or data) so that it is of the required length or (of a line of type or data) to fit exactly

### know

VERB: (also intransitive; may take a clause as object); to be or feel certain of the truth or accuracy of (a fact, etc.); to be acquainted or familiar with; to have a familiarity or grasp of, as through study or experience; (also intransitive; may take a clause as object); to understand, be aware of, or perceive (facts, etc.); (followed by how) to be sure or aware of (how to be or do something)

### labor

NOUN: physical or mental exertion; work; toil; a specific task; piece of work; all wage-earning workers as a group; management; all manual workers whose work is characterized largely by physical exertion; the work accomplished by or the role in production of all workers, esp. workers for wage

VERB: to work; toil; to work hard; exert oneself to get or do something; strive; to move slowly and with difficulty; to pitch and roll heavily; to be afflicted or burdened with a liability or limitation (with under); to labor under a delusion; to undergo, and suffer the pains of, childbirth; to spend too much time and effort on; develop in too great detail

**land**

NOUN: the solid part of the surface of the earth as distinct from seas, lakes, etc.; ground, esp. with reference to its use, quality, etc.; rural or agricultural areas as contrasted with urban ones; farming as an occupation or way of life; law, any tract of ground capable of being owned as property, together with any buildings on it, extending above and below the surface; any hereditament, tenement, or other interest; realty

VERB: to transfer (something) or go from a ship or boat to the shore; to come to or touch shore; to come down or bring (something) down to earth after a flight or jump; to come or bring to some point, condition, or state; angling; to retrieve (a hooked fish) from the water; informal; to win or obtain

**last**

ADJECTIVE: (often prenominal); being, happening or coming at the end or after all others; being or occurring just before the present; most recent; only remaining

ADVERB: after all others; at or in the end; most recently; (in combination) "last-mentioned"; (sentence modifier); as the last or latest item

NOUN: "the last"; one's last moments before death; the last thing a person can do (esp. in the phrase breathe one's last); the final appearance, mention, or occurrence

**lastly**

ADVERB: at the end or at the last point; sentence connector; in the end; finally

**law**

NOUN: a rule or set of rules, enforceable by the courts; regulating the government of a state; the relationship between the organs of government and the subjects of the state; and the relationship or conduct of subjects towards each other; a rule or body of rules made by the legislature; statute law a rule or body of rules made by a municipal or other authority; bylaw, the condition and control enforced by such rules; (in combination); lawcourt; a rule of conduct; one of a set of rules governing a particular field of activity

**laws**

NOUN: all the rules of conduct established and enforced by the authority, legislation, or custom of a given community, state, or other group; any one of such rules; the condition existing when obedience to such rules is general; the branch of knowledge dealing with such rules; jurisprudence; the system of courts in which such rules are referred to in defending one's rights, securing justice, etc.; to resort to law to settle a matter; all such rules having to do with a particular sphere of human activity; business law' common law, as distinguished from equity; the profession of lawyers, judges, etc.; a sequence of events in nature or in human activities that has been observed to occur; with unvarying uniformity under the same conditions; the formulation in words of such a sequence; as in "the law of gravitation", "the law of diminishing returns"; any rule or principle expected to be observed; inherent tendency; instinct

**left**

ADJECTIVE: (usually prenominal) of or designating the side of something or someone that faces west when the front is turned towards the north; (usually prenominal) worn on a left hand, foot, etc.; (sometimes capital) of or relating to the political or intellectual left; radical or progressive, esp. as compared to less radical or progressive groups, persons, etc.

ADVERB: on or in the direction of the left

NOUN: a left side, direction, position, area, or part; (often capital) the supporters or advocates of varying degrees of social, political, or economic change, reform, or revolution designed to promote the greater freedom, power, welfare, or comfort of ordinary people; to the left; boxing, a blow with the left hand

**liberty**

NOUN: the power of choosing, thinking, and acting for oneself; freedom from control or restriction; the right or privilege of access to a particular place; freedom (often plural); a social action regarded as being familiar, forward, or improper; (often plural) an action that is unauthorized or unwarranted in the circumstances; authorized leave granted to a sailor (as modifier)

**live**

VERB: (mainly intransitive); to show the characteristics of life; be alive; to remain alive or in existence; to exist in a specified way; to live poorly; (usually followed by in or at); to reside or dwell; (often followed by on)

ADJECTIVE: (prenominal) showing the characteristics of life; (usually prenominal) of, relating to, or abounding in life; (usually prenominal) of current interest; controversial; actual, informal

ADVERB: during, at, or in the form of a live performance

**long**

ADJECTIVE: having relatively great extent in space on a horizontal plane; having relatively great duration in time; (postpositive) of a specified number of units in extent or duration; (in combination); having or consisting of a relatively large number of items or parts; having greater than the average or expected range; being the longer or longest of alternatives

ADVERB: for a certain time or period; for or during an extensive period of time; at a distant time; quite a bit of time

NOUN: a long time (esp. in the phrase for long); a relatively long thing, such as a signal in Morse code

**long-awaited**

ADJECTIVE: (of an event) anticipated for a considerable time

**made**

VERB: the past tense and past participle of make[1]

ADJECTIVE: artificially produced; (in combination) produced or shaped as specified handmade;

**Mahdi**

NOUN: The Self-Guided One; Guide, Leader; A ruler who shall in the last days appear upon the Earth. The Mahdi is prophesied to fill the Earth with equity and justice, even as it has been filled with tyranny and oppression.

**maintain**

VERB: to continue or retain; keep in existence; to keep in proper or good condition, to maintain a building; to support a style of living, the money maintained us for a month; (takes a clause as object) to state or assert. i.e. "He maintained that Talbot was wrong"; to defend against contradiction; uphold, i.e. "she maintained her innocence"

**make**

VERB: to bring into being by shaping, changing, or combining materials, ideas, etc.; form or fashion; create; i.e. "to make a chair from bits of wood"; to draw up, establish, or form, i.e. "to make a decision"; to cause to exist, bring about, or produce, i.e. don't make a noise; to cause, compel, or induce, i.e. please make him go away; to appoint or assign, as to a rank or position, i.e. they made her president; to constitute, i.e. one swallow doesn't make a summer; to come or cause to come into a specified state or condition, i.e. to make merry, make someone happy; to be or become through development, i.e. he will make a good teacher; to cause or ensure the success of, i.e. your news has made my day; to amount to, i.e. twelve inches make a foot;

**man**

NOUN: an adult male human being; a member of the species Homo sapiens or all the members of this species collectively, without regard to sex; the human individual as representing the species, without reference to sex; the human race; humankind;

**mankind**

NOUN: human beings collectively; humanity; men collectively, as opposed to womankind; You can refer to all human beings as mankind when considering them as a group. Some people dislike this use.

**many**

DETERMINER: (sometimes preceded by a great or a good), a large number of, i.e. "many coaches, many times", (as pronoun; functioning as plural), i.e. "many are seated already"; (followed by a, an, or another, and a singular noun), each of a considerable number of i.e. "many a man"; (preceded by as, too, that, etc.), a great number of i.e. "as many apples as you like"; (as pronoun; functioning as plural), i.e. "I have as many as you";

**master**

NOUN: a man in a position of authority, ownership, or control, such as the head of a household; Related adjective: magistrate; a person with exceptional skill at a certain thing, i.e. "a master of the violin"; (as modifier), i.e. "a master thief"; (often capital), a great artist, esp. an anonymous but influential artist; a person who has complete control of a situation; an abstract thing regarded as having power or influence, i.e. "they regarded fate as the master of their lives"; a workman or craftsman fully qualified to practice a trade and to train others in it; (as modifier), i.e. "master carpenter"

**may**

AUXILIARY VERB: might; used to express ability or power now generally replaced by can; used to express possibility or likelihood, it may rain; used to express permission; used to express contingency, as in clauses of purpose, result, concession, or condition; used in exclamations and apostrophes to express a wish, hope, or prayer

**mean**

VERB: to intend to convey or express; to intend, i.e. "I didn't mean to hurt you"; (may take a clause as object), to say or do in all seriousness, i.e. "the management mean what they say about strikes"; (often passive; often followed by for), to destine or design (for a certain person or purpose), i.e. "she was meant for greater things"; (may take a clause as object), to denote or connote; signify; represent, examples help show exactly what a word means

**membership**

NOUN: the members of an organization collectively; the state of being a member

**men**

NOUN: the plural of man

**mental**

ADJECTIVE: of or involving the mind or an intellectual process; occurring only in the mind. mental calculations

**Messiah**

NOUN: The Hebrew word for "Anointed One." In the Old Testament it was sometimes applied in a general sense to prophets or priests (Exodus 30:30), but more specifically it referred to the coming of one who would usher in a period of righteousness and conquer sin and evil (Daniel 9:26)

**millions**

PRONOUN: an extremely large but unspecified number, quantity, or amount that is greater than one million.

**minerally rich**

ADJECTIVE: used to describe countries, areas, etc. that contain a lot of minerals; "Mineral wealth" means natural mineral substances contained in the depths in solid, liquid or gaseous state (including ground water and therapeutic muds) fit for usage in material production, or hydrocarbons.

**mixing**

VERB: to put or blend together in a single mass, collection, or compound; to make by putting ingredients together; to join; combine; to cause to join or associate; to hybridize

**mob**

NOUN: a riotous or disorderly crowd of people; rabble; (as modifier), "mob law, mob violence"; often derogatory, a group or class of people, animals, or things; Australian and New Zealand, a flock (of sheep) or a herd (of cattle, esp. when droving); often derogatory, the masses; slang, a gang of criminals

**more**

ADJECTIVE: greater in amount, degree, or number often used as the comparative of much, or many; additional; further

**most**

ADJECTIVE: greatest in amount, quantity, or degree greatest in number; in the greatest number of instances

**Muhammad**

NOUN: The Name of the Holy Prophet Muhammad; literally meaning one who is worthy of praise; commendable; highly lauded

**Muslim**

NOUN: Muslim means a person who has surrendered, who obeys God and His commandments; to be a Moslem—the one who lives 'Islam'—is to achieve tranquility, peace, security, and happiness; to be well-mannered and to possess splendid moral conduct; to attain perfection, liberation, and fulfillment by purifying oneself and unification.

**must**

AUXILIARY VERB: used to express compulsion, obligation, requirement, or necessity; used to express probability i.e. "you must be my cousin"; used to express certainty or inevitability, all men must die; they knew they must die

**name**

NOUN: a word or term by which a person or thing is commonly and distinctively known; mere outward appearance or form as opposed to fact (esp. in the phrase in name), "he was a ruler in name only"; a word, title, or phrase descriptive of character, usually abusive or derogatory, "to call a person names"; reputation, esp., if unspecified, good reputation, "she's made quite a name for herself"; a famous person or thing, "a name in the advertising world"

**nation**

NOUN: an aggregation of people or peoples of one or more cultures, races, etc., organized into a single state, "the Australian nation"; a community of persons not constituting a state but bound by common descent, language, history, etc., "the French-Canadian nation"; a federation of tribes, esp. of Native Americans; the territory occupied by such a federation

**nationalities**

NOUN: the state or fact of being a citizen of a particular nation; a body of people sharing common descent, history, language, etc.; a nation; a national group; national character or quality; the state or fact of being a nation; national status

**nearly**

ADVERB: not quite; almost; practically.

**necessary**

ADJECTIVE: that cannot be dispensed with; essential; indispensable; resulting from necessity; inevitable; that must be done; mandatory; not voluntary; inherent in the situation; undeniable; unavoidable from the premises; being essential, indispensable, or requisite

**need**

NOUN: necessity or obligation created by some situation; a lack of something useful, required, or desired; something useful, required, or desired that is lacking; want; requirement

**needs**

PLURAL NOUN: what is required; necessities

**negro**

NOUN: a word for a Black person, which was used frequently in the past and is now extremely offensive; deriving through the rules of morphology from the Latin "necro" meaning of or relating to death or the dead

**new**

ADJECTIVE: never existing before; appearing, thought of, developed, made, produced, etc. for the first time; existing before, but known or discovered for the first time

**next**

ADJECTIVE: immediately following; immediately adjoining; closest to in degree; next-best thing

ADVERB: at a time or on an occasion immediately to followed

**no**

SENTENCE SUBSTITUTE: used to express denial, disagreement,

refusal, disapproval, disbelief, or acknowledgment of negative statements; used with question intonation to query a previous negative statement, as in disbelief.

**north**

NOUN: one of the four cardinal points of the compass, at 0° or 360°, that is 90° from east and west and 180° from south; the direction along a meridian towards the North Pole; the direction in which a compass needle points; magnetic north

**not**

ADVERB: used to negate the sentence, phrase, or word that it modifies, I will not stand for it; (in combination), they cannot go; See not that

SENTENCE SUBSTITUTE: used to indicate denial, negation, or refusal

**nothing**

PRONOUN: no thing; not anything, as of an implied or specified class of things; a matter of no importance or significance; indicating the absence of anything perceptible; nothingness; indicating the absence of meaning, value, worth, etc.,

ADVERB: in no way; not at all, "she looked nothing like her brother"

NOUN: informal; a person or thing of no importance or significance

**now**

ADVERB: at or for the present time or moment; at this exact moment; immediately; in these times; nowadays; given the present circumstances,

**obligated**

ADJECTIVE: formal; having the feeling that it is one's duty to do something, or that one is legally bound to do it; having the feeling that it is one's duty to look after or do something for someone

**of**

PREPOSITION: from; derived or coming from; resulting from; caused by; through; proceeding as a product from; by; resulting from an operation or process involving; is what was done, expressed, etc. by; belonging to

**offer**

VERB: to present or proffer (something, someone, oneself, etc.) for acceptance or rejection; to present as part of a requirement; to provide or make accessible; to present itself if an opportunity should; to show or express willingness or the intention (to do something)

**on**

PREPOSITION: in contact or connection with the surface of; at the upper surface of, an apple on the ground; attached to; carried with; in the immediate vicinity of; close to or along the side of; within the time limits of a day or date, we arrived on Thursday

ADVERB: (often used as a particle); in the position or state required for the commencement or sustained continuation, as of a mechanical operation

ADJECTIVE: functioning; operating,

**one**

DETERMINER: single; lone; not two or more; distinct from all others; only; unique, a specified (person, item, etc.) as distinct from another or others of its kind; a certain, indefinite, or unspecified (time);

PRONOUN: an indefinite person regarded as typical of every person, "one can't say any more than that"; any indefinite person: used as the subject of a sentence to form an alternative grammatical construction to that of the passive voice, "one can catch fine trout in this stream"

NOUN: the smallest whole number and the first cardinal number; unity

**only**

ADJECTIVE: unique by virtue of being superior to anything else; peerless.

ADVERB: without anyone or anything else being included; alone,

SENTENCE CONNECTOR: but; however: used to introduce an

exception or condition, play outside: only don't go into the street

**open**

ADJECTIVE: not closed or barred; affording free passage, access, view, etc.; not blocked or obstructed; not sealed, fastened, or wrapped; having the interior part accessible; extended, expanded, or unfolded,

VERB: to move or cause to move from a closed or fastened position, to render, be, or become accessible or unobstructed, to open a road, to open a parcel; to come into or appear in view,

**opportunity**

NOUN: a favorable, appropriate, or advantageous combination of circumstances; a chance or prospect

**or**

CONJUNCTION (coordinating); used to join alternatives; used to join rephrasings of the same thing; used to join two alternatives when the first is preceded by either or whether

**other**

DETERMINER:  different (one or ones from that or those already specified or understood), "they found some other house"; additional; further, "there are no other possibilities"; (preceded by every), alternate; two, "it buzzes every other minute"

PRONOUN: another, additional or further ones

ADVERB: (usually used with a negative and followed by than), otherwise; differently, "they couldn't behave other than they do"

VERB: in sociology, to regard and treat (a person or people) as different from oneself or one's group

**others**

PRONOUN: used to indicate that people or things are not the ones already mentioned, but different ones.

**our**

PROGRESSIVE PRONOMIIAL ADJECTIVE: of, belonging to, or associated in some way with us

**ourselves**

PRONOUN: the reflexive form of we or us; (intensifier), used instead of we or us in compound noun phrases`

**own**

ADJECTIVE: belonging, relating, or peculiar to oneself or itself; of, pertaining to, or belonging to oneself or itself (usually used after a possessive to emphasize the idea of ownership, interest, or relation conveyed by the possessive)

**parents**

NOUN: a father or mother, a person acting as a father or mother; guardian; an ancestor; a source or cause; an organism or organization that has produced one or more organisms or organizations similar to itself; (as modifier), a parent organism

**part**

NOUN: a piece or portion of a whole; an integral constituent of something; an amount less than the whole; bit; (as modifier); one of several equal or nearly equal divisions; an actor's role in a play, the speech and actions which make up such a role, a written copy of these

**participate**

VERB: to take part, be or become actively involved, or share (in)

**peace**

NOUN: the state existing during the absence of war; a treaty marking the end of a war; a state of harmony between people or groups; freedom from strife; law and order within a state; absence of violence or other disturbance

**people**

NOUN: persons collectively or in general; a group of persons considered together; the persons living in a country and sharing the same nationality.

VERB: to provide with or as if with people or inhabitants

**person**

NOUN: an individual human being; the body of a human being, sometimes including his or her clothing; a human being or a corporation recognized in law as having certain rights and obligations; in philosophy, a being characterized by consciousness, rationality, and a moral sense, and traditionally thought of as consisting of both a body and a mind or soul

**physical**

ADJECTIVE: of or relating to the body, as distinguished from the mind or spirit; of, relating to, or resembling material things or nature, "the physical universe"; involving or requiring bodily contact; of or concerned with matter and energy; of or relating to physics

**place**

NOUN: a particular point or part of space or of a surface, esp. that occupied by a person or thing; a geographical point, such as a town, city, etc.; a position or rank in a sequence or order

VERB: to put or set in a particular or appropriate place; to find or indicate the place of; to identify or classify by linking with an appropriate context

**plan**

NOUN: a detailed scheme, method, etc., for attaining an objective; (sometimes plural), a proposed, usually tentative idea for doing something; a drawing to scale of a horizontal section through a building taken at a given level; a view from above an object or an area in orthographic projection; an outline, sketch, etc.; (in perspective drawing) any of several imaginary planes perpendicular to the line of vision and between the eye and object depicted

VERB: to have in mind as a purpose; intend; to arrange a method or scheme beforehand for (any work, enterprise, or proceeding)

**police**

NOUN: the members of such a force collectively; any organized body with a similar function, security police; the regulation and control of a community, esp. in regard to the enforcement of law, the prevention of crime, etc.; the department of government concerned with this

VERB: to regulate, control, or keep in order by means of a police or similar force; to observe or record the activity or enforcement of, a committee was set up to police the new agreement on picketing; US, to make or keep (a military camp, etc.) clean and orderly

**poor**

ADJECTIVE: lacking financial or other means of subsistence; needy; (as collective noun; preceded by the), the poor; characterized by or indicating poverty; deficient in amount; scanty or inadequate; badly supplied (with resources, materials, etc.)

**possible**

ADJECTIVE: capable of existing, taking place, or proving true without contravention of any natural law; capable of being achieved; having potential or capabilities for favorable use or development; feasible but less than probable.

**powerful**

ADJECTIVE: having great power, force, potency, or effect; extremely effective or efficient in action, large or great, a powerful amount of trouble

ADVERB: dialect, extremely; very, he ran powerful fast

**prevent**

VERB: to keep from happening, esp. by taking precautionary action; to keep (someone from doing something); hinder; impede; to interpose or act as a hindrance; to anticipate or precede

**prisons**

NOUN: a public building used to house convicted criminals and accused persons remanded in custody and awaiting trial, penitentiary, reformatory; any place of confinement or seeming confinement

**problems**

NOUN: anything, matter, person, etc., that is difficult to deal with, solve, or overcome; (as modifier in mathematics), a statement requiring a solution usually by means of one or more operations or geometric constructions; designating a literary work that deals with difficult moral questions, a problem play

**produce**

VERB: to bring (something) into existence; yield; to bring forth (a product) by mental or physical effort; make; to give birth to; to manufacture; to give rise to

**professed**

ADJECTIVE: avowed or acknowledge; alleged or pretended; having taken vows of a religious order

**prohibited**

VERB: to forbid by law or other authority; to hinder or prevent

**proper**

ADJECTIVE: appropriate or suited for some purpose, in its proper place; correct in behavior or conduct; excessively correct in conduct; vigorously moral; up to a required or regular standard; (immediately postpositive) ;(of an object, quality, etc.) referred to or named specifically so as to exclude anything not directly connected with it

**prophet**

NOUN: a person who speaks for God or a god, or as though under divine guidance; a religious teacher or leader regarded as, or claiming to be, divinely inspired; a person who foretells or predicts what is to come;

**protected**

ADJECTIVE: (of animals, plants, areas of land, etc.) forbidden by law to be harmed, destroyed, or damaged, a protected zone of national forest, home to protected animal and plant species

**prove**

VERB: to establish or demonstrate the truth or validity of; verify, esp. by using an established sequence of procedures or statements; to establish the quality of, esp. by experiment or scientific analysis; law, to establish the validity and genuineness of (a will); to show (oneself) able or courageous.

**provide**

VERB: to put at the disposal of; furnish or supply; to afford; yield, "this meeting provides an opportunity to talk"; to take careful precautions (over); to supply means of support (to), esp.

financially, to provide for one's family; (in statutes, documents, etc.) to determine (what is to happen in certain contingencies), esp. by including a proviso condition

## question

NOUN: a form of words addressed to a person in order to elicit information or evoke a response; interrogative sentence; a point at issue, "it's only a question of time until she dies", "the question is how long they can keep up the pressure"; a difficulty or uncertainty; doubtful point, "a question of money", "there's no question about it"; an act of asking; an investigation into some problem or difficulty; a motion presented for debate by a deliberative body

VERB: to make (something) the subject of dispute or disagreement; to express uncertainty about the validity, truth, etc., of (something); doubt

## Qur'an

NOUN: the book of scripture of the Muslims; According to conventional Islamic belief, the Qur'ān was revealed by the angel Jabril (Gabriel) to the Prophet Muhammad in the West Arabian towns Mecca and Medina beginning in 610 and ending in 632 CE. The word Qur'an, which occurs already within the Islamic scripture itself (e.g., 9:111 and 75:17–18), is derived from the verb qara'a— "to read and recite or proclaim"

## race

NOUN: a contest of speed, as in running, swimming, driving, riding, etc.; any competition or rivalry; rapid or constant onward movement; any of the different varieties or populations of human beings distinguished by a) physical traits such as hair, eyes, skin color, body shape, etc.: traditionally, the three primary divisions are Caucasoid, Negroid, and Mongoloid, although many subdivisions of these are also called races b) blood types c) genetic code patterns d) all their inherited characteristics which are unique to their isolated breeding population; a human population partially isolated reproductively from other populations, whose members share a greater degree of physical and genetic similarity with one another than with other humans

VERB: to engage in a contest of speed with (another); to engage (oneself or one's representative) in a race, esp. as a profession or pastime, "to race pigeons"; to move or go as fast as possible; to run (an engine, shaft, propeller, etc.) or (of an engine, shaft, propeller, etc.) to run at high speed, esp. after reduction of the load or resistance

## realizing

VERB: to become conscious or aware of (something); to bring (a plan, ambition, etc.) to fruition; make actual or concrete; to give (something, such as a drama or film) the appearance of reality; (of goods, property, etc.) to sell for or make (a certain sum), "this table realized $800"; to convert (property or goods) into cash

## receive

VERB: to take (something offered) into one's hand or possession; to have (an honor, blessing, etc.) bestowed; to accept delivery or transmission of (a letter, telephone call, etc.); to be informed of (news or information); to hear and consent to or acknowledge (an oath, confession, etc.)

## recognize

VERB: to perceive (a person, creature, or thing) to be the same as or belong to the same class as something previously seen or known; know again; to accept or be aware of (a fact, duty, problem, etc.), "to recognize necessity"; to give formal acknowledgment of the status or legality of (a government, an accredited representative, etc.); mainly US and Canadian: to grant (a person) the right to speak in a deliberative body, debate, etc.; to give a token of thanks for (a service rendered, etc.)

## regardless

ADJECTIVE: (usually followed by of); taking no regard or heed; heedless

ADVERB: in spite of everything; disregarding drawbacks, to carry on regardless

## reinterpreted

VERB: to interpret (an idea, etc.) in a new or different way

## reject

VERB: to refuse to accept, acknowledge, use, believe, etc.; to throw out as useless or worthless; discard; to rebuff (a person); (of an organism) to fail to accept (a foreign tissue graft or organ transplant) because of immunological incompatibility

NOUN: someone or something rejected as imperfect, unsatisfactory, or useless

**rejected**

VERB: to refuse to accept, acknowledge, use, believe, etc.; to throw out as useless or worthless; discard; to rebuff (a person); (of an organism) to fail to accept (a foreign tissue graft or organ transplant) because of immunological incompatibility

NOUN: someone or something rejected as imperfect, unsatisfactory, or useless

**relief**

NOUN: a feeling of cheerfulness or optimism that followed the removal of anxiety, pain, or distress; deliverance from or alleviation of anxiety, pain, distress, etc.; help or assistance, as to poor, needy, or distressed people; (as modifier), "relief work"; short for tax relief; something that affords a diversion from monotony

**religion**

NOUN: belief in, worship of, or obedience to a supernatural power or powers considered to be divine or to have control of human destiny; any formal or institutionalized expression of such belief, the world's major religions; the attitude and feeling of one who believes in a transcendent controlling power or powers

**respect**

NOUN: an attitude of deference, admiration, or esteem; regard; the state of being honored or esteemed; a detail, point, or characteristic; particular, "he differs in some respects from his son"; reference or relation (esp. in the phrases in respect of, with respect to); polite or kind regard; consideration, respect for people's feelings

VERB: to have an attitude of esteem towards; show or have respect for, to respect one's elders; to pay proper attention to; not violate, to respect; to show consideration for; treat courteously or kindly, to concern or refer to

**respected**

ADJECTIVE: admired, esteemed,

**resurrected**

VERB: to rise or raise from the dead; bring or be brought back to life; to bring back into use or activity; revive; to renew (one's hopes, etc.)

**resurrection**

NOUN: a supposed act or instance of a dead person coming back to life; belief in the possibility of this as part of a religious or mystical system; the condition of those who have risen from the dead, "we shall all live in the resurrection"; the revival of something, "a resurrection of an old story"

**return**

VERB: to come back to a former place or state; (transitive); to give, take, or carry back; replace or restore; to repay or recompense, esp. with something of equivalent value, return the compliment; to earn or yield (profit or interest) as an income from an investment or venture; (intransitive); to come back or revert in thought or speech, "I'll return to that later"

NOUN: the act or an instance of coming back; something that is given or sent back, esp. unsatisfactory merchandise returned to the maker or supplier or a theatre ticket sent back by a purchaser for resale; the act or an instance of putting, sending, or carrying back; replacement or restoration; (often plural); the yield, revenue, or profit accruing from an investment, transaction, or venture; the act or an instance of reciprocation or repayment (esp. in the phrase in return for)

**revealed**

VERB: to make known; disclose; divulge; to lay open to view; display; exhibit; to expose to view or show (something concealed)

**rich**

ADJECTIVE: well supplied with wealth, property, etc.; owning much; (as collective noun; preceded by the), the rich; (when postpositive, usually followed by in); having an abundance of natural resources, minerals, etc., a land rich in metals; producing abundantly; fertile, rich soil; (when postpositive, usually followed by in or with); well supplied (with desirable qualities); abundant (in), a country rich with cultural interest; of great worth or quality; valuable, a rich collection of antiques

**righteous**

ADJECTIVE: characterized by, proceeding from, or in accordance with accepted standards of morality, justice, or uprightness; virtuous; morally right; fair and just

**schooling**

NOUN: education, esp. when received at school; the process of teaching or being taught in a school; the training of an animal, esp. of a horse for dressage; an archaic word for reprimand

**school**

NOUN: a place or institution for teaching and learning; establishment for education; the building or buildings, classrooms, laboratories, etc. of any such establishment

**scriptures**

NOUN: Also called: Holy Scripture, Holy Writ, i.e. "the Scriptures Christianity", the Old and New Testaments; any book or body of writings, esp. when regarded as sacred by a particular religious group

**see**

VERB: to perceive with the eyes; mentally understand, i.e. "I explained the problem but he could not see it"; to perceive with any or all of the senses; to be aware of in advance; foresee; to ascertain or find out (a fact); learn

NOUN: the diocese of a bishop, or the place within it where his or her cathedral or procathedral is situated

**self**

NOUN: the distinct individuality or identity of a person or thing; a person's usual or typical bodily make-up or personal characteristics, i.e. "she looked her old self again"; one's own welfare or interests, i.e. "he only thinks of self"; an individual's consciousness of his or her own identity or being

**sent**

VERB: the past tense and past participle of send

**sentence**

NOUN: a sequence of words capable of standing alone to make an assertion, ask a question, or give a command, usually consisting of a subject and a predicate containing a finite verb; the judgment formally pronounced upon a person convicted in criminal proceedings, esp. the decision as to what punishment is to be imposed; an opinion, judgment, or decision; in music another word for period; any short passage of scripture employed in liturgical use, "the funeral sentences"

VERB: to pronounce sentence on (a convicted person) in a court of law, the judge sentenced the murderer to life imprisonment

**separate**

VERB: to act as a barrier between; to put or force or be put or forced apart; to part or be parted from a mass or group; to discriminate between, "to separate the men from the boys"; to divide or be divided into component parts; sort or be sorted

ADJECTIVE: existing or considered independently, "a separate problem"; disunited or apart; set apart from the main body or mass; distinct, individual, or particular

**separated**

ADJECTIVE: no longer living with one's spouse; away or apart from someone.

**separation**

NOUN: the act of separating or state of being separated; the place or line where a separation is made; in family law, the cessation of cohabitation of a married couple, either by mutual agreement or under a decree of a court, divorce; the act of jettisoning a burnt-out stage of a multistage rocket; the instant at which such a stage is jettisoned

**shall**

VERB: past tense should); used as an auxiliary to make the future tense, "we shall see you tomorrow"; used as an auxiliary to indicate determination on the part of the speaker, as in issuing a threat, "you shall pay for this"; used as an auxiliary to indicate compulsion, now esp. in official documents, "the Tenant shall return the keys to the Landlord"; used as an auxiliary to indicate certainty or inevitability, "our day shall come"; (with any noun or pronoun as subject, esp. in conditional clauses or clauses expressing doubt); used as an auxiliary to indicate nonspecific futurity, "I don't think I shall ever see her again", "he doubts whether he shall be in tomorrow"

**should**

VERB: the past tense of shall: used as an auxiliary verb to indicate that an action is considered by the speaker to be obligatory "you should go" or to form the subjunctive mood with I or we "I should like to see you"

**simply**

ADVERB: in a simple manner; merely; only; absolutely; altogether; really, "a simply wonderful holiday"; (sentence modifier); frankly; candidly

**since**

PREPOSITION: during or throughout the period of time after, "since May it has only rained once"

CONJUNCTION (subordinating): (sometimes preceded by ever); continuously from or starting from the time when, "since we last met, important things have happened"; seeing that; because, "since you have no money, you can't come"

**slave**

NOUN: a person legally owned by another and having no freedom of action or right to property; a person who is forced to work for another against his or her will; a person under the domination of another person or some habit or influence, a slave to television; a person who works in harsh conditions for low pay; a device that is controlled by or that duplicates the action of another similar device (the master device); (as modifier), slave cylinder

VERB: to work like a slave; an archaic word for enslave

**snared**

NOUN: a device for trapping birds or small animals, esp. a flexible loop that is drawn tight around the prey; a surgical instrument for removing certain tumors, consisting of a wire loop that may be drawn tight around their base to sever or uproot them; anything that traps or entangles someone or something unawares

VERB: to catch (birds or small animals) with a snare; to catch or trap in or as if in a snare; capture by trickery

**so**

ADVERB: (followed by an adjective or adverb and a correlative clause often introduce by that); to such an extent, "the river is so dirty that it smells"; (used with a negative; it replaces the first as in an equative comparison); to the same extent as, "she is not so old as you"; (intensifier), "it's so lovely, I love you so"; in the state or manner expressed or implied, "they're happy and will remain so"; (not used with a negative; followed by an auxiliary verb or do, have, or be used as main verbs; also; likewise, "I can speak Spanish and so can you"

**so-called**

ADJECTIVE: (prenominal); designated or styled by the name or word mentioned, esp. (in the speaker's opinion) incorrectly, (i.e. "a so-called genius")

**society**

NOUN: the totality of social relationships among organized groups of human beings or animals; a system of human organizations generating distinctive cultural patterns and institutions and usually providing protection, security, continuity, and a national identity for its members; such a system with reference to its mode of social and economic organization or its dominant class, middle-class society; those with whom one has companionship; an organized group of people associated for some specific purpose or on account of some common interest, a learned society

**solution**

NOUN: the act, method, or process of solving a problem; the answer to a problem; an explanation, clarification, etc.; a homogeneous mixture of two or more substances in which the molecules or atoms of the substances are completely dispersed. The constituents can be solids, liquids, or gases; the act or process of forming a solution; the state of being dissolved (esp. in the phrase in solution); a mixture of two or more substances in which one or more components are present as small particles with colloidal dimension; colloid, a colloidal solution; a specific answer to or way of answering a problem

**some**

DETERMINER: certain unknown or unspecified, "some idiot drove into my car", "some people never learn"; (as pronoun; functioning as sing or plural), "some can teach and others can't"; an unknown or unspecified quantity or amount of, "there's some rice on the table", "he owns some horses"; (as pronoun; functioning as sing or plural), "we'll buy some"; a considerable number or amount of, "he lived some years afterwards"; a little, "show him some respect"; (usually stressed) informal; an impressive or remarkable, "that was some game!"; a certain amount (more) (in the phrases "some more" and (informal) "and then some")

ADVERB: to a certain degree or extent, "I guess I like him some"

**something**

PRONOUN: an unspecified or unknown thing; some thing; an unspecified or unknown amount.

ADVERB: to some degree; a little; somewhat, "to look something like me"; (followed by an adjective) informal; (intensifier)," it hurts something awful"

**south**

NOUN: one of the four cardinal points of the compass, at 180° from north and 90° clockwise from east and anticlockwise from west; the direction along a meridian towards the South Pole

ADJECTIVE: situated in, moving towards, or facing the south; (esp. of the wind) from the south

ADVERB: in, to, or towards the south

**state**

NOUN: the condition of a person, thing, etc., with regard to main attribute; the structure, form, or constitution of something, "a solid state"; any mode of existence; position in life or society; estate; ceremonious style, as befitting wealth or dignity, "to live in state"

VERB: may take a clause as object); to articulate in words; utter; to declare formally or publicly to state one's innocence; to resolve

**status**

NOUN: a social or professional position, condition, or standing to which varying degrees of responsibility, privilege, and esteem are attached; the relative position or standing of a person or thing; a high position or standing; prestige,

**subsist**

VERB: to be sustained; manage to live; to continue in existence;(followed by in); to lie or reside by virtue (of); consist; philosophy; to exist as a concept or relation rather than a fact; to be conceivable; (transitive) obsolete, to provide with support

**such**

ADJECTIVE: of the kind mentioned or implied "a man such as his father"; of the same or a similar kind; like "pens, pencils, crayons, and such supplies"; certain but not specified; whatever "at such time as you go"; so extreme, so much, so great, etc. used, according to the context, for emphasis "embarrassed by such praise"

**sudden**

ADJECTIVE: occurring or performed quickly and without warning; marked by haste; abrupt; rare, rash; precipitate

NOUN: archaic; an abrupt occurrence or the occasion of such an occurrence (in the phrase on a sudden); See all of a sudden; ADVERB; mainly poetic, without warning; suddenly

**suffering**

NOUN: the pain, misery, or loss experienced by a person who suffers; the state or an instance of enduring pain, etc.

**supply**

VERB: to furnish with something that is required, "to supply the community with good government"; (often followed by to or for); to make available or provide (something that is desired or lacking), "to supply books to the library"; to provide for adequately; make good; satisfy, "who will supply their needs?"; to serve as a, substitute, usually temporary, in (another's position, etc.), "there are no ministers to supply the pulpit"; British; to fill (a vacancy, position, etc.)

NOUN: the act of providing or something that is provided; (as modifier); a supply dump; (often plural); an amount available for use; stock; (plural); food, equipment, etc., needed for a campaign or trip; economics; willingness and ability to offer goods and services for sale; the amount of a commodity that producers are willing and able to offer for sale at a specified price

**suppression**

NOUN: the act or process of suppressing or the condition of being suppressed; to put an end to; prohibit; to hold in check; restrain; to withhold from circulation or publication;

**sweat**

NOUN: the secretion from the sweat glands, esp. when profuse and visible, as during strenuous activity, from excessive heat, etc.; commonly also called perspiration

VERB: to secrete (sweat) through the pores of the skin, esp. profusely; to make wet or stain with sweat; to give forth or cause to give forth (moisture) in droplets; to collect and condense moisture on an outer surface; (of a liquid) to pass through a porous surface in droplets.

**system**

NOUN: a group or combination of interrelated, interdependent, or interacting elements forming a collective entity; a methodical or coordinated assemblage of parts, facts, concepts, etc., "a system of currency", "the Copernican system"; any scheme of classification or arrangement, "a chronological system"; a network of communications, transportation, or distribution; a method or complex of methods, "he has a perfect system at roulette"; orderliness; an ordered manner

**take**

VERB: to gain possession of (something) by force or effort; to appropriate or steal, "to take other people's belongings"; to receive or accept into a relationship with oneself, to take a wife; to pay for or buy; to rent or lease, to take a flat in town; tampered

**taught**

VERB: the past tense and past participle of teach

**taxation**

NOUN: the act or principle of levying taxes or the condition of being taxed; an amount assessed as tax; a tax rate; revenue from taxes

**teach**

VERB: to help to learn; tell or show (how), "to teach someone to paint", to teach someone how to paint; to give instruction or lessons in (a subject) to (a person or animal), to teach French, to teach children, she teaches; (tr; may take a clause as object or an infinitive); to cause to learn or understand, experience taught him that he could not be a journalist; Also: teach someone a lesson informal to cause (someone) to suffer the unpleasant consequences of some action or behavior

**teacher**

NOUN: a person whose occupation is teaching others, esp. children; a personified concept that teaches, "nature is a good teacher";

**territory**

NOUN: any tract of land; district; the geographical domain under the jurisdiction of a political unit, esp. of a sovereign state; a protectorate or other dependency of a country; the district for which an agent, etc. is responsible; an area of knowledge

**text**

NOUN: the main body of a printed or written work as distinct from commentary, notes, illustrations, etc.; the words of something printed or written; (often plural); a book prescribed as part of a course of study; computing; the words printed, written, or displayed on a visual display unit; the original exact wording of a work, esp. the Bible, as distinct from a revision or translation

VERB: to send a text message to (someone) using a mobile phone

**that**

DETERMINER: (used before a singular noun); used preceding a noun that has been mentioned at some time or is understood, "that idea of yours"; (as pronoun), "don't eat that". "that's what I mean"; used preceding a noun that denotes something more remote or removed, "that dress is cheaper than this one", "that building over there is for sale"; used to refer to something that is familiar, "that old chap from across the street"; See and that; See at that

CONJUNCTION (subordinating): used to introduce a noun clause, "I believe that you'll come"; Also: "so that, in order that"; used to introduce a clause of purpose, "they fought that others might have peace"; used to introduce a clause of result, "he laughed so hard that he cried"; used to introduce a clause after an understood sentence ; expressing desire, indignation, or amazement "oh, that I had never lived!"

ADVERB: used with adjectives or adverbs to reinforce the specification of a precise degree already mentioned, "go just that fast and you should be safe"; Also: "all that" (usually used with a negative) informal; (intensifier), "she wasn't that upset at the news"; dialect; (intensifier), "the cat was that weak after the fight"

PRONOUN: used to introduce a restrictive relative clause, "the book that we want"; used to introduce a clause with the verb to be to emphasize the extent to which the preceding noun is applicable, "genius that she is, she outwitted the computer"

**the**

DETERMINER (article): used preceding a noun that has been previously specified; used with a qualifying word or phrase to indicate a particular person, object, etc., as distinct from others; used preceding certain nouns associated with one's culture, society, or community; used preceding present participles and adjectives when they function as nouns; used preceding titles and certain uniquely specific or proper nouns, such as place names.

**their**

DETERMINER: of, belonging to, or associated in some way with them, "their finest hour", "their own clothes", "she tried to combat their mocking her"; belonging to or associated in some way with people in general not including the speaker or people addressed, "in many countries they wash their clothes in the river"; belonging to or associated in some way with an indefinite antecedent such as one, whoever, or anybody, "everyone should bring their own lunch"

## them

PRONOUN: (objective); refers to things or people other than the speaker or people addressed, "I'll kill them", "what happened to them?"; (objective); refers to a person whose gender cannot or need not be specified, "find someone you trust and ask them to advise you"

DETERMINER: a nonstandard word for those, "three of them oranges"

## there

ADVERB: in, at, or to that place, point, case, or respect, we never go there, I'm afraid I disagree with you there

PRONOUN: used as a grammatical subject with some verbs, esp. be, when the true subject is an indefinite or mass noun phrase following the verb as complement, "there is a girl in that office", "there doesn't seem to be any water left"

ADJECTIVE: (postpositive); who or which is in that place or position, "that boy there did it"

## therefore

SENTENCE CONNECTOR: thus; hence: used to mark an inference on the speaker's part, "those people have their umbrellas up: therefore, it must be raining"; consequently; as a result, "they heard the warning on the radio and therefore took another route"

## these

DETERMINER: the form of this used before a plural noun, "these men"; (as pronoun), "I don't much care for these"

## they

PRONOUN (subjective): refers to people or things other than the speaker or people addressed, "they fight among themselves"; refers to unspecified people or people in general not including the speaker or people addressed, "in Australia they have Christmas in the summer" ; not standard, refers to an indefinite antecedent such as one, whoever, or anybody, "if anyone objects, they can go"

**this**

DETERMINER: (used before a singular noun); used preceding a noun referring to something or someone that is closer: distinct from that, "this dress is cheaper than that one", "look at this picture"; (as pronoun), "this is Mary and that is her boyfriend", "take this"; used preceding a noun that has just been mentioned or is understood, "this plan of yours won't work"; (as pronoun), "I first saw this on Sunday"; used to refer to something about to be said, read, etc., "consider this argument"; (as pronoun), "listen to this"; the present or immediate, "this time you'll know better"; (as pronoun), "before this, I was mistaken" ; informal often used in storytelling, an emphatic form of a, the, "I saw this big brown bear"

**those**

PRONOUN or ADJECTIVE: pl. of that

**thousands**

PLURAL NOUN: a very large but unspecified number, amount, or quantity, "Thousands of refugees are packed into over-crowded towns and villages", "Hundreds have been killed in the fighting and thousands made homeless", "I must have driven past that place thousands of times."; the numbers 2000–9999

**throughout**

PREPOSITION: right through; through the whole of (a place or a period of time), throughout the day

ADVERB: through the whole of some specified period or area

**time**

NOUN: the continuous passage of existence in which events pass from a state of potentiality in the future, through the present, to a state of finality in the past; in physics; a quantity measuring duration, usually with reference to a periodic process such as the rotation of the earth or the vibration of electromagnetic radiation emitted from certain atoms. In classical mechanics, time is absolute in the sense that the time of an event is independent of the observer. According to the theory of relativity it depends on the observer's frame of reference. Time is considered as a fourth coordinate required, along with three spatial coordinates, to specify an event;

VERB: to ascertain or calculate the duration or speed of; to set a time for; to adjust to keep accurate time; to pick a suitable time for; sport; to control the execution or speed of (an action, esp. a shot or stroke) so that it has its full effect at the right moment;

**to**

PREPOSITION: used to indicate the destination of the subject or object of an action, "he climbed to the top"; used to mark the indirect object of a verb in a sentence, "telling stories to children"; used to mark the infinitive of a verb, "he wanted to go"; as far as; until, "working from Monday to Friday"; used to indicate equality; "ounces to the pound"

ADVERB: towards a fixed position, esp. (of a door) closed

**together**

ADVERB: with cooperation and interchange between constituent elements, members, etc., "we worked together"; in or into contact or union with each other, "to stick papers together"; in or into one place or assembly; "with each other", "the people are gathered together"; at the same time, "we left school together"; considered collectively or jointly, "all our wages put together couldn't buy that car"

ADJECTIVE: slang; self-possessed and well-organized; mentally and emotionally stable, "she's a very together lady"

**toward**

ADJECTIVE: in progress; afoot; about to happen; imminent; promising or favorable

PREPOSITION: a variant of towards

**train**

VERB (transitive): to guide or teach (to do something), as by subjecting to various exercises or experiences, "to train a man to fight"; to control or guide towards a specific goal, "to train a plant up a wall"; to do exercises and prepare for a specific purpose, "the athlete trained for the Olympics"; to improve or curb by subjecting to discipline, "to train the mind"; to focus or bring to bear (on something), "to train a telescope on the moon"

NOUN: a line of coaches or wagons coupled together and drawn by a railway locomotive; a sequence or series, as of events, thoughts, etc., "a train of disasters"; a procession of people, vehicles, etc., travelling together, such as one carrying supplies of ammunition or equipment in support of a military operation; a series of interacting parts through which motion is transmitted; a train of gears' a fuse or line of gunpowder to an explosive charge, etc.

**trained**

ADJECTIVE: (in combination); having been trained by a specified person or organization, "an American-trained lawyer", "French-trained troops"

**treatment**

NOUN: the application of medicines, surgery, psychotherapy, etc., to a patient or to a disease or symptom; the manner of handling or dealing with a person or thing, as in a literary or artistic work; the act, practice, or manner of treating; cinema; an expansion of a script into scquence form, indicating camera angles, dialogue, etc.

**tried**

VERB: the past tense and past participle of try

**truth**

NOUN: the quality of being true, genuine, actual, or factual, "the truth of his statement was attested"; something that is true as opposed to false, "you did not tell me the truth"; a proven or verified principle or statement; fact, "the truths of astronomy"; (usually plural); a system of concepts purporting to represent some aspect of the world, "the truths of ancient religions"; fidelity to a required standard or law

**truthful**

ADJECTIVE: telling or expressing the truth; honest or candid; realistic, a truthful portrayal of the king

**trying**

ADJECTIVE: upsetting, difficult, or annoying, "a trying day at the office"

**two**

NOUN: the cardinal number that is the sum of one and one. It is a prime number

**under**

PREPOSITION: directly below; on, to, or beneath the underside or base of, "under one's feet"; less than, "under forty years"; lower in rank than, "under a corporal"; subject to the supervision, jurisdiction, control, or influence of; subject to (conditions); in (certain circumstances

ADVERB: below; to a position underneath something

**unemployed**

ADJECTIVE: without remunerative employment; out of work; (as collective noun; preceded by the), the unemployed; not being used; idle

**united**

ADJECTIVE: produced by two or more persons or things in combination or from their union or amalgamation, "a united effort"; in agreement; in association or alliance

**universal**

ADJECTIVE: of, relating to, or typical of the whole of humankind or of nature; common to, involving, or proceeding from all in a particular group; applicable to or affecting many individuals, conditions, or cases; general; existing or prevailing everywhere; applicable or occurring throughout or relating to the universe; cosmic.

**university**

NOUN: an educational institution of the highest level, typically, in the U.S., with one or more undergraduate colleges, together with a program of graduate studies and a number of professional schools, and authorized to confer various degrees, as the bachelor's, master's, and doctorate.

**unless**

CONJUNCTION: except under the circumstances that; except on

the condition that, "they'll sell it unless he hears otherwise"

PREPOSITION: except

**up**

PREPOSITION: indicating movement from a lower to a higher position; at a higher or further level or position in or on.

**upon**

PREPOSITION: another word for on; indicating a position reached by going up, "climb upon my knee"; imminent for, "the weekend was upon us again"

**us**

PRONOUN: refers to the speaker or writer and another person or other people; refers to all people or people in general; an informal word for me, when used by editors, monarchs, etc., a formal word for me; mainly in United States a dialect word for ourselves.

**want**

VERB : to feel a need or longing for, "I want a new hat"; to wish, need, or desire (something or to do something); "he wants to go home"; to be lacking or deficient (in something necessary or desirable), the child wants for nothing; to feel the absence of, lying on the ground makes me want my bed; to fall short by (a specified amount)

NOUN: the act or an instance of wanting; anything that is needed, desired, or lacked, to supply someone's wants; a lack, shortage, or absence, for want of common sense; the state of being in need; destitution, the state should help those in want; a sense of lack; craving

**wars**

NOUN: open armed conflict between two or more parties, nations, or states Related adjectives: belligerent, martial; a particular armed conflict, "the war between Sparta and Athens"; the techniques of armed conflict as a study, science, or profession; any conflict or contest, "a war of wits", "the war against crime"; (modifier); of, relating to, resulting from, or characteristic of war, "a war hero", "war damage", "a war story"

**way**

NOUN: a manner, method, or means, "a way of life", "a way of knowing"; a route or direction, "the way home"; a means or line of passage, such as a path or track; (in combination); waterway; space or room for movement or activity (esp. in the phrases "make way", in the way, out of the way); distance, usually distance in general, "you've come a long way"

ADVERB: informal; at a considerable distance or extent, "way over yonder"; very far, "they're way up the mountain"; informal; by far; considerably, "way better"; slang; truly; genuinely, "they have a way cool site"

**we**

PRONOUN : refers to the speaker or writer and another person or other people, "we should go now"; refers to all people or people in general, "the planet on which we live"; when used by editors or other writers, and formerly by monarchs, a formal word for I; (as noun), "he uses the royal we in his pompous moods"; informal; used instead of you with a tone of persuasiveness, condescension, or sarcasm, "how are we today?"

**well**

ADVERB: better or best; (often used in combination); in a satisfactory manner, "the party went very well"; (often used in combination); in a good, skillful, or pleasing manner, "she plays the violin well"; in a correct or careful manner, "listen well to my words"; in a comfortable or prosperous manner, "to live well"; (usually used with auxiliaries); suitably; fittingly, "you can't very well say that"

ADJECTIVE: (usually postpositive) (when prenominal, usually used with a negative); in good health, "I'm very well, thank you", "he's not a well man"; satisfactory, agreeable, or pleasing; prudent; advisable, "it would be well to make no comment"; prosperous or comfortable; fortunate or happy, "it is well that you agreed to go";

EXCLAMATION; an expression of surprise, indignation, or reproof; an expression of anticipation in waiting for an answer or remark

**were**

VERB:  the plural form of the past tense (indicative mood) of "be" and the singular form used with "you". It is also used as a subjunctive, esp. in conditional sentences

**what**

PRONOUN: as an interrogative: which thing, event, circumstance, etc.? used to ask for the specification of an identity, quantity, quality, etc.,

**wherein**

ADVERB: in what place or respect?

PRONOUN:  in which place, thing, etc.; whether;

CONJUNCTION (subordinating): used to introduce an indirect question or a clause after a verb expressing or implying doubt or choice in order to indicate two or more alternatives, the second or last of which is introduce by or whether; (subordinating; often followed by or not); used to introduce any indirect question,

**which**

PRONOUN: what one (or ones) of the number of persons, things, or events mentioned or implied? i.e. "which of the men answered?" "which do you want?"

**white**

ADJECTIVE: having no hue due to the reflection of all or almost all incident light; a color without hue at one extreme end of the scale of grays, opposite to black.

**whites**

PLURAL NOUN: plural of white

**who**

PRONOUN: what or which person or persons used to introduce a direct, indirect, or implied question i.e. "who is he? "I asked who he was"; "I don't know who he is"

**whose**

DETERMINER:  the possessive case of who used as an adjective

PRONOUN: that or those belonging to whom used without a following noun i.e. "whose is this? "whose will look best?"

**will**

NOUN; the faculty of conscious and deliberate choice of action; volition; desire; wish; determined intention, where there's a will there's a way

VERB: used as an auxiliary to express resolution on the part of the speaker; used as an auxiliary to indicate willingness or desire; used as an auxiliary to express compulsion; used as an auxiliary to express capacity or ability,

**with**

PREPOSITION: using; by means of, "he killed her with an axe"; accompanying; in the company of, "the lady you were with"; possessing; "having, a man with a red moustache"; concerning or regarding, "be patient with her"; in spite of, "with all his talents, he was still humble"

**without**

PREPOSITION: not having; not accompanied by; not making use of, (followed by a verbal noun or noun phrase), not, while not, or after not

ADVERB: formal; outside; outwardly

CONJUNCTION: not standard; unless, i.e. "don't come without you have some money"

**woman**

NOUN: an adult female human being; (modifier); female or feminine, "a woman writer"; women collectively; womankind; traditionally feminine qualities or virtues; a female member of a group, team, etc.; informal; a wife, girlfriend, etc.

**women**

NOUN: the plural of woman

**worst**

ADVERB: in the most extreme or bad manner or degree; least well, suitably, or acceptably; (in combination); in or to the smallest degree or extent; least, worst-loved

ADJECTIVE: the superlative of bad

NOUN:(often preceded by at); the most poor, unpleasant, or unskilled quality or condition, "television is at its worst these days"; the greatest amount of damage or wickedness of which a person or group is capable, "the invaders came and did their worst"

## would

VERB: used as an auxiliary to form the past tense or subjunctive mood of "will"(with you, he, she, it, they, or a noun as subject); used as an auxiliary to indicate willingness or desire in a polite manner, "would you help me, please?"; used as an auxiliary to describe a past action as being accustomed or habitual, i.e. "every day we would go for walks"; "I wish, would that he were here."

## written

VERB:  the past participle of write

ADJECTIVE: taken down in writing; transcribed, written evidence, the written word

## years

PLURAL NOUN: a long time; time; period.

# For Book Sales, Speaking Engagements & Podcast Appearances

EMAIL: brotherdemetric@researchminister.com

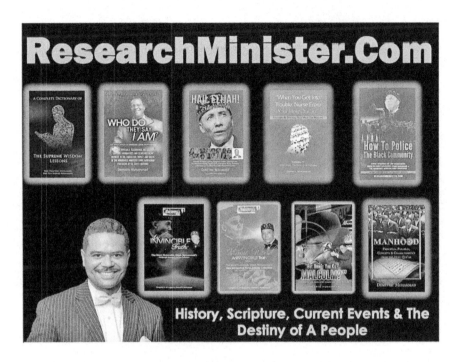

**Bulk Discounts Available for Large Orders**

# ResearchMinister.Com

Made in the USA
Columbia, SC
22 March 2025

55497484R00143